WHITE CARGO

WHITE CARGO

The Forgotten History of
Britain's White Slaves in America

DON JORDAN and MICHAEL WALSH

NEW YORK UNIVERSITY PRESS
Washington Square, New York

To Dian
and
To Eithne

First published in the U.S.A. in 2008 by
NEW YORK UNIVERSITY PRESS
Washington Square
New York, NY 10003

Library of Congress Cataloging-in-Publication Data

Jordan, Don.
  White cargo : the forgotten history of Britain's White slaves in America / Don
Jordan and Michael Walsh.
    p. cm.
  First published: Edinburgh : Mainstream Pub., 2007.
  Includes bibliographical references and index.
  ISBN 978-0-8147-4296-9 (alk. paper)
  1. Slavery--United States--History--17th century. 2. Slavery--United States--
History--18th century. 3. Whites--United States--Social conditions--17th century.
4. Whites--United States--Social conditions--18th century. 5. Indentured servants-
-United States--History. 6. United States--History--Colonial period, ca. 1600-1775.
7. Whites--Great Britain--Social conditions--17th century. 8. Whites--Great Britain-
-Social conditions--18th century. 9. Great Britain--Social conditions--17th century.
10. Great Britain--Social conditions--18th century. I. Walsh, Michael. II. Title.

E446.J665 2007
306.3′62097309034--dc22

                              2007037976

Typeset in Galliard

New York University Press books are printed on acid-free paper,
and their binding materials are chosen for strength and durability.

Manufactured in The United States of America

10 9 8 7 6 5 4 3 2 1

CONTENTS

INTRODUCTION

IN THE SHADOW OF THE MYTH

Slavery they can have everywhere. It is a weed that grows in every soil.

– Edmund Burke

That man who is the property of another, is his mere chattel, though he continue a man.

– Aristotle, *A Treatise on Government*

In the summer of 2003, archaeologists excavated a seventeenth-century site outside Annapolis, Maryland, and discovered the skeleton of a teenage boy. Examination showed the boy to have died sometime in the 1660s. He was about sixteen years old and had tuberculosis. His skull showed evidence of a fearful mouth infection, and herniated discs and other injuries to his back were synonymous with years of hard toil.

The youth was neither African nor Native American. He was northern European, probably English. His remains were found in what had been the cellar of a seventeenth-century house, in a hole under a pile of household waste. It was as if the boy was of so little account that after he died he was thrown out with the rubbish.

Forensic anthropologists believe the youth was probably an indentured servant – the deceptively mild label commonly used to describe hundreds of thousands of men, women and children shipped from Britain to America and the Caribbean in the 150 years before the Boston Tea Party in 1773. Most of these servants paid their passage to the Americas by selling the rights to their labour for a number of years. Others were forcibly exiled and sold in the colonies as servants for up to fourteen years. Many were effectively enslaved.

While the Spanish slaughtered in America for gold, the English in America had to plant for their wealth. Failing to find the expected mineral riches along the eastern seaboard, they turned to farming, hoping to make gold from tobacco. They needed a compliant, subservient, preferably free labour force and since the indigenous peoples of America were difficult to enslave they turned to their own homeland to provide. They imported Britons deemed to be 'surplus' people – the rootless, the unemployed, the criminal and the dissident – and held them in the Americas in various forms of bondage for anything from three years to life.

This book tells the story of these victims of empire. They were all supposed to gain their freedom eventually. For many, it didn't work out that way. In the early decades, half of them died in bondage. This book tracks the evolution of the system in which tens of thousands of whites were held as chattels, marketed like cattle, punished brutally and in some cases literally worked to death. For decades, this underclass was treated just as savagely as black slaves and, indeed, toiled, suffered and rebelled alongside them. Eventually, a racial wedge was thrust between white and black, leaving blacks officially enslaved and whites apparently upgraded but in reality just as enslaved as they were before. According to contemporaries, some whites were treated with less humanity than the blacks working alongside them.

Among the first to be sent were children. Some were dispatched by impoverished parents seeking a better life for them. But others were forcibly deported. In 1618, the authorities in London began to sweep up hundreds of troublesome urchins from the slums and, ignoring protests from the children and their families, shipped them to Virginia.[1] England's richest man was behind this mass expulsion. It was presented as an act of charity: the 'starving children' were to be given a new start as apprentices in America. In fact, they were sold to planters to work in the fields and half of them were dead within a year. Shipments of children continued from England and then from Ireland for decades. Many of these migrants were little more than toddlers. In 1661, the wife of a man who imported four 'Irish boys' into Maryland as servants wondered why her husband had not brought 'some cradles to have rocked them in' as they were 'so little'.

A second group of forced migrants from the mother country were those, such as vagrants and petty criminals, whom England's rulers wished to be rid of. The legal ground was prepared for their relocation by a highwayman turned Lord Chief Justice who argued for England's gaols to be emptied in America. Thanks to men like him, 50,000 to 70,000 convicts (or maybe more) were transported to Virginia, Maryland, Barbados and England's other American possessions before 1776. All manner of others considered undesirable by the British Crown were also dispatched across the Atlantic to be sold into servitude. They ranged from beggars to prostitutes, Quakers to Cavaliers.[2]

A third group were the Irish. For centuries, Ireland had been something of a special case in English colonial history. From the Anglo-Normans onwards, the Irish were dehumanised, described as savages, so making their murder and displacement appear all the more justified. The colonisation of Ireland provided experience and drive for experiments further afield, not to mention large numbers of workers, coerced, transported or persuaded. Under Oliver Cromwell's ethnic-cleansing policy in Ireland, unknown numbers of Catholic men, women and children were forcibly transported to the colonies. And it did not end with Cromwell; for at least another hundred years, forced transportation continued as a fact of life in Ireland.

The other unwilling participants in the colonial labour force were the kidnapped. Astounding numbers are reported to have been snatched from the streets and countryside by gangs of kidnappers or 'spirits' working to satisfy the colonial hunger for labour. Based at every sizeable port in the British Isles, spirits conned or coerced the unwary onto ships bound for America. London's most active kidnap gang discussed their targets at a daily meeting in St Paul's Cathedral. They were reportedly paid £2 by planters' agents for every athletic-looking young man they brought aboard. According to a contemporary who campaigned against the black slave trade, kidnappers were snatching an average of around 10,000 whites a year – doubtless an exaggeration but one that indicates a problem serious enough to create its own grip on the popular mind.[3]

Along with the vast numbers ejected from Britain and forced to slave in the colonies were the still greater multitudes who went of their own free will: those who became indentured servants in the Americas in return for free passage and perhaps the promise of a plot of land. Between 1620 and 1775, these volunteer servants, some 300,000, accounted for two out of three migrants from the British Isles.[4] Typically, these 'free-willers', as they came to be called, were the poor and the hopeful who agreed to sacrifice their personal liberty for a period of years in the eventual hope of a better life. On arrival, they found that they had the status of chattels, objects of personal property, with few effective rights. But there was no going back. They were stuck like the tar on the keels of the ships that brought them. Some, of course, were bought by humane, even generous, masters and survived their years of bondage quite happily to emerge from servitude to build a prosperous future. But some of the most abused servants were from among the free-willers.

It invites uproar to describe as slaves any of these hapless whites who were abused, beaten and sometimes killed by their masters or their masters' overseers. To do so is thought to detract from the enormity of black suffering after racial slavery developed. However, black slavery emerged out of white servitude and was based upon it. As the African-American writer Lerone Bennett Jr has observed:

> When someone removes the cataracts of whiteness from our eyes, and when we look with unclouded vision on the bloody shadows of the American past, we will recognize for the first time that the Afro-American, who was so often second in freedom, was also second in slavery.[5]

Of course, black slavery had hideous aspects that whites did not experience, but they suffered horrors in common, many of which were first endured by whites. In crude economic terms, indentured servants sold their labour for a set period of time; in reality they sold *themselves*. They discovered that they were placed under the power of masters who had more or less total control over their destiny.

The indentured-servant system evolved into slavery because of the economic goals of early colonists: it was designed not so much to help would-be migrants get to America and the Caribbean as to provide a cheap and compliant workforce for the cash-crop industry. Once this was established, to keep the workforce in check it became necessary to create legal sanctions that included violence and physical restraint. This is what led to slavery: first for whites, then for blacks.

It has been argued that white servants could not have been truly enslaved because there was generally a time limit to their enforced labour, whereas black slavery was for life. However, slavery is not defined by time but by the experience of its subject. To be the chattel of another, to be required by law to give absolute obedience in everything and to be subject to whippings, brandings and chaining for any show of defiance, to be these things, as were many whites, was to be enslaved. Daniel Defoe, writing in the early 1700s, described indentured servants as 'more properly called slaves'. Taking his cue, we should call a slave a slave.

How many of those whites who migrated from Britain were subject to the abuses we associate with slavery – 100,000, 200,000, 300,000? It is impossible to know. No one did compile, nor could they have compiled, such statistics. All we can be sure of is that the numbers were considerable. Time and again, the evidence shows this to be the case. Too many white servants ran from their masters, too many instances of ill treatment surfaced, and there were too many damaging admissions throughout the years of British rule for white slavery to be a rarity or a localised aberration that was quickly corrected. In 1663, about the time the wretched sixteen year old buried in that Annapolis cellar breathed his last, the Virginia Assembly warned that 'the barbarous usage of some servants by cruel masters' was giving the colony such a bad name that immigrants would stop coming voluntarily. As the cases in this book confirm, that barbarous usage was widespread and prolonged on the American mainland and in Britain's Caribbean colonies.

Throughout the colonial period, those who were sold into servitude or who sold themselves as servants formed the majority of immigrants, but they have often had short shrift from historians. In the words of the social historian Gary B. Nash, 'Most depictions of early America as a garden of opportunity airbrush indentured servants out of the picture while focusing on the minority who arrived free.'[6] A creation myth has flourished in which early American settlers are portrayed as free men and women who created a democratic and egalitarian model society more or less from scratch.

The truth could not be more different. The freedoms of modern American society evolved only gradually from enforced labour and penal servitude. Many of those instrumental in planning the earliest colonies were, like the reputedly richest man in Elizabethan England, Sir Thomas Smythe, ruthless and oblivious to the misery they caused. They were nonetheless often men of vision and extraordinary resilience. The tale of the white slave trade unfolds through their exuberant lives no less than through those who were their victims. European slavery in early America is contained within two centuries and between three continents: from the tiny band of Englishmen who established Jamestown in 1607, to the slave ports of Africa and finally to Captain Cook feeling his way along the shores of what was to become New South Wales in 1770.

The 1607 expedition laid the foundations for English settlement in America and when American independence closed the mainland colonies to the dumping of convicts and undesirables, Australia provided a new penal colony. In between, the stream of humanity flowed in a vast current across the Atlantic but has since been diverted from its place in the histories of the British Empire and of the United States.

As soon as the new nation of America was born, it became commonplace to deny the central part played in its establishment by key sections of founding fathers, mothers, sons and daughters.

Those who chose to ignore the place of both the villain and the ill-used in this new country's history included contemporary apologists whose motivation was to create both social cohesion and status. In Virginia, the Old Dominion, where ideals of freedom flourished and where America's aristocracy was rooted, it was unacceptable for jailbirds to be discovered lurking in the family tree. Just ten years after the Declaration of Independence, this is what Thomas Jefferson wrote about convicts:

> The malefactors sent to America were not sufficient in number to merit enumeration as one class out of three which peopled America . . . I do not think the whole number sent would amount to two thousand, and being principally men, eaten up with disease, they married seldom and propagated little. I do not suppose that themselves and their descendants are at present four thousand, which is little more than one-thousandth part of the whole inhabitants.[7]

In fact, at the time of the Declaration nearly 1,000 convicts a year were being dumped in America, mostly in Maryland and Virginia. A convict dealer intimated that in the 1700s more than 30,000 convicts had been sold in Maryland alone.

The numbers of convicts and their descendants in the period when Jefferson was writing were not, as he would have it, 'one-thousandth part of the whole inhabitants' but in reality the much more significant one in a hundred. However, there continued to be those who denied that large-scale dumping of the vicious, the irredeemable, the wicked and the plain unlucky had gone on in anything like either the numbers or over the period that we know occurred. Sydney George Fisher, writing in 1898, claimed that Virginia had avoided 'convicts, paupers and inferior nationalities'.[8] The very different reality has been exposed by the pioneering work of leading American historians such as Edmund S. Morgan, David W. Galenson and A. Roger Ekirch. Nevertheless, right up to the present day, many Americans have difficulty reconciling themselves to the true nature of their antecedents. The truth is that in Virginia and Maryland a significant proportion of the early settlers was composed of convicts. The fact that wealth and nobility could grow from such material is testimony not to the importance of bloodstock but to social evolution.

This book features some of the great names of American history who were the masters of white slaves as well as black. It tracks the ruthless kingpins of the white servant trade who bought and sold their human wares, sometimes disguising convicts as regular servants, sometimes hawking servants from settlement to settlement. And it tells the stories of those they sold and of those who sold themselves. Some refused to be victims and fought the system by running away, by rebellion and even by murder. Many others succumbed to disease or exploitation or to attack from Native Americans. Some thrived and laid down roots.

The book has mainly been designed along simple chronological lines; here and there, however, the reader will discover occasional digressions or side-steps to take a closer look at particular fields of inquiry.

We have chosen to limit what would otherwise be quite a lengthy work to describing what occurred in a small but important group of geographic areas. We concentrate on Virginia and Maryland, for example, where the indentured-servant system was created and where its poisonous bloom flowered most widely. The very many colonies in the Caribbean are largely ignored in favour of dealing in detail with Barbados, so providing a clear account of one important colony, unencumbered by multitudes of regional variations. We hope that this approach also helps to clarify the defining difference between the enterprise carried out on the sugar islands and the colonisation of the American mainland. Broadly, the primary purpose of the settlements on Caribbean islands was to make money. There was little thought of Empire. This role fell to the enterprises in America, where profit and empire building went hand in hand. In the great open spaces of America, indentured servants were theoretically expected to survive bondage and prosper in a growing society; on the island of Barbados, freed workers became an embarrassment.

The *Oxford Dictionary* defines as slaves persons who are the legal property of another or others and bound to absolute obedience:

in short, 'human chattels'. By this definition white servants were the first slaves in America and it is upon their labour, and later that of African-American slaves, that the nation was initially built. Today, tens of millions of white Americans are descended from such chattels. It is a shame that few in America claim these largely forgotten men and women of the early frontier as their own.

CHAPTER ONE

A PLACE FOR THE UNWANTED

Slavery's introduction to the New World took place much as serfdom left the Old: stealthily and hesitantly; its sly arrival over a few decades hardly noticed except by a few vigilant pamphleteers and its mainly silent victims.

The seeds of the new colonial serfdom were planted in the 1570s, when English pride in social freedoms was strong enough for Shakespeare's favourite historian, Raphael Holinshed, to boast:

> As for slaves and bondsmen, we have none. Nay, such is the privilege of our country by the especial grace of God and the bounty of our princes that if anyone come hither from other realms so soon as they set foot on land they become so free . . . all note of servile bondage is utterly removed from them.[1]

Even as Holinshed was celebrating his notion of England, forces were at work that would soon produce a very different prospect for tens of thousands of freeborn English men, women and children who sailed to America either willingly or involuntarily. Within a generation, a system of slave labour would evolve in America that would deprive them of those very freedoms in which Holinshed gloried.

One of the catalysts for the white slave trade was the fear that

England was in danger of being overwhelmed by the poor and the lawless, a perception of insecurity still all too recognisable today. In the course of a few generations, the population had risen by a third. In 1509, Henry VIII came to the throne to inherit a kingdom of around three million souls. By the time his daughter Elizabeth faced the Spanish Armada eighty years later, she ruled over a population nearer to four million.[2]

For landowners fattened by church lands acquired during the Reformation and common lands grabbed through the first Enclosure Acts, it was a time of gallivanting Renaissance luxury. But at the other end of the scale, life in the mid-sixteenth century was pitted and disfigured by poverty. Recurring harvest disasters, the enclosures and economic depressions had left hordes of peasants and labourers dispossessed and on the margins of survival. Once, the monasteries would have offered some succour but Henry had closed them down and now the poor roamed the countryside and cluttered the towns. In 1570, 2,000 beggars were reported in Coventry alone. A crowd of 20,000 poor people gathered at the funeral of one rich magnate, begging for alms. In London, between 1560 and 1601, there was an eightfold increase in the number of vagrants ending up in the old Bridewell Palace, which had become a house of correction.[3]

Inevitably, lawlessness increased. A statute of 1572 begins with the lament:

> All the parts of this realm of England and Wales be presently
> with rogues, vagabonds, and sturdy beggars exceedingly
> pestered, by means whereof daily happeneth in the same
> realm horrible murders, thefts, and other great outrage,
> to the high displeasure of Almighty God, and to the great
> annoyance of the common weal.[4]

One of the most bloodstained figures of the age, Humphrey Gilbert, half-brother of Walter Raleigh, promoted the idea of finding a solution in America. Gilbert has been left in the historical shade by his brilliant sibling but he was as much a Renaissance Man as Raleigh. He was born into minor gentry in the West Country and began his career as a page to the future Queen Elizabeth, before taking to soldiering, whereupon he gained a reputation for cold-blooded ruthlessness. However, he was also a poet, classical scholar and visionary who inspired a generation of fellow Englishmen with thoughts of empire in America.

Humphrey Gilbert made his mark during the religious wars that gripped France in the early 1560s. This was a saga of massacre, torture and atrocity exemplified by the Huguenot captain who wore a necklace of priests' ears around his neck. Nearly a century later, Pascal wrote of this conflict: 'Men never do evil so completely and cheerfully as when they do it from religious conviction.' While still in his early twenties, Gilbert headed a contingent of 1,000 English Protestants fighting on the Huguenot side. He exhibited dash and bravery but cruelty, too, making a practice of taking no prisoners. Those who were captured were invariably hanged. Impressed as always by young daredevils, in 1569 the Queen put him in command of English troops in Munster, where the English responded to a revolt by launching an ethnic-cleansing campaign to replace the native Irish with plantations of English Protestants.

In this gory arena, the ambitious young firebrand demonstrated an implacability unsurpassed by either Oliver Cromwell or William of Orange a century later. In every stronghold that offered resistance, Gilbert slaughtered wholesale, scouring the countryside for anyone who got away. 'I slew all those . . . that did belong to, feed, accompany or maintain any outlaws or traitors . . . how many lives whatsoever it cost putting man, woman and child to the sword.' The severed heads of his victims were stuck on rows of pikes on either side of the path leading to his tent. Gilbert explained that it brought 'great terror to the people when they saw the heads of their fathers, brothers, children, kinfolk and friends'. Tens of thousands died; Humphrey Gilbert was knighted.[5]

It is one of the paradoxes of human nature that the most ruthless often have a well-developed sense of the romantic. And so it was with Sir Humphrey. In France, he is thought to have met seafarers who had crossed the Atlantic and to have developed a fascination with America. Marriage to a Kentish heiress called Anne Aucher in 1570 enabled him to retire from the Queen's service, buy a seat in

Parliament and devote himself to what soon became his obsession.

Gilbert believed the North American continent was an island and – like a number of contemporaries – burned to prove the existence of a North-West Passage to China through the Arctic Circle. After studying every manuscript and classical text that he could find, he produced a scholarly-looking discourse to support his own theory and with it – almost as an aside – the first detailed blueprint for English colonisation of North America.[6] It was said that, 'His geography, if learned and often ingenious, was mostly preposterous.'[7] However, it was convincing enough for the Queen and her council, and in 1578 Gilbert was granted leave to go ahead. He was given six years to found a colony.

His motives weren't, of course, purely altruistic. For Gilbert – as for so many empire builders – personal aggrandisement and the national interest happily went hand in hand. He ordered up written versions of the stories of a sailor called David Ingram who'd been shipwrecked in Florida and spent two years trekking through North America. Ingram had just returned with fantastical tales of native women wearing 'plates of gold like armour', men decorated with 'pearls as big as one's thumb' and houses 'upheld by pillars of gold, silver, and crystal'. If gold there was, Gilbert aimed to grab the lion's share. In his scheme, the envisaged territory would be a fiefdom of the Crown that he would rule, taking an eighty per cent share of any gold or silver. The humble servant would retain twenty per cent for his Queen.

Gilbert's blueprint covered everything, from the size of the first colony (a mere nine million acres), right down to street layouts and the number of churches. In retrospect, the most significant part of his plan was the suggestion of where to find the colony's manpower. He proposed transporting 'such needy people of our country which now trouble the commonwealth and through want here at home are forced to commit outrageous offences whereby they are daily consumed with the gallows'.[8] It is difficult to reconcile the humanity infusing this passage with the butcher of Munster. One historian has suggested that Gilbert was mellowed by his experiences in Ireland. A more reliable explanation may be that self-interest hid behind altruism's lofty mask.

There were precedents for Gilbert's scheme. Convict labour had featured from the earliest European forays into the Americas. In Spain, the difficulties of persuading free men to try their luck in the unknown had prompted King Ferdinand and Queen Isabella in 1497 to promise a pardon to convicts facing death if they would agree to go on Christopher Columbus's third expedition. Half a century later, the Marquis de la Roche, an old adversary of Gilbert's, took his pick from the Breton jails to man successive expeditions to parts of the New World that Gilbert had an eye on. It was said that de la Roche's ships were 'deep freighted with vice'.[9]

At first, the Queen was reluctant to let Gilbert go. She was anxious to keep her former page close at hand to stamp down further eruptions in Ireland. But Gilbert was backed by his persuasive half-brother Walter Raleigh, Elizabeth's emerging favourite, and she finally agreed. The letters patent allowed him to claim vast tracts of America in the Queen's name. Only those areas to the south already ruled by 'Christian princes' were officially precluded, i.e. those already invaded by the Spanish and Portuguese. However, with her habitual eye on the main chance, Elizabeth secretly gave Gilbert the go-ahead to plunder the Spanish and Portuguese wherever he found them. In an equally typical move, the Queen would not fund the venture. Gilbert had to raise the money from friends and relations and any adventurous spirits who agreed to accompany him. He recorded how he only managed to fit out his fleet of ten ships after 'selling the clothes off my wife's back'.[10]

In 1578, he set sail with a large fleet and 500 men, including at least one convict who had been reprieved from execution and handed over to him. His 27-year-old half-brother Walter furnished his own ship and came too. For Gilbert, it must have been a mouth-watering prospect. The royal licence entitled him to total control over a land expected to be awash with gold and silver just like the Spanish American colonies. But a combination of bad luck, infighting, bad weather and bad leadership turned the expedition into a disaster when it was barely out of English waters. A decimated fleet returned home without even crossing the Atlantic.

Undeterred, Gilbert tried again in 1583. Without Raleigh this time, he followed in the track of the fishing fleets to the Grand

Banks and made landfall at the bleak fishing outpost of St John's in Newfoundland. The Basque, Portuguese and French fishermen already at anchor there were no doubt bewildered as Gilbert flourished his royal commission and claimed Newfoundland as English. He then issued licences for them all to continue fishing and just as suddenly departed. His fleet headed west and south, casting along the dangerous eastern seaboard for a site to settle. It was not to be, however. 'Foul weather increased with fogs and mists' and Gilbert's largest ship foundered and was lost.[11] Morale collapsed and demands grew for a return home. Most of the great Elizabethan seafarers at one time or another were threatened by mutiny in similar situations and most faced down the threat. Gilbert, however, could not. He reluctantly conceded an immediate return but lest anyone think him a coward he announced that he would brave the storms on the journey home by sailing on the smallest, most vulnerable ship, a ten-ton brig called the *Squirrel*. It was a typical act of Elizabethan braggadocio – and fatal.

The *Squirrel* was overloaded with guns, tackle and provisions. When the fleet encountered heavy seas, Gilbert was urged to transfer to the comparative safety of his flagship the *Golden Hind* but refused. He vowed that he would not desert the shipmates with whom he had faced so many perils. A storm developed and the *Squirrel* began to founder. Gilbert's last recorded words, shouted to the *Golden Hind*, had a fatalism that made him more famous in England than anything he had previously done.

'We are as near to heaven by sea as by land,' he called and resumed reading his book as waves broke over the tiny vessel.[12] The book was said to have been Thomas More's *Utopia*. The manner of his death made Gilbert a national hero. Three centuries later, the image of the visionary adventurer swept away under the waves was still being immortalised in verse by Longfellow:

> Alas! the land-wind failed,
> And ice-cold grew the night;
> And nevermore, on sea or shore,
> Should Sir Humphrey see the light.

Walter Raleigh waited just long enough to be sure that Gilbert had indeed drowned, then seized his half-brother's mantle and made the American project his own. The Queen, already showering favours on Raleigh, was prevailed upon to grant him the same free hand given to Gilbert, and Raleigh set to work selling America to would-be backers. Some later romantics would portray Raleigh as one of their own. But essentially, as the historian David Beers Quinn puts it: 'He was an acute and hard-dealing businessman. Colonization was a business which he undertook to promote.'[13] His first step was to commission what was effectively a market report on the New World.

The man he employed to undertake it was Richard Hakluyt, then at the start of a career that would make him the world's leading geographer. A clergyman by profession, Hakluyt had become fascinated as a student with the 'discoveries' that were opening up the furthest oceans. He made himself an expert in the field by translating every work of navigation and exploration he could find and interviewing every explorer and seafarer he could track down. Like a sixteenth-century paparazzo, he pounded from port to port to greet the Drakes and Hawkinses and Gilberts returning from their latest trips of piracy in order to cast an eye over their ships' logs.

Hakluyt had just published his first major work on geography when Raleigh, with his rare eye for young talent, hired him to write about America. The result was a persuasive piece of propaganda, the *Discourse Concerning Western Planting*. Echoing Gilbert's theme of an England being engulfed by the lawless poor and America as her salvation, Hakluyt claimed that the country was so populous that people were 'ready to eat up one another'. In their desperation, so many had turned to crime that 'all the prisons of the land are daily pestered and stuffed full of them, where either they pitifully pine away or . . . are miserably hanged'. How much better, Hakluyt suggested evangelically, to put the wretches to work in a colony overseas. He reeled off a list of America's resources and set out the different industries that should flourish there. There were more than forty of them, ranging from tar making, gold mining and cotton picking to diving for pearls. It is a mark of Hakluyt's judgment that almost all would one day thrive in America.

While Hakluyt was still writing, two of Raleigh's ships were probing the estuaries of what is now South Carolina for a possible settlement site. In 1584, they sent home reports ranging from the heartening to the ecstatic:

> The goodliest soil under the cope of heaven . . . we have found here maize . . . whose ear yielded corn for bread four hundred upon one ear, and the cane makes very good and perfect sugar . . . it is the . . . most pleasing territory of the world. The territory and soil of the Chesapeake . . . for pleasantness of seat, for temperature of climate, for fertility of soil and for the commodity of the sea . . . is not to be excelled by any other whatsoever.[14]

The next year, a fleet of settlers was dispatched. The story of Raleigh's 'lost colony' is well known: the fateful selection of the mosquito-ridden island of Roanoke as a site; Raleigh's celebrated naming of the colony Virginia after Elizabeth, the Virgin Queen; the three-year struggle to sustain this precarious foothold; the disastrous failure to re-supply the colonists during the war with Spain; the colonists' unexplained disappearance and the futile expeditions launched by Raleigh in later years to try to find his lost people.

Queen Elizabeth's beneficence had made Raleigh wealthy: he is reported to have appeared at court encrusted with jewels from head to foot. But the American ventures drained his resources. He reputedly spent £40,000 on his voyages – equivalent to approximately £6 million in today's money – and, although he remained obsessed with Virginia, in 1590 he leased out the patent entitling him to colonise it, retaining the right to twenty per cent of all gold or silver discovered – the same cut he had agreed to pay the Queen when his hopes were higher. He also retained the right to veto any other would-be colonists in Virginia.

The new holders of the patent included three of his friends: Richard Hakluyt, John White, the nominal Governor of Raleigh's colony who had returned to Britain before the colonists vanished, and Thomas Smythe, a young man destined to play a big role in bringing white slavery to Virginia. Smythe had his own vision of the New World and would become the driving force in the Virginia project.

Like Gilbert and Raleigh, Smythe had made his mark in war, both in Ireland and on the Continent, and, like them, he was much more than a simple soldier. He was a financial genius and no Englishman better fits the title 'merchant prince'. He could be called England's – or, indeed, America's – first tycoon.

Smythe's father, also a Thomas, was a rich merchant who during the reign of Bloody Mary had secured one of the most lucrative franchises in the country. He became chief collector of customs duties, called the 'farmer of customs'. This involved paying an agreed annual sum to the royal exchequer and then collecting what he could. 'Customer Smythe', as he became known, kept the job when Elizabeth came to the throne, and made a fortune. Some of the proceeds were used to back the piratical expeditions of Drake and later of Raleigh, his son's friend. Both would have been hugely successful investments.

However, young Thomas left the Customer standing. This was the era of the first joint stock companies, those harbingers of capitalism that opened up world trade and would eventually make Britain the dominant world commercial power. Smythe Junior would play a leading role in almost all of them. Wherever England traded in the late Elizabethan and Jacobean eras, Smythe left his fingerprints. In a ruthless, cut-throat age, he conjured deals with rulers across the globe, from the Emperor of Japan to the Tsar of Russia. Just about every major English company that started up in a thirty-five-year period was either initiated or run by him – the East India Company, the Muscovy Company, the Levant Company, the Somers Island Company, the North-West Passage Company, the Merchant Adventurers and, eventually, the Virginia Company. By the time Thomas Smythe bought into the Virginia enterprise he was well on his way to becoming the wealthiest merchant in London.

With money and commercial success went power. Smythe rose

through the ranks of London aldermen to become city auditor, Sheriff of the City of London and captain of the city's trained bands (London's militia), giving him command of 2,000 men. He also succeeded his father as collector of customs, reportedly increasing the take by 100 per cent.

Smythe was at the centre of the debates over the lawless and the poor that raged during the 1590s. The decade had started with record harvests but England was soon hit by the gravest agrarian crisis since the Black Death two centuries earlier. For five successive years, the skies opened and the harvest failed. The price of corn doubled and starvation and plague spread across the nation. Following what was supposed to be a triumphal tour of the realm to mark victory over the Spanish Armada, the Queen complained that 'paupers are everywhere'. Magistrates were ordered to take control of corn supplies and profiteers were punished. In Colchester in Essex, aldermen were required to donate loans of £20, and councillors £10, to buy corn to feed the poor. A baker was appointed in every ward to bake 'three seams of bread' a day to give to the hungry.

Parliament's response was to introduce another new law in the late 1590s to control the poor. One of the most daunting and corrupt of Elizabeth's ministers, her Lord Chief Justice, Sir John Popham, drew up the bill; Smythe served on the grand committee that debated it. The ferocious measure required parishes to support the 'impotent poor' (the old, disabled and sick) but specified severe punishment for the able-bodied, those 'rogues and vagabonds' who, in the view of the better placed, should be able to look after themselves. Tinkers, gypsies, begging scholars, palm readers, wandering musicians and actors were all defined as vagabonds. One William Shakespeare, who had possibly been a wandering actor not many years before, must have felt relieved that his aristocratic patronage would have protected him from the act.

Among the punishments was transportation. The new law decreed that those

> who would not be reformed of their roguish kind of life . . .
> shall be banished out of this realm and . . . shall be conveyed

into such parts beyond the seas as shall be at any time hereafter for that purpose assigned by the Privy Council.

But transported where? At this stage, it evidently didn't matter. The imperative was simply to get rid of undesirables. Sir John Popham announced that the act would be used 'to drive from here thieves and traitors to be drowned in the sea'. But as the Elizabethan era drew to a close, the legislation lay in abeyance, unused for several years while the country became consumed with the succession to the throne.

During the plotting that developed in the Queen's last years, Smythe's contribution to history was nearly cut short. He seems to have been a thoroughly political creature, with a reassuring, all-things-to-all-men persona that he deployed to recruit allies where he could. One friendship he established was with Elizabeth's greatest favourite: the flamboyant, vain Robert Devereux, Earl of Essex.

In 1596, the budding merchant prince emerged from his counting house to join the Earl of Essex in an expedition that climaxed in the famous attack on Cadiz. There was no military or political purpose; it was simply a raid for plunder and it was a financial triumph. The city was sacked and the raiders returned home laden with booty. One report has Essex knighting Smythe for bravery on the Spanish dockside.

Given their rapport, it was hardly surprising that when Essex tried to mount a coup d'état against Elizabeth in 1601 he might have expected support from Smythe and his city militia. He was to be disappointed. On the morning of the coup, Essex arrived at Smythe's door with armed supporters, only to find the clearly agitated merchant refusing to help. Grabbing the bridle of the Earl's horse, Smythe urged his friend to give himself up and then retreated into his mansion.

Essex surrendered later that day and was swiftly executed. Thomas Smythe nearly followed him. Under interrogation, the Earl's supporters claimed that Smythe had egged Essex on and vowed to deploy his militia in support. Suspicions were heightened by a report that an emissary from the Earl had delivered a letter to

Smythe's wife just before the coup. There was also the matter of the Earl's arrival at Smythe's house. Smythe and his wife were hauled off to the Tower of London. Denying everything, Smythe claimed he had had no communication with the Earl for years and that he met him on the fateful morning merely to pass on a message from the Lord Mayor.

As stories go, it was a lamer excuse than told by many a commoner condemned for treason and sent to Tyburn's triple tree, there to be castrated, disembowelled, hanged, beheaded and dismembered. Smythe was spared, perhaps because he had lent Elizabeth £31,000 to help equip the fleet that defeated the Spanish Armada, perhaps because it was thought not to be financially prudent to kill the richest man in the country. Whatever the reason, Smythe was deprived of all his offices and ordered to pay a substantial fine. In the language of the Privy Council, Thomas Smythe had 'forgotten his duty to her Majesty'.

The great merchant did not languish long in disgrace. In March 1603, the 69-year-old Elizabeth was overcome by an illness that signalled the end of her long reign. Her successor, James I, was generous to all those who had been linked to the Essex rebellion, including Thomas Smythe. The main reason was that James himself had plotted with Essex. Within a month of assuming the English throne, James not only restored Smythe to all his offices but also knighted him. Sir Thomas Smythe would be James I's chief adviser on trade, with a special interest in the colonisation of the New World. Smythe would hold this position for the rest of his life and use it to ensure that when England's new colony was eventually planted in America it would survive, whatever the human cost in life or liberty. He had taken the first step three years later when he joined a race to plant the first permanent colony in Virginia and found that his rival was the most feared man in the realm, Sir John Popham.

CHAPTER TWO

THE JUDGE'S DREAM

The Kennebec River runs gently down through the wooded uplands of Maine to the sea. Its source is Moosehead Lake, a stretch of water so large that it was once mistaken for the China Sea. From this great lake, the Kennebec flows 150 miles through New England before draining into the North Atlantic near a windy point of land called Sabino Head. It was here that 400 years ago a fortress was built by Englishmen used by other Englishmen as their chattels or slaves.

Fort St George would be formidable had it survived. A blueprint discovered nearly 300 years later shows it with thick battlements, great crenellated gates, several mansions, a church, fifty other buildings and a walled garden. A dozen cannon point towards the sea. Construction was well under way when the settlement was suddenly deserted, leaving the fort to crumble back into the earth.

Today, the fort exists as the merest outline etched in the landscape, revealing little of the philosophy or vision that impelled men to build it. The settlement was the project of Sir John Popham, one of the most powerful men in the government of Queen Elizabeth I. Popham was the first to put to the test Sir Humphrey Gilbert's proposal for colonising America with the dregs of England. What Popham tried would one day be one of the most hated features of English rule in America; ambitions buried at Fort St George were to live on and change the face of North America.

Work on the short-lived fortress had begun in August 1607. It was to be the centrepiece of a new colony. A charter issued the previous year by King James I restated England's claim to 'Virginia' – the entire length of the eastern American seaboard from Canada to Florida – and authorised the establishment of two colonies. One, under the aegis of Sir Thomas Smythe, was to be in the south, between the thirty-eighth and forty-first parallels. The other, under the guidance of the Lord Chief Justice Sir John Popham, was to be located to the north, in New England.

The charter signalled a new approach to England's hoped-for conquest and share in the New World. Hitherto, all England's colonial ventures in America had been individualistic forays, each one ultimately dependent on the vision, finances and staying power of one man. By the early 1600s, this was starting to be recognised as a fatal weakness. An anonymous broadside circulating at the time reflected on twenty years of failure: 'Private purses are cold comfort to adventurers, and have ever been found fatal to all enterprises hitherto undertaken by the English, by reason of delays, jealousies, and unwillingness to back that project which succeeded not at the first attempt.'[1]

The broadside argued for 'a stock', a joint stock company that could take a long view and ride the kind of setbacks that had been the ruin of so many previous ventures. Joint stock companies were relatively new entities in which individuals owned shares they could sell without reference to their fellow stockholders. These companies were opening the far corners of the globe to English trade, so why not a joint stock company to fund the next big English push to colonise America?

Interest in America had been largely dormant since 1590, when the financial drain persuaded Walter Raleigh to give up his Roanoke adventure. Twelve years went by and then a new round of exploration began. It was led by Bartholomew Gosnold, a friend of Richard Hakluyt and Raleigh. Accompanied by Bartholomew Gilbert, one of Sir Humphrey Gilbert's six sons, Gosnold landed in New England in 1602 and stayed for several months, trading and exploring.

They returned with sensational reports that rhapsodised over the natural riches of the New World:

> The soil is fat and lusty . . . Cherry trees like ours, but the stalks bear the blossom or fruit which are like a cluster of Grapes . . . all sorts of fowls, whose young ones we took and ate at our pleasure . . . Grounds nuts as big as eggs.[2]

Gosnold summed up their reaction as they caught the first sight of all this plenty: 'We stood a while as ravished.'

The following year, a merchant from Bristol, Martin Pring, landed in Virginia looking for the sassafras tree, the root of which was then used to treat the 'French pox' and is today, in a marvellous piece of serendipity, used in the perfumery trade. Two years after Pring, George Waymouth came looking for a settlement site in what is now Maine. Pring and Waymouth were down-to-earth seamen with none of Gosnold's descriptive flair. But they did enough to stoke the fires of enthusiasm for America still more. 'The land is full of God's Good blessings,' said Pring.[3] Waymouth made the same point more graphically, returning with intriguing samples of plant and animal life and five captured Native Americans all London wanted to see.

Despite the fact that Gosnold and the other mariners had found not a scrap of evidence for the existence of gold mines, these expeditions sparked new speculation about gold waiting to be discovered in America. The fantastical stories of 'golden cities' brought back three decades earlier by that wandering seaman David Ingram had not been forgotten and American gold became the talk of the taverns and counting houses. The Spanish dream of *El Dorado*, the golden man, had led to the discovery of fantastic treasures in South America. The English, it was argued, would find theirs in the northern continent.

A taste of the fantastic hopes that developed can be had from Ben Jonson's satire on gold fever, *Eastward Ho!*, staged at the same time as Shakespeare was putting on *Macbeth*. Jonson imagines the lost Roanoke colonists marrying into the local population and living in a society literally covered in gold. 'Why, man,' exclaims a character, 'all their dripping-pans are pure gold, and all the chains with which they chain up their streets are massy gold; all the prisoners they take are fettered in gold; and for rubies and diamonds they go forth on holidays and gather 'em by the seashore!'

It was in this atmosphere that the charter authorising the two new forays to America was drawn up and two joint stock companies of 'knights, gentlemen, merchants and other adventurers' created for the purpose. The two principal aims were announced as 'bringing infidels and savages, living in those parts, to human civility' and 'the mining of gold, silver and copper'. Three of the Crown's leading councillors helped draft the document: Robert Cecil, Chief Secretary of State; Sir Edward Coke, Attorney General; and the fearsome Lord Chief Justice, Sir John Popham.

Cecil emerged as principal patron of the company that was allocated the southern territory, lying roughly between what is now Florida and New York. It was composed of men drawn mainly 'from our city of London' and inevitably became known as the London Company, and later the Virginia Company. The key post of treasurer of the company, equivalent to managing director, was taken by Sir Thomas Smythe.

Sir John Popham was the principal investor in the second company, drawn from 'our cities of Bristol and Exeter and of our town of Plymouth' and allocated New England. It came to be known as the Plymouth Company. Popham was a man whose character was written in his face. In one portrait, he appears a physical giant, the scarlet robes of the High Court clutched around his bulk, a heavy, ugly face glaring out, cold eyes cunning and suspicious: the face of a calculating, unstoppable bully. In his voluminous *Lives of the Chief Justices of England*, Lord Campbell refers to the portrait and adds decorously: 'I am afraid he would not appear to great advantage in a sketch of his moral qualities, which lest I do him an injustice I will not attempt.'[4]

Sir John was the man who had passed the death sentence on Sir Walter Raleigh, telling him, 'It is best for man not to seek to climb too high, lest he fall.' He had participated in the trial of Mary, Queen of Scots and condemned to death Guy Fawkes and hundreds more. The miracle was that he did not join them on the gallows himself. Before he occupied one by one most of the great legal offices of state, John Popham had been a highwayman and, according to one rumour, 'probably a garrotter', too.

Popham was born in 1531 into an affluent Somerset family. He read law at Balliol College, Oxford, and in his twenties he was called to the Bar and respectably married. Even then, however, he was exhibiting a different side to his character. He was a heavy drinker and a gambler, and according to Lord Campbell, 'either to supply his profligate expenditure or to show his spirit', Popham

> frequently sallied forth at night from a hostel in Southwark with a band of desperate characters and, planting themselves in ambush on Shooter's Hill, or taking other positions favourable for attack and escape, they stopped travellers and took from them not only their money but any valuable commodities they carried with them – boasting that they were always civil and generous and that to avoid serious consequences they went in such numbers as to render resistance impossible.[5]

Popham's antics continued right through his twenties. Amazingly, he was never caught. In his thirties, he decided he could make as much money from the law as from highway robbery and developed an extensive practice in south-west England that brought him to the attention of the Queen. With her rare ability to pick ruthless talent that could be used one day, Elizabeth arranged a seat in Parliament for him. The former highwayman became Speaker of the House, then Attorney General and, finally, Lord Chief Justice.

'He was a hanging judge,' says Campbell. 'Ordinary larcenies and, above all, in highway robbery there was little chance of acquittal.' It was the same with those who did not fit the Protestant orthodoxies the Crown was trying to mould. Sir John pursued outspoken Puritans and Catholic priests to the scaffold. Under him, hundreds of Jesuits and suspected sympathisers were sent to Tyburn or Smithfield to be hanged, drawn and quartered, or, if a woman, perhaps to be crushed to death or strangled before being burnt at the stake.

When it came to the rich, Sir John could be lenient if the price was right. There was no more corrupt age than the Elizabethan and the future Lord Chief Justice proved himself as buyable as any. In the 1580s, a midwife's story horrified all who heard it. She told of being taken blindfolded in a closed coach to attend the delivery of a child in a great house, and after the birth seeing a masked man seize the newborn infant and cast it into the fire, where it perished. When the story became known, a hue and cry was raised for the perpetrator of what Lord Macaulay called this 'horrible and mysterious crime'.[6] The murderer was tracked down, only to be let off after he paid the judge in the case a truly massive bribe in the shape of his mansion, Littlecote Hall in Wiltshire. John Popham was the judge. By this and other means he became a very rich man. 'He left behind him the greatest estate that has ever been amassed by any lawyer.'[7]

This intimidating man was involved in colonialism years before the Plymouth Company was created. In the 1580s, the Queen decided to stamp out rebellion for ever in Munster by confiscating the vast estates there of the Desmond family and repopulating them with English Protestants. Catholic Irish were ordered out and the land was offered at tuppence an acre to English landlords who would undertake to 'plant' it with tenants from England. Popham was one of many who saw himself accumulating a huge Irish estate. He assembled more than eighty families and dispatched them to Munster. However, another English worthy was already off the mark and had tenanted the land, leaving Popham's tenants no choice but to return home. A few decades later, a not dissimilar scheme called the headright system would be introduced in America and the wealthy would become still richer by obtaining grants of land for importing the poor to settle the New World.

The experience in Munster did not deter Popham from such schemes and his Lordship was soon propelled towards the far more ambitious project of colonising America. He was now in his late fifties, so why did the New World consume him in the last years of his life? The avarice of a rapacious old man certainly played a part, but for Popham it was also about the pursuit of a dumping ground for the criminals that even he, the draconian law officer, could never eradicate.

As we have seen, social conditions had produced levels of crime that frightened the gentry. Now, as the century ended, a new crime wave swept over England. This was the price of peace with Spain, for, as ever, when a major war ended, newly released soldiers and mariners spread across the realm. Many of these men had been criminals beforehand and returned to their former profession. In Plymouth, London, Bristol and York, they had taken the Queen's shilling as an alternative to the rope. In the late 1590s, when war with Spain wound down and peace negotiations began, 'The land then swarmed with people who had been soldiers, who had never gotten (or else quite forgotten) any other vocation . . . too proud to beg, too lazy to labour. These infected the highways with their felonies.'[8]

In 1597, the year before the Treaty of Vervins officially ended the war, Popham had pushed through Parliament the tough new Vagrancy Act described in the previous chapter, under which persistent rogues could be banished to 'parts beyond the seas' at the behest of members of the Privy Council. The act was a prelude to what was to come.

Five years later, Popham drew up an Order in Council identifying those 'parts beyond the seas' where England's unwanted could be dumped: 'Newfoundland, the East and West Indies, France, Germany, Spain and the Low Countries or any of them'. As will be seen, some of these were meant in all seriousness. Virginia would soon be added to the list.

At this point, an enigmatic character entered Popham's life. Sir Ferdinando Gorges was 'captain and keeper' of Plymouth Castle. He was said to be a vain, 'very avaricious man' hardly any more attractive than Sir John.[9] The two met in 1601 during that most tangled of Tudor dramas, the attempted coup by Robert Devereux, Earl of Essex. Gorges was supposedly an Essex supporter. When the coup began, Essex entrusted him with guarding three members of the Queen's council who were being held in Essex House, the Earl's sumptuous Thameside palace. Popham was among the captives. To their surprise, Gorges turned out to be their rescuer rather than jailer and he had the party rowed upriver to Whitehall and safety. It later transpired that from the beginning Gorges had leaked details of the plot to Essex's long-time rival Walter Raleigh, who in turn kept the Queen constantly updated. Gorges was the key witness against Essex when the former royal favourite was tried for treason, condemned and sent to the block on Tower Hill.

While his part in the plot was investigated, Gorges was imprisoned in the Tower. As that other recurrent figure in our story Sir Thomas Smythe had learned, any involvement in the Essex plot, however slight, damned you in the old Queen's eyes. Sir Ferdinando found himself held for nine months and deprived of his military post in Devon. When James I succeeded to the throne, he was immediately reinstated and held in high favour.

Gorges backed George Waymouth's 1605 expedition to the North Atlantic coast. Upon his return, Waymouth presented him with five members of the Wabanaki and Pemaquid tribes he had captured. The idea was to exhibit them around England to drum up interest in the colonial enterprise. The captives demonstrated their skill in handling a dugout canoe on the River Thames, and, according to the Spanish ambassador, Don Pedro de Zuniga, they were quickly taught English so they could 'say how good that country [America] is for people to go there and inhabit it'.[10]

Gorges wanted Popham's help in his American ventures and presented the Lord Chief Justice with two of his Native Americans. The two men were soon partners and they aimed to bring together burghers from London and Plymouth, and members of the gentry who had previously invested in expeditions. Top of the list would have been great merchants like Smythe and aristocrats like Henry Wriothesley, the brilliant Earl of Southampton who was William Shakespeare's patron. Most of the lobbying appears to have taken place in the vast new banqueting hall of the Middle Temple, under the coats of arms of Tudor knights that still hang there today over the heads of other ambitious lawyers.

In the winter of 1605–06, Popham approached the Attorney General, Sir Edward Coke. He laid the emphasis not on the riches to be had in America but on England's desperate need for a dumping ground for criminals. Coke reported their conversation:

My Lord Chief Justice, foreseeing in the experience of his place the infinite number of cashiered captains and soldiers, of poor artisans that would and cannot work, and of idle vagrants that may and will not work, whose increase threatens the state, is affectionately bent to the plantation of Virginia.[11]

He explained that the judge wanted the go-ahead 'to call the undertakers, gentlemen, merchants etc unto him and by their advices set down the best manner of project, which being agreed upon shall be speedily returned to your lordships because the best season for the journey approaches'.

More talks followed, with a great deal of haggling over who was to be in control. Eventually the Virginia Company was chartered with two divisions: a London Company and a Plymouth Company.

The charter helped to give birth to a myth. Ostensibly, it was a remarkable document from a King who espoused the divine right to rule and conceded no powers without a struggle. In a section on how the colonies were to be governed, James stated:

I do . . . declare and order that my loving subjects in America shall forever . . . enjoy the right to make all needful laws for their own government provided only that they be consonant with the laws of England.

Two hundred and sixty years later, when the American Civil War – the war to end slavery – had been won by the northern states, the New England historian John A. Poor traced the region's belief in human rights back to James's charter: 'This charter of liberties was never revoked,' he crowed.

It was a decree of universal emancipation and every man of any colour from any clime was by this Act of King James redeemed, regenerated, disenthralled the moment he landed on the soil of America between the thirty-fourth and forty-fifth degrees . . . 150 years before the decree of Lord

Mansfield [threw] off the chains and fetters of Africans in England.[12]

It was bunkum. There would be forms of both white and black slavery even in New England throughout the colonial period.

Once the charter was issued for his Plymouth Company, Popham wasted no time. 'His position as Chief Justice gave him a controlling influence in all the jails and penitentiaries in the realm.'[13] Although there is no chapter and verse on his use of convicts, snippets of information from contemporaries leave little doubt that Popham exploited his power. 'He stocked Virginia out of all the gaols of England,' reported John Aubrey, the seventeenth century's master of the biographical sketch.[14] Popham sent out men who were 'pressed to that enterprise endangered by the law', wrote the Earl of Stirling, a confidant of Gorges and later a colonist himself.[15] The image lingers in the mind's eye of the hatchet-faced Popham handing down rough justice, offering convicts facing execution the option that would become commonplace in later decades – slave for years in exile in America, possibly to die there, or go to the gallows. This choice had the happy effect not only of saving lives but of aiding Sir John's financial endeavours. Likely-looking specimens for transportation – the young and strong – would no doubt have been paraded before Sir John for inspection. It is difficult to imagine the Lord Chief Justice of England vetting each felon and vagabond in the notorious foulness of Jacobean gaols.

The Spanish Ambassador to London, Don Pedro de Zuniga, was worried about the threat to Spanish interests in America. He complained to Popham and was assured that colonisation aimed only 'to drive thieves out of England'. They were then to be 'drowned in the Sea'.

In May 1606, Popham and Gorges organised a trial voyage. A vessel called the *Richard* was dispatched across the Atlantic with twenty-nine men to establish a bridgehead. Also on board were two of the captured Native Americans sent along to act as guides. The expedition put Popham eight months ahead of the rival London Company, which was fitting out its small fleet in the Port of London as Christmas approached.

The *Richard* never made landfall. Her captain, Henry Challons, ignored instructions to sail directly west and took the more traditional, and supposedly safer, route south, hugging the African coast before turning the helm westwards. He ran straight into a Spanish fleet off Santa Domingo and the *Richard* was captured. Her ship's company and her would-be colonisers ended up as galley slaves.

It is thought significant by historians that Popham made no effort to free his colonists. 'It must be admitted,' says his biographer, that 'he was not full of urgency about the men's recovery.'[16] One reason suggested was that, 'If they were . . . criminals it was natural that he should leave them to their fate.' In a letter to Robert Cecil, Popham wrote: 'If the natives were to be had again in my opinion it would serve to good purpose', but he made no remarks about the others from the *Richard*.

A year later, the judge was ready to try again, with a much larger expedition. In May 1607, 120 men shipped out from Plymouth. They sailed in two vessels: the *Mary and John*, captained by Raleigh Gilbert, a son of Sir Humphrey Gilbert; and the wonderfully named *Gift of God*, a shallow-draughted 'flyboat' designed to navigate shallow unexplored rivers. She was captained by Popham's nephew, George, who was appointed leader of the expedition. Their orders were secret, not to be revealed until they arrived in the New World. Skidwarres, one of the tribesmen captured by Waymouth, was sent as a guide. Sir Ferdinando Gorges was still very much involved in the venture but it was now so much the Lord Chief Justice's project that the colony they planned would be known by everyone – and by history, too – as the Popham colony.

Sir Ferdinando, it seems, contented himself with dreaming of his profits. One of his early biographers, the one-time Governor of Massachusetts, James Sullivan, described Gorges as wanting a colony run on feudal lines in which he 'expected to enjoy the profits at his ease without crossing the Atlantic . . . his expectations were very great'.[17]

The *Gift of God* arrived at the mouth of the Kennebec on 13 August and the *Mary and John* followed three days later. The 120 colonists were rowed ashore to the windy headland and gathered together for what was first business of every European expedition to the New World – a service of thanks on dry land. The group thanked the Lord for a safe delivery. Next came the moment all those present had been waiting for – their orders. A list of secret instructions issued by Sir John Popham was taken from the sealed chest in which it had travelled. George Popham read them out.

Few details survive but the imperative was undoubtedly the search for gold. The 'discovery of mines was the main intended benefit', reported William Strachey, secretary of the Virginia Company who wrote a history of Virginia in 1612.[18] Woe betide all if gold wasn't found. According to historian George Chalmers, Judge Popham's instructions 'imperiously required that the interior should be explored for gold and threatened that in the event of failure the colonists should . . . remain as banished men in Virginia'.[19]

Convicts probably weren't employed on the search but laboured to construct a star-shaped fort. From surviving records, it appears the fort was thrown up at a furious pace, mostly by unskilled labour. Walls, church, storehouse and around fifty wattle-and-daub dwellings were completed by winter. The trick, it seems, was to use simple building techniques demanding mainly muscle and sweat. George Popham was in charge. He was said to be 'timorously fearful to offend' his peers but not, one would suspect, the gangs of men toiling on the banks of the Kennebec that autumn. The very name of Popham would have put the fear of God into most of them.

Plans began to go awry early. The search for 'mines' of gold or silver was led by 24-year-old Raleigh Gilbert. Week after week, they found nothing. Skidwarres deserted back to his people and relations with the local Wawenoc, Canibas and Arosaguntacook peoples – initially promising – turned sour. The colonists' behaviour was to blame. After one incident when four tribesmen were dragged by their hair aboard the *Gift of God*, an attack was mounted and fourteen colonists were killed. Then an inordinately grim winter descended. And all the time not a speck of gold.

A sudden piece of dramatic news appeared to have transformed their fortunes. Members of the Abenake tribe told Popham and Gilbert about a huge stretch of water just seven days' walk away.

George Popham wrote a breathless letter to King James claiming the greatest discovery of the new century: 'This cannot be other than the Southern ocean reaching to the regions of China.' They had, he claimed, found the fabled North-West Passage. It was, of course, nonsense. The tribesmen were almost certainly referring to Moosehead Lake.

What became known as the 'ill-fated Popham colony' soon ended. After less than a year and a terrible winter, George Popham died, believing he had established a permanent foothold in the New World and would go down in history. 'I die content,' he wrote. 'My name will always be associated with the first planting of the English race in the New World. My remains will not be neglected away from the home of my fathers and my kindred.'[20]

George Popham was wrong. He was forgotten and so, almost, was the colony. Raleigh Gilbert took over the leadership, supposedly with great plans for expansion. Instead, he packed up and went home. His change of heart surprised everyone, but not for long. The *Mary and John* had just returned from England packed with provisions – and with news: Gilbert's brother, Sir John Gilbert, was dead. Raleigh was heir to his estate and title. It must have been a bombshell for the youngest of seven children, forced to seek his fortune in the New World, but he did not hesitate. He was going home.

There had been another death, too. This was the news that really gripped the colony: Sir John Popham had died. The ogre was no more. No retribution for failure awaited them on the quay at Plymouth. Everybody could now go home, and everybody did. The Popham colony decamped for England en masse, leaving the fort to decay.

The colony had lasted little more than a year and the colonists returned with little more than a few hundred furs. Most of those involved blamed the dreadful winter. Across the northern hemisphere it had been the worst in memory. 'All our hopes have been frozen to death,' wrote Sir Ferdinando Gorges.[21] The returning colonists reported that America was 'over cold, and in respect of that not habitable by our nation'. In years to come, some patriotic American historians expressed relief that the venture had failed. 'The abortion of Sagadahocke was the first, the last, the only attempt of the English Corporation to fasten a moral pestilence on our northern shores,' declared the nineteenth-century historian, John Wingate Thorton.[22]

The Popham colony might have failed but its philosophy would be revived many miles to the south, where the rival colony, named Jamestown, succeeded in putting down permanent roots. Within a decade, convicts and other representatives of England's cast-offs would begin to arrive in the New World with the King's blessing.

CHAPTER THREE

THE MERCHANT PRINCE

Six hundred and fifty miles south of the Popham colony, the London Company had secured its own precarious foothold in Virginia. Its settlers would face far worse than Popham's men and they would survive, though only just. It would be here, along the James River, that England would begin to dump its unwanted and treat them like livestock. One eighteenth-century writer would call conditions in the colony 'a worse than Egyptian bondage'.

The London Company's expedition was led by a fierce one-armed veteran. Christopher Newport had made his reputation more than a decade earlier, plundering and burning on the Spanish Main as one of Sir Walter Raleigh's captains. He was grizzled and gruff and could have accumulated enough money to retire long before the London Company approached him. In 1592, he helped to capture the *Madre de Dios*, the huge Spanish treasure ship seized off Santa Domingo. Captain Newport sailed her back to England, the richest prize that English privateers ever recorded. She carried gold and silver worth about £15 million at today's prices. It is not known what Christopher Newport's share was. As well as bullion, the *Madre de Dios* was said to be carrying a fabulous hoard of precious stones. The gems had vanished by the time Newport dropped anchor in home waters and welcomed visitors aboard. Every member of the crew is thought to have shared in them, presumably the captain amongst them.

The London Company put Christopher Newport in command of a difficult group of men on board three ships. There was a 120-ton merchantman named the *Susan Constant* and two smaller vessels, the *Godspeed* and the *Discovery*. Spread among them were 120 men and boys. A few were craftsmen and twenty were listed as labourers. The biggest group comprised young 'gentlemen' of one sort or another who had contracted to stay with the company for seven years as tenants. They included young bloods dreaming of easy riches and troublesome ne'er-do-wells dispatched by their families to get rid of them or teach them a lesson. One member of the party described them as 'unruly gallants . . . sent to Virginia to escape ill destinies'. This voyage into the unknown was, he suggested, a chance for parents to 'disburden themselves of lascivious sons, masters of bad servants and wives of ill husbands'.[1] Later, the alleged misbehaviour of this gallant band would be used to justify the suspension of individual rights for the majority of colonial settlers.

On this first voyage, it was the behaviour of the leaders that most threatened the enterprise. They were domineering, fractious characters. There was Newport's number two, the aggressively self-confident Bartholomew Gosnold, whose own expedition five years earlier had done so much to turn English eyes towards America again. There was the former soldier Edward Maria Wingfield, who had mortgaged his estate to take a block of shares in the venture. He was the only major stockholder coming along to risk his life as well as his money. There was Captain John Martin, the son of London's leading goldsmith, who was obsessed with finding gold; and George Percy, the arrogant brother of the Duke of Northumberland. Most disruptive of all was the turbulent adventurer John Smith, a yeoman farmer's son who, according to his own account, would one day be saved from death by the Native American princess Pocahontas. Smith was a vividly persuasive writer who portrayed himself as the heroic saviour of the colony and perhaps he was. He would certainly go down in history as one of the most significant players in the American story.

Of the rest of the party, the histories of some gentlemen on board are known but nothing about the 'fry' – the scattering of servants and the twenty labourers brought to do the manual work. In the 1600s, there was no Robert Tressell to record their stories. All we know is that they were 'waged men' and that there would soon be complaints that there weren't nearly enough of them to build a colony.

The flotilla set sail from London in Christmas week 1606, watched wistfully, no doubt, by an eminent prisoner in the Tower, the inspiration of them all, Sir Walter Raleigh. The battlements of his prison must have afforded a fine view of the three ships as they upped anchor and made their way downstream. Of all the spectators who witnessed them depart, Raleigh was among the few who could have had an inkling of how momentous the event taking place might prove to be.

It was a meticulously planned expedition, equipped with mining and building tools, large stocks of arms and ammunition and food calculated to feed everyone for a year. Carried in Christopher Newport's cabin was a sealed list of instructions from the Royal Council for Virginia that were to be opened within twenty-four hours of landing. In five pages, the instructions covered everything from relations with the 'natural people of the country' to who should lead the hunt for gold. The document also contained the names of seven men picked to form an administrative council that would choose a president and rule the colony. Not even those named yet knew who they were.

Newport's problems began when, like Henry Challons, he chose the longer route to America via the Azores. A series of setbacks en route saw the party spend nineteen fractious weeks at sea, eating into their food supplies and into their tempers. Long claustrophobic days at sea could have fatal results. On both the first circumnavigation of the world by Ferdinand Magellan and the second by Sir Francis Drake, shipboard relations took such terrible turns that the commanders hanged good friends, on both occasions crying mutiny. Newport found himself similarly placed, as the collection of super-sized egos around him clashed. Finally, at a stopover in the Azores, he erected gallows, fully intending to execute John Smith.

Although Newport relented and postponed the execution, the

rancour and bickering continued up to the moment of landing. When the flotilla finally sighted mainland America, at what should have been a moment for rejoicing, a row broke out. It was just after dawn on a Sunday in April 1607. The ships had been blown by a storm to the mouth of Chesapeake Bay. When Newport opted to make for the invitingly sheltered waters of the bay, he was furiously criticised by Bartholomew Gosnold, who insisted it was a bad decision and tried to force Newport to head out again and steer northwards. Newport indignantly refused.

They entered the bay and anchored, sending a party of twenty men ashore to scout around. According to John Smith, the party was met with a shower of arrows from the natives. A volley of musket fire from the *Susan Constant* put the attackers to flight but it was a bad start.

What followed in the Chesapeake would be far grimmer than anything experienced by Sir John Popham's colonists. The latter would be lambasted for scurrying back home after a harsh winter and a small number of deaths. Disease, desertion and attack by Native Americans cut the London Company's numbers far more savagely over a similar period – and cut them again and again after reinforcements arrived. As a modern British historian puts it: 'The more the early history of Virginia is studied the more it must (and did) appear miraculous that the colony survived.'[2]

Sir Thomas Smythe and the other members of the Royal Council of Virginia had not expected the expedition to be anything less than hard going, as was evident from the secret instructions. They were the foundations for what Richard Hakluyt would later call 'a prison without walls'.[3] One instruction barred anyone from quitting the colony: 'Suffer no man to return but by passport.' Another banned all communication with the homeland. And one warned of 'disorder', directing that in laying out the settlement every street should be wide and straight so that with 'low field pieces you may command every street throughout'.

It is doubtful that all the instructions were read out to every one of the 120 men and boys in the party. If they had been read out, it is unlikely that many would have been especially bothered. Most of the young adventurers were too gripped by gold fever to worry about much else. They spent several weeks exploring, endowing every striking spur and landmark with an English name, usually of a British royal or a Protestant saint, like tomcats marking their territory. Finally, they identified what seemed the ideal location for a fort, on an easily defensible island on the James River, and so Fort James was established. It would later become known as Jamestown. The site proved anything but ideal.

The fragility of the project was swiftly brought home to them – or should have been. Having picked the site for their fort, the most capable leaders, Gosnold and Newport, left others to begin constructing it and took men off on a week-long search for gold. While they were gone, an attack by Algonquin tribesmen almost overwhelmed those left behind. The colonists were busy clearing the ground and were so oblivious to danger that firearms had not even been distributed. When the attack came, it was claimed that 200 or more tribesmen were involved. As the Algonquin charged out of concealment in the woods, several 'gentlemen' with guns just managed to hold them off but it took cannon and musketry from the *Susan Constant* to turn the attackers back. It was a close call: 'Most of the Council was hurt, a boy slain in the pinnace and thirteen or fourteen more hurt.'[4] For days, the future Jamestown was under virtual siege.

On–off war with the local inhabitants became par for the course. Little was known in England about the Algonquin people who had named the great inlet around which they lived, Chesapeake, 'Great Shellfish Bay'. The secret instructions called for 'great care' to be taken not to offend the 'natural people of the country' but also assumed the worst. The colonists were instructed that if they shot at 'the naturals', they should employ the best marksmen: 'If you miss, they will think your weapons not so terrible.' No doubt the still greater shock-and-awe capacity of a *Susan Constant* broadside was added comfort for the colonists.

One of the other forces undermining the colonists – disease – struck almost as quickly as the Algonquin. The riverside site chosen for Jamestown was on top of a mosquito-ridden swamp, used by some of the party as a latrine and drinking well. Within a month of the departure of Christopher Newport's flotilla for England in

July for supplies and new recruits, the colonists began to die in ones and twos. The suffering has been depicted with gothic gusto by later historians but the roll call of death recorded by one of the colonists is coldly eloquent:

> The sixth of August there died John Asbie of the bloody Flux. The ninth day died George Flower of the swelling. The tenth day died William Brewster, gentleman, of a wound given by the Savages. The fourteenth day Jerome Alikock, ancient, died of a wound, the same day Francis Midwinter, Edward Morris, Corporal, died suddenly. The fifteenth day there died Edward Browne and Stephen Galthrope. The sixteenth day there died Thomas Gower, gentleman. The seventeenth day there died Thomas Mounsley. The eighteenth day there died Robert Pennington and John Martine, gentlemen. The nineteenth day died Drew Piggase, gentleman. The two and twentieth day of August there died Captain Bartholomew Gosnold one of our Council.[5]

More than half would be dead by the time Christopher Newport returned in October. He had left 104 alive. Forty-eight were still living on his return. Most of the reinforcements he brought would soon die, too; so would the majority of the following year's intake because hunger followed on disease. Too little food had been sent, too much consumed in the early days and too much lost to rats that had migrated with the settlers to the New World.

There had been a belief that sufficient supplies could be traded from the Native Americans to tide the colony over till its own crops were harvested. This was a terrible mistake. In 1608, the rats devoured the first crop of English corn and the fledgling community was driven 'alternately to negotiate, trade, or raid for foodstuffs'. But none of that was sufficient and famine set in. The 'starving time' was approaching.

As conditions worsened, the leaders on the ruling council squabbled and connived and replaced one another. One was hanged for mutiny. In this sorry atmosphere, some young bloods vanished and somehow made their way back to England. But others were still hypnotised by gold and they remained. It was the same with the colony's backers in London. The company kept the money flowing on the premise that gold and other rich minerals, principally copper, would be found eventually.

They thought they had found gold on several occasions. A report by an Irishman, Francis Magill, obtained by the Spanish Council of State, claimed that rich samples of gold, silver and copper had been sent to England. Magill reckoned the authorities blocked all communications home not to prevent bad news getting out but quite the opposite – to prevent the outside world knowing that immense wealth was there for the taking.

One of the most embarrassing episodes in the search for gold occurred after a mineral expert from England noticed a glittering clay-like substance used by one of the local tribes to daub their bodies. The expert thought the glitter came from specks of gold. A party of colonists, led by an Algonquin guide, trekked into the hills to locate the mine from which the gold-bearing clay was extracted. They returned with a barrel load of the stuff. An excited Christopher Newport assumed that he was about to become a very rich man and hurried back to England in the *Susan Constant* with the barrel of clay and the minerals expert.

The impact of the news of the 'gold' on those of the settlers who were still alive was described succinctly by John Smith: 'There was now no talk, no hope, no work, but dig gold, wash gold, refine gold, load gold.'[6] Smith was a lone voice on the council urging other priorities.

In England, Newport and his expert presented the barrel and its glittering contents to Sir Walter Cope, the Chancellor, who was a member of the Royal Council of Virginia. An ecstatic Cope passed the news to Robert Cecil. 'There is but a barrel full of the earth,' he said, 'but there seems a kingdom full of the ore.' He counselled Cecil that even digging down a couple of spadefuls 'the ore appears on every part as a solid body, a treasure endlessly proportioned by God'.[7]

Almost immediately, Sir Walter had to swallow his words. 'This other day we sent you news of gold, and this day we cannot return you so much as copper. Our new discovery is more like to prove the land of Canaan than the land of Ophir.' Four tests by the most experienced men in London showed it was fool's gold. In the end, 'all turned to vapour'.

It is not known whether the rethink in London was prompted by this episode or by the increasing number of disaster stories coming from the colony – the deaths and desertions – or by the drain on funds, but rethink there was. The thrust of it was set out in the Jacobean equivalent of a position paper drawn up for Sir Thomas Smythe, treasurer of the London Company, in the early weeks of 1609, under the heading 'The Colonising of Virginia'. Running to nearly 12,000 words, the unsigned document was an assessment of Virginia by someone closely attuned to James I's prejudices and ambitions. It urged that gold should be forgotten and a trading colony developed. 'Trade . . . is the best mine and the greatest wealth which a prince can possess,' it argued. The anonymous author asserted that trade had transformed England into a wealthy power over the previous century and promised greater things yet if the natural wealth of America was harnessed properly.[8]

The King evidently listened. In May 1609, he issued a new charter that exchanged royal control of Virginia for commercial control by the merchants of the London branch of the Virginia Company. The squabbling colonial executive in Jamestown was abolished. In its place, the colony was to be brought under a governor with dictatorial powers. Above him in London was a new Royal Council and the London Company's court, or board of directors. Above them all was the guiding hand of the company's treasurer, Sir Thomas Smythe. And it would be his hand that planted the seeds of white slavery.

Few Englishmen could have appeared better qualified than Smythe to turn Virginia into a success. He is a strangely forgotten figure now but for centuries his commercial stature was recognised by historians. The great Victorian Alexander Brown said of him: 'He was . . . the head of every one (and a founder of most of them) of the English companies directly interested in foreign colonies and commerce, which have ever since been the chief sources of the wealth and power of Great Britain.'[9]

In Muscovy, the Tsar publicly acknowledged Smythe's eminence.

When the merchant arrived at the head of an English mission, he was allowed to remain hatted in the royal presence, a signal honour. In Agra, the Great Mogul had a portrait of Smythe hanging in his palace. In the Cape, men of the Khoi tribe reportedly chanted, 'Sir Thomas Smid! English ship!' whenever a ship flying the red-and-white striped flag of the East India Company anchored in Table Bay.

Smythe combined astute risk-taking with ruthlessness and the wooing of princes. In India, he learned that the Great Mogul and his son were heavy drinkers and regularly supplied the Mogul with the best burgundy. Smythe also sent the Mogul a full-sized replica of the Lord Mayor of London's coach – like that used to this day to lead the Lord Mayor's annual procession.

Smythe constantly cultivated the Court of St James. After the King developed an interest in exotic mammals and birds, Smythe had his captains return with parakeets and monkeys, big cats and bears for the royal cages. When James expressed interest in the flying squirrels rumoured to exist in America, the order went out to Smythe's ships to bring some back.

King James was also fascinated by ships, so in 1610 Smythe invited him to launch one of his Indiamen, a 1,200-ton monster called the *Trades Increase*. The event gives a glimpse of the style of the man and his relationship with the King. On the day of the launch, James, together with the Queen, the heir to the throne, Prince Henry and other members of the royal family, were rowed in the royal barge to Deptford, where the ship had been built. Other members of the court followed in what must have been, in the manner of the times, a splendid cavalcade stretching downstream from the Palace of Whitehall to Deptford. After the launch came a 'bountiful banquet', with all kinds of 'delicates in fine china dishes' and then a royal presentation. 'The King,' it was reported, 'graced Sir Thomas Smythe, the Governor, with a very faire chain of gold . . . with a jewel wherein was the King's picture hanging at it; and the King put it about his neck with his own hands.'[10]

A few months before the *Trades Increase* was launched, Smythe took over the direction of Virginia. An immediate and crucial decision was the appointment of the right calibre of men to take control of the colony on the ground. Whoever was picked as governor would have autocratic powers and an almost monarchical status. The choice eventually fell on 34-year-old Thomas West, Baron De La Warr. He and Thomas Smythe were old comrades. They had fought alongside each other in the raid on Cadiz, where both had been commended for bravery, and both had later been caught up in the Essex rebellion but survived. They had much in common and no doubt were of a mind on how to revive fortunes in America.

Smythe appointed three seasoned fighting men to serve under De La Warr: Sir George Somers, who had fought under Walter Raleigh, was made admiral of a new fleet to relieve the colony; Sir Thomas Gates, a veteran of war in the Netherlands, was appointed Deputy Governor; and Sir Thomas Dale, another veteran of the Dutch wars, was made High Marshal.

The next requirement was to reinstall a belief in the Virginia project in the public mind and raise money. The damage done by the stories of death and disaster filtering across the Atlantic can be gauged from a broadside published in rebuttal a few years later. It attacked the 'malicious and looser sort . . . who wet their tongues with scornful taunts' about the colony and asserted: 'There is no common speech nor public name of anything this day (except it be the name of God) which is more wildly depraved, traduced and derided by such unhallowed lips than the name of Virginia.'[11]

The company launched a vigorous promotional campaign. Clerics were commissioned to urge congregations to 'go forward to assist this noble action'. All the merchants connected with the company went to work on their friends. The little printing shops huddled around St Paul's churchyard were paid to pump out broadsides and circulars lauding Virginia as 'an earthly paradise', a 'delicious land' with 'gentle natives', and 'one of the goodliest countries under the sun'.

Smythe played on the patriotism and self-interest of Jacobean England. A broadside dedicated to him read:

> The eyes of all Europe are looking upon our endeavours to
> spread the Gospel among the heathen people of Virginia, to

plant an English nation there, and to settle a trade in those parts, which may be peculiar to our nation, to the end we may thereby be secured from being eaten out of all profits of trade by our more industrious neighbours [the Dutch].[12]

It became a priority to attract skilled workers rather than another batch of gentlemen adventurers. Every person that 'hath a trade or a body able to endure days labour' was promised 100 acres of land at the end of seven years' service. Smythe, who clearly had no problems mixing with the low as well as the high, had a letter circulated that invited 'workmen of whatever craft . . . who have any occupation' to meet him at his house in Philpot Street. There, in his Cheapside mansion, the richest man in England was waiting to offer sawyers, tile makers, soap-ash men, pearl drillers, ploughmen, carpenters, blacksmiths and sturgeon dressers and all the other craftsmen and tradesmen, housing, food, clothes, a cash payment and land if they would sign up for the New World.

The net was cast wide. Glass makers and wine makers were recruited from France and potash workers from Poland. Ministers of religion were on the recruitment list, too. The company issued instructions for Native American children to be kidnapped so they could be made into good Protestants.

Whether Smythe followed Popham's lead by recruiting from the gaols at this early stage is not known but efforts were made to persuade the City of London to subsidise the relocation of the surplus poor. Two of those promoting the Virginia Company, Robert Johnson and Robert Gray, put the case for relocation, using the arguments about an England drowning in vagrants. Johnson warned that unless the 'swarms of idle persons' were found foreign employment, they would 'infect one another with vice and villainy worse than the plague itself'.[13]

The idea of an American solution to the problem of the poor appealed to the burghers of London. The very mention of the ragged masses who packed the tenements of Whitefriars, Aldgate and Southwark prompted shivers of distaste and apprehension. When the Virginia Company offered to transport one poor 'inmate' from the metropolis for every new share in the company purchased by the burghers, the Lord Mayor responded encouragingly. However, little appears to have come of this proposal. Nothing more would be heard of the idea of shipping out the adult poor for more than a decade.

When not interviewing colonists, Sir Thomas trod the cobblestones between the halls of the great livery companies. He banked on their financial support, making an offer of either a cash dividend from the gold or other valuable commodities the Company was bound to amass, or a dividend in land. Either way, it would be payable after seven years. An investor buying a single £12 10s share could look forward eventually to a return of at least 500 acres.

It was not an easy task to persuade his fellow merchants. The timing was appalling, for another venture was just being launched. This was the Ulster plantation and the King let it be known that he regarded support for this Irish project as a patriotic obligation. Smythe, therefore, had an uphill struggle. His own livery company, the Skinners, bought only £62 of shares. The Fishmongers' offer was so paltry it 'was scornfully refused'.[14] All told, the livery companies invested only a quarter of what he expected. In the end, more than thirty companies and 650 individuals took Virginia's £12 10s shares but that brought in only £18,000. Smythe had hoped for £30,000.

Despite the problems, a fleet was assembled to relieve and re-supply Jamestown. It represented one of the largest colonial expeditions so far mounted by a European power. Nine ships with 600 settlers, including a scattering of women, set sail from Plymouth in the early summer of 1609. It was led by Sir Thomas Gates and Sir George Somers and would be known as the 'Third Supply'. The new Governor of the colony, Lord De La Warr, was to follow on later.

Luck was not with them. Off the Azores, a hurricane scattered the fleet. The flagship *Sea Venture*, carrying Somers, Gates and another 150 passengers, was blown hundreds of miles off course. The storm was graphically described by one of the passengers, William Strachey. 'The sea swelled above the clouds,' said Strachey, 'and gave battle unto Heaven.' A huge wave enveloped the vessel 'like a garment or a vast cloud'. From almost every joint, the ship 'spewed out her okam' so that water rose swiftly in the hold. Terror 'turned the blood' of even the bravest mariners.[15]

For three days, Somers was constantly at the helm, with everyone else bailing and plugging and throwing stores overboard to keep the *Sea Venture* afloat. The battered vessel eventually found herself in the Bermuda archipelago, dreaded by mariners as 'the isles of devils'. Around these reefs, they said, you could hear the howling of the demons who lurked awaiting the sight of a sail to whip up a maelstrom. It was assumed that none caught in their seas could possibly survive. Against all odds, the *Sea Venture* stayed intact until Somers was able to beach her on one of the islands. She ended up in what we know today as Discovery Bay, Bermuda.

The island was uninhabited. But a previous shipwreck had marooned a number of hogs there. The pigs had multiplied enormously and were easy to hunt down. A diet of pork, grapefruit and wild berries kept the survivors going. But they did not confine themselves just to catching food to survive. Somers and Gates were determined men. Amongst the marooned were skilled carpenters and a shipwright. They were put to work to design and build a ship to take the party on their interrupted journey. Using oak salvaged from the *Sea Venture* and cedar wood from the island, the survivors built not one but two pinnaces to carry them on to Virginia. The *Patience* and the *Deliverance* set sail forty-two weeks after the *Sea Venture* was wrecked. Their voyage took ten weeks.

When the news of their epic story reached London, it caused a sensation. During the time on the island, Gates and Somers had imposed a ruthless regime, executing a group of men who questioned their authority. That was ignored; instead, England celebrated what was seen as something truly miraculous. William Shakespeare immortalised the saga, drawing on it for his last great play, *The Tempest*. In Act I, Shakespeare has his magician king Prospero order up a storm so terrible that 'not a soul but felt the fever of the mad', only to relent after the intercession of his daughter Miranda and tell her:

Wipe thou thine eyes, have comfort
The direful spectacle of the wreck, which touch'd
The very virtue of compassion in thee,
I have with such provision in mine art
So safely ordered, that there is no soul –
No, not so much perdition as an hair
Betid to any creature in the vessel
Which thou heard'st cry, which thou saw'st sink.

No doubt some of the leading lights in the Virginia Company watched the first performance of *The Tempest* on Hallowmass night in November 1611, in the presence of the King. Shakespeare's patron, the Earl of Southampton, was a founder member of the Virginia Company and Shakespeare himself was an investor. Were the Earl and his friend Sir Thomas Smythe among the courtiers applauding on that first night in the Palace of Whitehall?

In Jamestown, there was nothing to applaud. When Sir Thomas Gates and Sir George Somers and the other survivors of the *Sea Venture* finally made the Jamestown settlement in 1610, they found that the colony marketed as an earthly paradise by Sir Thomas Smythe was more akin to hell. The ships of the Third Supply were supposed to have brought relief, with adequate supplies and reinforcements. Six of the vessels, though battered by the hurricane, did make port at Jamestown. But they had few supplies and didn't stay long. Four left inside a month, taking with them the only man who had shown real ability as a leader, John Smith.

As food supplies again ran out in Jamestown, the 'starving time' had set in. Just how bad it was will always be unclear. A rush of self-serving and contradictory reports muddied the waters then and for ever. What is certain is that when the survivors of the *Sea Venture* finally arrived at Jamestown from Bermuda, they found a ghost town. Behind the palisades there were broken-down dwellings, a ruined church and filthy, rubble-strewn streets. Sir Thomas Gates, the senior commander, decided that it was pointless to start again and decided to abandon the settlement, taking the remaining colonists, numbering between forty and sixty. Gates was preparing to make for Newfoundland when De La Warr appeared with a relief fleet and turned him back.

The new Governor no doubt heard many explanations as to what had happened to the settlers. One eyewitness account was from George Percy, the last president of the colonial council, who later wrote up his recollections. He had seen near-constant fighting with the Native Americans, who made it impossible to stray much beyond the palisades, and then mass starvation set in, the prelude to a grim descent into cannibalism. After supplies of fish and corn ran out, 'horses and other beasts' were eaten by colonists. Next they caught 'vermin . . . dogs and cats and rats and mice', then they ate 'boots, shoes or any other leather'. There were frantic forays into the woods, which netted a few snakes and some 'wild and unknown roots'. Finally, they dug up corpses. 'Famine began to look so ghastly and pale in every face that nothing was spared to preserve life,' Percy recalled. One man murdered his wife and 'chopped her in pieces and salted her for his food'.[16] The man was discovered with her partly eaten corpse and, on Percy's orders, hung up by his thumbs till he confessed and then was executed.

The colonists themselves were blamed for their troubles and blamed each other. Stories of theft, murder and mutiny emerged and of astonishing lassitude and torpor. Too many of the settlers were 'drunken, gluttonous loiterers'. Too many were 'of the vulgar and viler sort who went thither for ease and idleness, profit and pleasure and found contrawise . . . that they must labour or not eat'.[17]

Before the Governor could do anything much to put the colony to rights, he himself apparently became a victim of Jamestown. Six months after landing, he reportedly collapsed. What was wrong with him was never satisfactorily explained. The suspicion lingers that it might have been as much the daunting task he faced in rescuing the colony rather than the bite of an insect that disabled him. Whatever the truth, he ordered a ship to take him away from the Chesapeake to the healthier climes of the Caribbean. From there, he eventually went back to England. In an age when people firmly believed in auguries, this was not a good one.

His Lordship was never officially replaced as Governor. In his place, Sir Thomas Dale, followed by Sir Thomas Gates, then Sir Thomas Dale again, served as acting Governor. They would be credited with rescuing the colony and setting it on the path to prosperity. The most indelible mark was left by Dale. The High Marshal has been described as 'a sturdy watch-dog tearing and rending with a cruelty equal to his zeal every offender against the common-weal'.[18] He began to acquire that reputation from day one. On arrival in Jamestown after Lord De La Warr's departure, he announced a new legal code for the colony, of which the Taliban would have approved.

The 'Laws Divine, Moral, and Martial' were most probably drawn up by De La Warr, Gates and Dale in consultation with Smythe. They would become known as Dale's Code because it was he who implemented them.[19] They were based on a code designed by a Dutch prince to keep his troops in order and required unquestioning obedience in everything:

> No manner of Person whatsoever, contrary to the word of God . . . shall detract, slander, calumniate, murmur, mutiny, resist, disobey, or neglect the commandments, either of the Lord Governor, and Captain General, the Lieutenant General, the Martial, the Council, or any authorised Captain, Commander or public Officer upon pain for the first time so offending to be whipped thirty times, and upon his knees to acknowledge his offence, asking forgiveness upon the Sabbath day in the assembly of the congregation, and for the second time so offending to be condemned to the Galley for three years: and for the third time so offending to be punished with death.

Even 'intemperate railings' against authority was a capital offence carrying the same punishment as murder or sodomy.

Along with murder, sodomy, rape and lese-majesty, the code made blasphemy and irregular attendance at church capital crimes. Everyone had to attend church twice a day. On Sundays, a bell sounded half an hour before the first service. The gates of Jamestown were barred and guarded while search parties went into every building looking for anyone not in church. Those caught missing church three times faced execution. Special moral guards – four per preacher – were to be appointed to spy and report on what went on at other times. Englishmen had probably experienced nothing like it since their ancestors were made serfs by their Norman conquerors five and a half centuries before.

Trading with the Native Americans was a capital crime, as was leaving the colony without permission or selling anything to visiting sailors. Pilfering a few potatoes could get you executed and so, in theory, could the plucking of a rose.

> What man or woman shall rob any garden, public or private,
> being set to weed the same, or wilfully pluck up therein any
> root, herb, or flower . . . or gather up the grapes, or steal any
> ears of the corn growing . . . shall be punished with death.

Almost everything was to be communal. Meals were all to be eaten in refectories. There was no private ownership. All work was for the company. Overseers stood over you to ensure that no one was 'negligent and idle'. Tools and implements, even your own, had to be handed in when a drum or whistle sounded to end the day. The one mitigating factor was that the official working day was considerably shorter than in England, perhaps because of the climate or to allow for military duties.

Not everyone had to labour. 'The extraordinary men, divines, governors, ministers of state and justice, knights, gentlemen, physicians and such as be men of worth for special purposes' were not required to work. As ever, England's class system automatically transferred across the seas.

Dale enforced the laws to the hilt. Though a deeply pious man, he must have struck fear into friends as well as foes. On one occasion, he lost his temper with Christopher Newport, grasped the veteran captain by his beard and shouted that he would execute him. Newport's mistake, it seems, was to have sounded too wildly positive about Virginia. George Percy was a witness to the exemplary punishments Dale handed out on the capture of half a dozen colonists who deserted after being ordered to help build a new fort. The fugitives had headed south in an attempt to reach Spanish-held territory 1,000 kilometres away in Florida. The High Marshal employed Native Americans to track down the fugitives and bring them back. Percy reported: 'Some he appointed to be hanged, some burned, some to be broken upon wheels, others to be staked and some to be shot to death.'

Thieves faced a more protracted death. They were bound to trees and left there to suffer the attentions of a roaming bear or to starve. Similar treatment was meted out to anyone infringing the religious requirements. One blasphemer had a red-hot bodkin plunged through his tongue before he was chained to a tree and left to his fate. Another miscreant was similarly mutilated and then forced through a 'guard of forty men' to be butted by each one and then kicked out of the fort, no doubt to perish.

Dale was less than a year into his term in the colony when he took the momentous step of calling on the Crown to provide convict labour. In desperate need of settlers, Virginia's hard man addressed the matter in his typically blunt way. In a personal letter to King James in August 1611, he vowed that if he could be furnished with 2,000 men by the following April he would overcome the Algonquin tribes and completely settle the colony within two years. Recognising the impossibility of raising so many men so quickly, he urged the King to 'banish hither all offenders condemned to die out of common gaols' for the next three years. 'It would be a ready way to furnish us with men and not always with the worst of men, either for birth, for spirit, or body.' Dale added that this was how 'the Spaniards do people the Indies'.[20]

Francis Bacon, the future Attorney General, led the opposition to the 'scum' of England being allowed to infect the colony. The views of this body of opinion had previously been summed up in one of the broadsides issued in 1609 during the company's promotional campaign: 'It would be a scandal and a peril to accept as settlers, idle and wicked persons . . . the weeds of their native country,' the broadside warned. They 'would act as poison in the body of a tender, feeble, and yet unformed colony'. What were needed were men who could show 'a character for religion and considerate conduct in his relations with his neighbours'.[21]

Others, not least in the Privy Council, were insistent that some way had to be found to dispose of convicts and the country's 'swarms' of vagrants. They argued that famine and pestilence would only disappear from England if all the unwanted could be shipped abroad.

King James certainly took this line. He was a timid man, who wore specially padded doublets to protect against the assassin's knife. After succeeding to the throne in March 1603, his first appearance in London coincided with a devastating outbreak of plague in the capital. As always, it struck first and worst in the Liberties and other slums where vagrants concentrated. The new monarch arrived to find the merchants and gentry of London escaping en masse to the countryside in search of safety. Their King immediately followed suit and fled the capital. He took with him the lesson that the poor had to go.

Sir Thomas Smythe was not one to argue with the King. A broadside dedicated to Smythe carried exactly the message James wanted to hear. It warned that unless somewhere far away was found for the swarms of the 'lewd and idle', more prisons would have to be built. One recurring proposal to rid the land of convicts was to exchange them with Christian galley slaves held by the Turkish or North African corsairs. Four convicts for one galley slave was the suggested exchange rate. Another proposal was to seek a remote unpopulated location somewhere far away where England's felons could be dumped, provided with seeds to plant and left there to sink or swim. Sir Thomas Smythe led the search for a site and initially considered South Africa rather than America.

A letter written to Smythe in 1609 by one of his agents, Thomas Aldworth, put the case for a site at the Cape of Good Hope. Aldworth had anchored in Table Bay while he was en route for India and liked what he saw. An earlier European visitor had carved a huge cross on the steep mountain overlooking the bay. The vegetation grew lushly on the narrow peninsula and the natives seemed friendly. Aldworth reported enthusiastically to Smythe that the Cape had 'courteous and tractable folk' and was just the place to send convicts. The area could take 'one hundred English convicts a year', he estimated.[22]

Always cautious, Smythe decided to send just ten convicts to see how they fared. How and where he obtained them, we do not know. However, they included a highwayman called James Crosse, whose name we know because the company listed him as the men's leader in the Cape. Crosse and the other nine were duly landed at Table Bay and presented with what Smythe's men deemed sufficient for their survival: 'half a peck of turnip seeds', a few other seeds, 'and a spade to dig the ground'.[23] Unsurprisingly, the experiment was a failure.

Crosse and the other convicts had been left with no arms with which to protect themselves and they were terrified when they saw tribesmen from the local Khoi people in the distance. Maybe they had heard how Portuguese traders had once been massacred here after falling out with the Khoi. The convicts hid and managed to evade the natives. Somehow, they reached a rocky island just off Table Bay. It was a refuge that would one day be notorious as Robben Island, the prison where Nelson Mandela and so many other fighters against apartheid were held three centuries later. Here, the ten Englishmen eked out a miserable existence, probably living on shellfish or the seals that basked on the shore. Eventually, a visiting ship took pity on them and took them off. Three of the convicts got back to England. Within hours they had become embroiled in a purse snatch and were arrested. They were later executed.

Smythe tried once more. He ordered another group of convicts to be sent to the Cape aboard one of his India-bound ships. When it reached Table Bay and anchored, the convicts begged the captain to hang them rather than leave them in Africa. He couldn't oblige. Following orders, they too were dumped on the shore. However, Lady Luck was with this group. Another passing ship took them off within a couple of days. Nearly two centuries would pass before England would again send convicts to the Cape.

The argument stirred up in 1611 by Sir Thomas Dale's call for convicts simmered for the next four years. Meanwhile, out of sight over in America, far bloodier contests were taking place as the Virginia Company's twin martinets, Sir Thomas Dale and Sir Thomas Gates, sent settlers out to build forts beyond the Chesapeake and deeper into Algonquin territory.

This was the period of Pocahontas. The fairy-tale story of the bewitching Native American princess who saved English colonists from massacre, was kidnapped by one of them and fell in love with another gripped contemporaries just as it gripped later generations. It also lent a welcome romance to the colonising process. The following, typically lyrical, description of Virginia in these years is from Mary Johnston's *Pioneers of the Old South*:

> As the Company sent over more colonists, there began to show, up and down the James though at far intervals, cabins and clearings made by white men, set about with a stockade, and at the river edge a rude landing and a fastened boat. The restless search for mines of gold and silver now slackened. Instead eyes turned for wealth to the kingdom of the plant and tree, and to fur trade and fisheries.[24]

The reality was bloody guerrilla warfare between white and red and between white and white. The Algonquin retreated before the superior firepower of the war parties dispatched by Dale and Gates. French settlements were also harried by the English. In 1613, Gates sent a 100-ton vessel called the *Treasurer* to the north to remove the French from Mount Desert Island. Its commander was Sam Argall, the man who had kidnapped Pocahontas. At Mount Desert Island, Captain Argall is said to have fired 'the first shots in the 150 years' war in America between France and England'.[25] He looted and burnt the settlement and set half the surviving Frenchmen adrift in an open boat. The rest were taken to Jamestown, where their reception must have made them long to be adrift with their comrades. 'As soon as Dale saw them he spoke of nothing but ropes and of gallows and of hanging "every one of them".'

For the English behind the palisades along the James River, life continued to be grim. An unflattering but not necessarily wholly inaccurate picture of life in Jamestown was drawn by a Spaniard who was held prisoner there between 1613 and 1614. Don Diego de Molina had been captured after his ship was driven into Chesapeake Bay. He wrote a letter that was sewn into the sole of a shoe and somehow smuggled out to Madrid. Referring to the Virginia Company, he wrote:

> The merchants have not been able to maintain this colony with as much liberality as was needed and so the people have suffered much want, living on miserable rations of oats or maize and dressing poorly . . . There is not a year when half do not die. Last year there were seven hundred people and not three hundred and fifty remain, because little food and much labour on public works kills them and, more than all, the discontent in which they live seeing themselves treated as slaves with cruelty.[26]

Recruitment and investment were not helped by a drip, drip, drip of complaints filtering back to England. Those who had pledged to invest now began to renege on their commitments. Gondomar, the Spanish minister, wrote to Philip III: 'Here in London this colony Virginia is in such bad repute that not a human being can be found to go there in any way whatever.'[27]

What made the days still darker for the colony was the emergence of the Bermudas as a rival. In 1612, a royal charter authorised a settlement and a party of sixty settlers landed. In honour of Sir George Somers, who had been so memorably marooned on the archipelago, it was renamed the Somers Islands and, like Virginia, promoted as a paradise but with no Native Americans to combat and a healthy climate, to boot. The numbers of settlers tumbled in Virginia but soared in Bermuda. By 1614, there were 600 colonists there, nearly twice as many as in the senior colony. The discovery of a gigantic piece of amber on a beach seemed to confirm that the islands rather than the mainland were the future.

A rumour circulated that the company was to close down all operations in Virginia and relocate everyone to the new colony. Sir Thomas Dale was so concerned that he wrote a personal appeal to Sir Thomas Smythe. Typically it pulled no punches:

> Let me tell you all at home this one thing, and I pray remember it; if you give over this country and loose [sic]

it, you, with your wisdoms, will leap such a gudgeon as our
state hath not done the like since they lost the Kingdom of
France . . . I protest to you, by the faith of an honest man,
the more I range the country the more I admire it. I have
seen the best countries in Europe; I protest to you, before
the Living God, put them all together, this country will be
equivalent unto them if it be inhabited with good people.[28]

Dale need not have worried. Smythe found the money to keep the
Virginia Company going. He staved off one crisis by persuading
the King to give him the go-ahead to do what the great Italian
merchants in Venice and Genoa did and raise money by 'lotto', a
lottery. It was the first lottery in fifty years and only the second in
England's history, netting a staggering £8,000, the equivalent of
£1 million today. But even that was not enough. In another crisis,
Smythe asked investors to forgo their first dividend and accept the
promise of a tract of forest somewhere in Virginia. Somehow, he
persuaded them. Meanwhile, he was constantly going to court to
pursue those who had reneged on investment pledges.

It was now seven years since the first batch of settlers had been
brought by Christopher Newport, which meant that survivors
were no longer tied to the company. They could go home or stay
on as tenants. Of those who stayed, a favoured group, whom Dale
referred to as farmers, were allotted a three-acre 'garden' apiece,
or twelve acres if they had families, and allowed to cultivate it as
they pleased. But the company wanted a rental of two and a half
barrels of corn an acre, plus thirty days' 'public service' every year.
The conditions imposed on a second larger group of stayers, the
'labourers', were even more onerous. In any year, they would have
to work for the company for eleven months, leaving just one month
in which to raise corn to feed themselves.

This was a far cry from what had been promised seven years
earlier but it was a start. Private ownership of land would begin
to spread rapidly. Ralph Hamor, Dale's secretary, caught the
importance of the change in a memorable comment once taught
to every American child:

When our people were fed out of the common store and laboured jointly together, glad was he who could slip from his labour, or slumber over his task he cared not how, nay, the most honest among them would hardly take so much true pains in a week, as now they themselves will do in a day.[29]

This dawning of private enterprise coincided with the discovery that a tobacco agreeable to the English palate could be cultivated in Virginia. In 1613, the planter John Rolfe, who later married Pocahontas, produced the colony's first commercial crop of 'tall tobacco' and it was shipped to England the following year. Gold hadn't been discovered but here was a cash crop that would prove as valuable as the mines that the settlers had dreamt of. But cultivating it would need masses of labour and would be so arduous that few could bear it for long – the manpower wastage would be enormous.

In London, the variety produced by Rolfe was an instant success. Very quickly other planters followed Rolfe's lead. But Virginia's grim reputation kept immigration low. A new initiative was needed. In 1614, the Virginia Company lawyer Sir Richard Martin outraged MPs when he was allowed to address the House of Commons on behalf of the company and roared at them to stop wasting time on trivial matters and concentrate on saving Virginia. Martin demanded they set up a committee to consider how to populate the colony. England had lost one chance of an American empire when Henry VII turned down a request for backing from Christopher Columbus. But when Martin urged them not to lose this second chance, he was forced to come back the next day to apologise.

Early in 1615, the Privy Council finally reached a decision on convicts. Francis Bacon's faction lost: convicts would be transported to the New World. In presenting the decision, the Privy Council trod carefully. It is difficult to picture the rich, hard-nosed advisers of James I being overly concerned about the rights of vagabonds and felons. But this was a period that was especially suspicious of arbitrary acts by the Crown against individuals. There was no law enabling the Crown to exile anyone, including the basest convict, into forced labour. According to legal scholars, the Magna Carta itself protected even them. The Privy Councillors therefore dressed up what was to befall the convicts and presented the decree authorising their transportation as an act of royal mercy. The convicts were to be reprieved from death in exchange for accepting transportation.

The Privy Council's decree read:

> Whereas it hath pleased his Majesty out of his singular clemency and mercy to take into his princely consideration the wretched estate of divers of his subjects who by the laws of the realm, are adjudged to die for sundry offences, though heinous of themselves not of the highest nature, so His Majesty, both out of his gracious clemency, as also for divers weighty considerations, could wish they might be rather corrected than destroyed and that in their punishments some of them might live and yield a profitable service to the commonwealth in parts abroad where it shall be found fit to employ them.[30]

To the extent that it is better to live than die, it was an act of mercy in some degree to send convicts to the colony rather than to the scaffold. Perhaps the 'scum' would prove useful members of the colonial community and one day even earn their freedom in Virginia. But that was not the underlying intention. Four years later, in 1619, the Privy Council made the intention clear. It ordered that convicts sent to 'parts abroad' were to be 'constrained to toil in such heavy and painful works as such servitude shall be a greater terror than death itself'.

To some, transportation did appear from the start to be worse than death. The Spanish Ambassador to London reported home that two prisoners destined for transportation to Virginia had – like the convicts left on an African beach – pleaded to be executed instead.

Immediately after the Privy Council's decision, seventeen convicts were assigned to Smythe, followed by a batch of five, then a group of six. It seems that Smythe was allowed to cherry-pick from the condemned and select those he thought would be most useful. One man was saved from death on account of being 'of the mystery of the carpenters'.

King James had rather different ideas about selection. In the early years of his reign, he built a palace near the village of Newmarket in East Anglia, seventy miles away from London, which he hated. It was the King's favourite bolt-hole. 'Away to Newmarket, away to Newmarket!' was the signal for extravaganzas of drunken feasting, masques, jousting and horse racing. At Newmarket, James paraded his homosexuality for all to see, as he indulged and openly fondled Robert Carr, George Villiers and other male lovers. Anyone disrupting the prolonged roistering invited an outburst of royal fury.

Sometime in 1617, rowdy youths began to make nuisances of themselves at the court. Various explanations have been offered as to the nature of these youths, among them being that they were young jobless men who made a practice of trailing round after the royal retinue, or that they were simply hoodlums or felons, or that they were the bastard sons of royal courtiers. Whatever they were, their crime is not recorded. Perhaps they specialised in baiting some of the ruffed and perfumed young men at court who hoped to catch the King's fancy? Whatever it was, something prompted James to explode and he had the youths arrested.

In January 1618, Sir Thomas Smythe received a letter from the King saying that 100 youths were being dispatched to him to dispose of in Virginia 'at the first opportunity'. They were described variously as 'dissolute' or convicts, though there is no record of their having been tried in any court of law. The King instructed Smythe to 'Take sure order that they be set to work' in the colony.

There were, however, no Virginia Company ships available in London or Bristol or Plymouth. And for all Thomas Smythe's worldwide trading interests, he had no vessels to spare either, or pretended he did not. But the King would brook no excuses. Robert Cecil's successor as Secretary of State, Sir George Calvert, summoned Smythe to Whitehall and banged the table. 'The King's desire admitted no delay,' he was told. Reluctantly, Smythe and his fellow merchants in the Virginia Company put aside £1,000 to pay for the miscreants to be held in a London gaol until transportation was arranged. Smythe feared that once they were at sea, the prisoners would break free and take over the ship. As we shall see, when convicts became a major business, with up to 200 shipped at a time, that is what happened again and again.

It was decided that the prisoners should be split into smaller, easily managed groups. At least four vessels were needed. While the company vacillated over their unwanted prisoners, three of the wealthiest stockholders saw an opportunity. The Earl of Warwick, Sir Edwin Sandys and John Ferrar had all acquired land in Virginia's sister colony, the Somers Islands. It appears they took advantage of the Newmarket affair to secure forced labour to work their plantations. The Virginia Company's minutes record the three applying for some of 'the dissolute [to be] sent to the Somers Islands . . . to be servants upon their land'. Their fellow stockholders agreed.

We do not know if all hundred convicts finally went but, given King James's determination to make an example of them, we can assume that they were dispatched to one or other colony, or perhaps to both, probably never to return. The door was opening for the transportation of Britain's unwanted to America. The first to come flooding through were street children.

CHAPTER FOUR

CHILDREN OF THE CITY

A visitor to London in the early 1600s looking south from St Paul's Cathedral would have seen a Renaissance palace on the near bank of the river Thames. It stood where Blackfriars Bridge is today, deep red in colour, bordered on the west by the rambling courts of the Temple and on the east by the Fleet ditch gushing the filth of London into the Thames. The onlooker would have noted the three vast courtyards, the sweep of long galleries enclosing them, the terrace facing over the river and the guards on the huge heavy gates.

This was Bridewell, the palace built nearly a century earlier by the young Henry VIII to house visiting rulers and ambassadors and sometimes the King himself. It was here at Bridewell that the Papal envoy stayed during the futile negotiations over Henry's divorce from Catherine of Aragon and here that Catherine learned that she was being replaced as Queen by Anne Boleyn. It was here that the greatest foreign monarch ever entertained in England, the Holy Roman Emperor Charles V, was invited to lodge.

But by 1618 it was utterly changed. The boy king Edward VI had donated Bridewell to the City of London as a hospital and it subsequently transmogrified into an infamous house of correction. 'Strumpets, night-walkers, pick-pockets, vagrant and idle persons' were brought here for exemplary punishment – a whipping and then a year or two in the prison workshop picking oakum or beating hemp.[1] Innocent and guilty, hundreds at a time were packed in to undergo the Jacobean equivalent of tough love.

Bridewell was the chosen holding pen when Thomas Smythe, his assistant Sir Edwin Sandys and the Lord Mayor of London agreed a plan to sweep London clear of street children and ship them to the colonies in the New World. It would later hold many others also destined for the colonies.

The round-ups began on 8 August when constables seized three boys and a girl and lodged them in Bridewell. They were told that they had been judged 'vagrants' and by court order were being 'held for Virginia'. Over the next six months, another 108 boys and twenty-eight girls, aged between eight and sixteen years old, were brought in to join them.[2] The following February, they were lined up in Bridewell so that representatives from the Virginia Company could take their pick and the shipments began. The first 100 children arrived in America around Easter time 1619, four months before the arrival of a shipment of black slaves that has attracted more attention than any other and which will be examined at the end of this chapter. Another 100 followed, then another shipment and another. Most of the children would die before they reached adulthood.

The idea of transporting vagrant children had been floated in the early days of Virginia when the company first came under pressure to provide a faraway dump for the unwanted. Hugh Lee, the English Consul in Lisbon, mooted it in 1609 in a letter to Thomas Wilson, secretary to the King's chief minister, Robert Cecil. Lee's reports usually concerned the suspected plotting of English Catholic refugees in Portugal. Child labour was a novel theme. Lee had been watching a fleet of carracks manoeuvre into the Tagus estuary one morning when he realised that they were packed with children. He started asking questions and discovered that boys and girls as young as ten were being transported to the East Indies to work on the plantations. The theory was that young bodies would acclimatise better than adult bodies to the searing heat of the tropics.

Considerable numbers were being shipped out: 1,500 on board the five carracks that had attracted Lee's attention. In his report to London, the Consul suggested that England take a leaf from the Portuguese book and try child labour in its own colony: 'It were no evil course to be followed in England for the planting of inhabitants in Virginia,' he told Wilson.[3]

In the event, the Portuguese stopped shipping children to the east because their outposts there fell to the all-conquering fleets of the Dutch. However, the idea was not forgotten in England. After 1615, when the door was opened for convict transportation, English eyes turned to street children and the possibility of getting rid of them, especially from overcrowded, plague-ridden, crime-ridden, booming London.

Street children were not, of course, unique to London in the sixteenth and seventeenth centuries. Venetians bewailed the 'enormous increase in the number of child rogues and beggars who wander around the squares of San Marco and the Rialto', while the Swedes were so concerned about child thieves that several hundred children were interned in Stockholm during Queen Christina's coronation. Frenchmen complained in Lyons about the noise of 'the great number of children crying and hooting with hunger day and night through the town'. They were 'making a marvellous racket' in the churches.[4]

Londoners would have heard the same sounds and seen similar scenes and on a larger scale. The city was teeming with homeless urchins and teenage runaways. A petition asking for action over them referred to the 'great number of vagrant boys and girls [who] lie in the streets . . . having no place of abode nor friends to relieve them'.[5] There is no knowing exactly how many street children there were. But in a city of 200,000 they must have totalled many, many thousands. Most of them would have survived hand to mouth through petty theft, begging and selling their bodies. One imagines them ragged, half-starved and impudent, lineal ancestors of the cockney urchins Dickens depicted two centuries later.

In 1617, councillors from 100 parishes were called to a meeting in St Paul's to discuss street children. There might have been a sense of urgency because the Privy Council had recently berated metropolitan officials over the 'infinite multitude of rogues and vagrants' at large in the Liberties. The council had warned that the King was thinking of appointing a man of his own, a provost marshal, to deal with the problem. The St Paul's meeting agreed to assess each parish with the aim of ridding the city of as many children as possible. Eyes turned to Virginia as the solution.

Under the Poor Law, a parish could get shot of some of its poor children by forcibly apprenticing them in another parish a few miles away, though it is thought only small numbers were ever involved. What was now proposed was very different: a mass street round-up ending on the other side of the world.

The Virginia Company appears to have been happy to cooperate. The company wanted the children both to work in the tobacco fields and as part of a developing strategy to promote family life in the colony. Company documents show that there were plans to import hundreds of women and offer an 'apprentice' as a bonus to every planter who married one of them.[6]

Talks between the City of London Aldermen and the Virginia Company began early in 1618. Sir Thomas Smythe and Sir Edwin Sandys, the Puritan politician, represented the company. Sandys, one of the leading figures in the House of Commons, was a major investor in the Virginia Company and had involved himself in its affairs as far back as 1609. He generally played a background role but after 1615, when Sir Thomas Smythe's health began to deteriorate, Sir Edwin became much more prominent in company affairs, deputising for Sir Thomas when the great merchant was absent.

After weeks of haggling with the Lord Mayor, agreement was reached on the street children. The city would pay the company £5 a head to take them off its hands and ship 100 out to America as 'apprentices'. It was agreed that all children would have to be between eight and sixteen years of age and have been born in London.

As with the decree authorising convict transportation, the arrangement was dressed up in bright humanitarian clothes. The Virginia Company was depicted as a saviour of starving children who would learn a trade in the colony, just as apprentices did in England, and one day they would be granted some land. The prolific letter writer John Chamberlain summed up the view of London's gentry when he wrote that shipping to Virginia 'a hundred young boys and girls that [had] been starving in the streets . . . is one of the best deeds that could be done'.[7]

However, it would turn out that few if any of these cockney apprentices would learn 'the mystery' of smithying or baking or tailoring or physicking or any of the other crafts an apprentice might learn in England. The agreement with the City gave the company carte blanche in deciding how to dispose of the children. One document stated that the children would be apprenticed 'in such trades and professions as the . . . company shall think fit'. Another required the children merely to be 'employed in some industrious courses'. In fact, most were destined for the tobacco plantations, where the only trade they learned was as field labourers.

In the summer of 1618, the round-ups began. The Lord Mayor ordered constables to 'walk the streets . . . and forthwith apprehend all such vagrant children, both boys and girls, as they shall find in the streets and in the markets or wandering in the night . . . and commit them to Bridewell, there to remain until further order be given'.[8]

The constables appear to have gone about it surreptitiously and with good reason, for a heavy hand in London's warren of back alleys could quickly incite a riot. Macaulay, describing the Whitefriars Liberty between St Paul's and the river, wrote:

> . . . no peace officer's life was in safety. At the cry of 'Rescue!' bullies with swords and cudgels, and termagant hags with spits and broomsticks, poured forth by hundreds; and the intruder was fortunate if he escaped back into Fleet Street, hustled, stripped, and pumped upon. Even the warrant of the Chief Justice of England could not be executed without the help of a company of musketeers.[9]

To avoid trouble, constables picked up children from the main thoroughfares and markets, one or two at a time. The first two, Robert King and John Bromley, were arrested by the beadle patrolling Britten Street, a road on the edge of Smithfield clogged with market stalls. The same day, a girl and boy, Jane Wenchman and Andrew Nuttinge, were picked up from Fleet Street, the most densely thronged highway in the metropolis. A single boy, Thomas Otley, was seized in Cheapside.

The net quickly spread out. Children were picked up from St Sepulchre's in the west, to Cripplegate and Bishopsgate in the east. For most of these children, the only existing record of them is a name in the Bridewell charge book. One of the few of whom we will hear more was Elizabeth Abbott, the third girl to be arrested.

By February 1619, 140 children were in Bridewell listed as 'held for Virginia'. No doubt they were lined up and the most robust selected by an official from the company, perhaps Sir Thomas Smythe himself. Seventy-four boys and twenty-three girls were picked out.

Three ships took them, sailing from London some time in the spring of 1619. One was called the *Duty*, another is thought to have been the *Jonathan*. On arrival in the colony, the children were sold for tobacco. Though they and other children shipped after them would ever after be known as the 'Duty Boys', one in four of that first consignment was a girl.

Before another batch of children could go, there was a seismic shift that appeared to change everything. Sir Thomas Smythe was forced out as treasurer of the Virginia Company and replaced by Sir Edwin Sandys, who promised a new deal to everyone, investors and settlers.

It is hard to fathom the relationship between Sir Edwin Sandys and Sir Thomas Smythe. They ended up poisonous enemies, each working for the destruction of the other. Given their characters and utterly different points of view, it is understandable that they clashed. Yet, before the crisis of 1619 they had worked together, seemingly harmoniously, for years.

Sandys, the son of an Archbishop of York, had sprung to prominence at the beginning of James I's reign as a Parliamentarian, and a brilliant one. In a foretaste of the bitter constitutional arguments that would eventually lead to Civil War, he led the attacks on the King's claim to divine right to rule. The monarch's right was solely through a contract with the people, Sir Edwin asserted. At James's accession, Sandys had been in such royal favour that he was among the first of the new King's subjects to be given a knighthood. But his views quickly turned the monarch into his enemy and he cemented himself into that position when he went on to organise the defeat in Parliament of James's pet project, the union of his two realms, England and Scotland.

Sir Edwin was a populist who revelled in taking on the powerful. He followed up his besting of the King by attacking one of the most envied and disliked groups in the land: London's merchant fraternity. Sandys arranged for himself to be elected chairman of a House of Commons committee on monopolies and went to war against the powerful merchants. There were, he said, 5,000 to 6,000 people engaged in trade in England but because of the monopolistic dealings of the governors of the capital's leading companies 'the whole trade of the realm is in the hands of 200 persons at most'.[10] He probably was not exaggerating. London's take in customs dues in one year was £110,000. That was more than six times the total take of £17,000 from the rest of the country.[11]

No merchant was wealthier or headed more monopolies than Sir Thomas Smythe. Yet from 1609 Smythe allowed Sandys, the merchants' enemy, into the inner councils of the Virginia Company to take a prominent role. The Virginia Company treasurer was also happy, it seems, to see the Puritan politician voted onto the governing councils of two other ventures, the Somers Islands and East India companies. Perhaps Sir Thomas was acting on the Lyndon Johnson principle of preferring your enemy inside the tent pissing out than outside the tent pissing in. Whatever his reasoning, after 1615, Smythe's health deteriorated and Sandys filled in for him when he was too ill to attend to Virginia business. In 1616, Sandys was officially appointed as Smythe's assistant. He handled such matters as the establishment of a second lottery and the negotiations with the Pilgrim Fathers, who wanted to settle in New England.

In 1618, as the street children were being rounded up, Sandys began to move against Sir Thomas Smythe. He emerged as leader of a group of discontented small investors who wanted an audit of Virginia Company finances. Once, Smythe would easily have seen Sir Edwin off. The great merchant had always been supported not only by other leading merchants on the Virginia Company's court of shareholders but by the aristocratic investors, who were known as the Court party. Now, though, the leader of the Court party, Robert Rich, Earl of Warwick, fell out with him.

The crucial issue between them was piracy. Warwick was an enthusiastic dabbler in privateering and was manoeuvring to use Virginia as a base from which to attack the Spanish. In 1617, a new Governor, Sam Argall, was appointed. He was in league with Warwick and allowed privateers into the Chesapeake. Company chiefs in London were told that, with Argall's connivance, Warwick's ship the *Treasurer*, 'manned with the ablest men in the colony was set out on roving in the Spanish dominions'.[12]

Complaints against Argall mounted. Smythe had instructed him to rule with a lighter hand but London was deluged with complaints about his tyranny. On one occasion he had sentenced a planter to death for attempting to free a group of time-served workers the Governor was refusing to liberate. Smythe ordered Argall home. The recall of his protégé and a row over another of his piratical ventures prompted Warwick to split from Sir Thomas Smythe. In 1619, he forged an alliance with Sir Edwin Sandys and Smythe was forced out.

Smythe attempted to save face by resigning before being pushed. He announced that the King had just appointed him Commissioner for the Navy and this would leave him no time for the Virginia Company. He died six years later, reportedly of the plague.

Sir Edwin Sandys's triumph enabled him to control the company, and thus the colony, for four momentous years and win plaudits from historians. He was, says the *Columbia Encyclopaedia*, 'responsible for many of the progressive features that characterized the last years of the company's control over Virginia'. Prime among these was the introduction of a representative assembly, the House of Burgesses. This was 'the beginning of freedom,' according to one modern historian.[13]

Freedom for some was not freedom for others. In November 1619, three months after the burgesses held their first meeting, Sir Edwin took the first step to resume the shipment of street children. In November 1619, he informed the Lord Mayor of London that the first 100 had arrived safely 'save such as died on the way' and the company wanted more. 'We pray your Lordship . . . in pursuit of your former so pious actions to renew your like favours and furnish us again with one hundred more for the next spring.'[14]

The Common Council of London, which Sandys expected to pay once again for these deportations, was a little more demanding this time. It required a written assurance that the apprenticeships were genuine and a commitment that eventually, in adulthood, the apprentices would be offered a plot of land each. Years later, some of those few apprentices who survived long enough to qualify for a plot found that the land apportioned to them was deep in Algonquin territory.

Round-ups of children resumed the following month. On Christmas Eve 1619, ten boys were brought into Bridewell. A week later, on New Year's Eve, a further thirty-four were delivered from the City and twenty-five from different parts of Middlesex. Others followed in dribs and drabs. Bridewell records tell us little about each child beyond a name and the destination – 'kept for Virginia'. Ages are not given but the odd comment in the charge book, such as Willie Laratt is 'a little boy who says his mother dwells in the country at Westminster', suggest that some were very young indeed.

The arrests of the children the previous year had not resulted in any problems. There were no recorded protests and the children appear to have gone quietly. No doubt they assumed they would spend a few months in a Bridewell prison workshop and then be released. Not this time. The grapevine of the streets knew what was afoot and the children did not come meekly. In late January, constables brought in more than fifty boys, half of them in a single day. Serious disturbances broke out, leading to a 'revolt' inside Bridewell.[15]

Then someone – perhaps a parent or a pamphleteer – raised the question: by what right was this being done? It emerged that no law permitted children to be forcibly transported. The 100 girls and boys who had been shipped to Virginia the previous year had been sent illegally. Edwin Sandys was forced to admit that the City lacked the authority to deliver, and the company to transport, the children against their will.

It did not matter: the 100 who had gone were history. Sandys moved rapidly to ensure that there would be no legal doubts about the next 100. On 28 January 1620, he wrote to the King's Secretary of State, Sir Robert Naunton, repeating the claim that child transportation was a great humanitarian exercise and asking for powers to deal with a hard core of the worst children who were refusing to go. He described them as those of 'whom the City is especially desirous to be disburdened' and asserted that 'under severe masters in Virginia they may be brought to good'.[16]

Three days later, the Privy Council replied. It paid obeisance to the humanitarian motives of the Common Council of London in 'redeeming so many poor souls from misery and ruin and putting them in a condition of use and service to the State' in Virginia. Then, with venom that King Herod might have approved, it turned to the children:

> We authorize and require . . . the City and the Virginia Company, or any of them, to deliver, receive, and transport into Virginia all and every the foresaid children as shall be most expedient. And if any of them shall be found obstinate to resist or otherwise to disobey such directions as shall be given in this behalf, we do likewise hereby authorize such as shall have the charge of this service to imprison, punish, and dispose any of those children, upon any disorder by them or any of them committed, as cause shall require, and so to ship them out for Virginia with as much expedition as may stand with conveniency.[17]

With this, children could now be transported without reference to their own or their parents' wishes. The second batch appears to have departed on the *Duty* in the spring of 1620. Simultaneously, the company was beginning to send so-called 'bridal boats' packed with women. This was part of the strategy devised by Sir Edwin Sandys to encourage planters to stay and marry. Sandys ordered company officials in the colony to publicise the coming of more marriageable 'maids' and also publicise the news that for the 'further encouragement' of men to marry them, those who did would each be offered the chance to buy an 'apprentice'.[18] The maids were to be offered for 120 pounds of tobacco each, the children for twenty pounds. It would become such a profitable business that Sir Edwin would later sink £200 of his own into a joint stock company concerned exclusively with marketing maids.

Two hundred metres from Bridewell, up in St Paul's Cathedral, the incoming Dean could see nothing but good in these departures to the New World. The Dean was John Donne, the poet. In a rousing sermon, he blessed the Virginia enterprise:

> . . . It shall sweep your streets, and wash your doors, from idle persons, and the children of idle persons, and employ them: and truly, if the whole country were but such a Bridewell, to force idle persons to work, it had a good use. But it is already, not only a spleen, to drain the ill humours of the body, but a liver, to breed good blood; already the employment breeds mariners; already the place gives essays, nay freights of merchantable commodities; already it is a mark for the envy, and for the ambition of our enemies.[19]

Few of those dispatched to Virginia lived long enough to reach adulthood. The muster records indicate that of the first 300 children shipped between 1619 and 1622, only twelve were still alive in 1624. Evidently, their bodies had not proved more adaptable to the blistering heat of the Chesapeake than those of adults.

While the fate of those youngsters rounded up from the streets of London has been largely forgotten, history would take a keen interest in the destiny of a group of men and women who arrived a few months after the first shipment of children in 1619. They arrived in a ship flying the orange, white and blue colours of the Dutch Republic and were mentioned in a letter to Edwin Sandys from John Rolfe, the husband and now widower of the Native American princess Pocahontas, who had died during a visit to England.

Rolfe wrote:

> About the latter end of August, a Dutch man of war of the burden of 160 tons arrived at Point Comfort. The Commander's name was Capt. Jope, his pilot for the West Indies one Mr. Marmaduke an Englishman . . . He brought not anything but 20 and odd Negroes, which the Governor and Cape Merchant [Virginia Company trading agent] bought for victuals (whereof he was in great need as he pretended) at the best and easiest rate they could buy.[20]

Much would be written over the next 400 years about the significance of this episode. But precious little was known about the ship or her cargo until the late 1990s, when painstaking research through Spanish records revealed where the Africans came from and who it was that sold them.[21]

The 'Dutch' man-of-war was, in fact, not Dutch but English. She was the *White Lion*, one of the deadly little vessels that Sir Francis Drake had employed against the Spanish Armada thirty years earlier. Her commander, 'Capt. Jope', was not Dutch but John Colwyn Jupe, a wild Cornishman who had inherited the vessel from one of Drake's captains.[22]

Jupe was an ordained Calvinist minister turned privateer. As with many ardent English Protestants, he married fervent belief in Scripture with fervent insistence on despoliation of the Spanish as God's holy work. He spent ten years renovating the *White Lion* and then took her to the Caribbean to prey on the Spanish treasure fleets heading home from Hispaniola. Portugal was at the time under Spanish rule and Jupe targeted Portuguese galleons as well as Spanish.

The *White Lion* flew Dutch colours to avoid charges of piracy. This was possible because the Dutch, unlike the English, were still at war with Spain. The wrath of King James I would descend on any captain attacking the Spanish while under the cross of St George.

It is not known when John Jupe brought the *White Lion* to the Caribbean. However, some time in the spring or summer of 1619 he joined forces there with Daniel Elfrith, skipper of the *Treasurer*. She was the privateer owned by the Earl of Warwick, whose piratical activities had so embarrassed the Virginia Company the previous year.

Spanish records report that in mid-July, 'English corsairs' waylaid and captured the Portuguese slaver *Sao Joao Bautista*. She had below decks some 370 Angolans, who had been taken prisoner during Portugal's bloody war of conquest in Luanda. They were being shipped into slavery at Vera Cruz. The English corsairs were undoubtedly the *Treasurer* and the *White Lion*. According to Spanish records, the two raiders made off with more than 200 Angolans.

Elfrith, whose ship was larger than Jupe's, evidently took aboard the bulk of them. Jupe's share seems to have been under thirty men and women.

Both captains then set course for Virginia, which had been such a haven for privateers under the governorship of Sam Argall. Jupe arrived first, four days ahead of the *Treasurer*, and then bartered his human booty.

When Elfrith appeared, he was less successful. Something caused him to up anchor almost immediately and take off before he could sell any of his Africans. He took them instead to Bermuda, where he could be sure of finding them a home – on estates belonging to his employer, the Earl of Warwick, owner of the *Treasurer*.

On the slender basis of those few words from John Rolfe describing the bartering of the 'twenty and odd Negroes' history moulded a story of a Dutch slave trader selling the first slaves to America. Book after book listed the barter at Point Comfort as the moment slavery began. In reality, the road to slavery was already being laid through indentured servitude and John Jupe's Africans were merely joining it, for they too were treated as indentured servants.

No flood of Africans followed them. The transaction was a one-off. Although the Dutch and Portuguese were bringing out slaves in their thousands from Africa, for the moment there was no market for them in Virginia. Six years later, in 1625, there were still only twenty-three Africans in the colony. Many decades later, there were still only a few hundred. That would change late in the century; but for the moment, the poor of England remained the colony's main source of chattel labour.

CHAPTER FIVE

THE JAGGED EDGE

When they first set foot in America, convicts and slum children from England must have felt trepidation and even dread. Equally, hope and expectation must have pumped through the veins of those making the trip voluntarily as indentured servants – but many had shipped into a nightmare. These volunteers would come to be called 'free-willers' but would discover that they were no more free than the convicts or the street urchins and were wide open to abuse. One of the better-treated servants amongst them would find that the price of bringing his wife and children to join him in Virginia was an extra stretch of bondage, either for him, or for his wife and his children.

The term 'indenture' derives from the Latin *indentere*, to cut with teeth. It was used in England from the Middle Ages to describe a contract duplicated on parchment and torn jaggedly in half – indented. Each party to the contract retained one half as evidence of what had been agreed. Land sale documents were called indentures. So were marriage settlements. Labour contracts were not. Generally they did not require indenturing, as a whole body of English law governed the master–servant relationship. That changed abruptly in 1618 when the Virginia Company introduced headrights and revolutionised the labour market.

The headright scheme was essentially an invitation to those with money to secure great tracts of Virginia by populating it with the poor. The brainchild of Sir Edwin Sandys, the headright was a grant of fifty acres for every new settler. This land went to whoever paid the settler's passage. News of the scheme led to a frantic scramble amongst speculators and planters to sign up hopeful young people willing to become their servants and be shipped to labour for them in Virginia. Indentures were used to tie them to the deal – and supposedly to tie the planter or speculator to it as well.

Invariably, it was a one-sided affair. Servants were asked to indent to work unwaged for enormous lengths of time – anything from three up to eleven years or more. In return, most were offered little more than their passage to Virginia and the promise of some of the wherewithal for a new life when servitude ended. Sometimes a strip of land was promised but few would ever own an inch of soil.

Such terms were terrible but in an England where enclosures had thrown so many off the land and where an agricultural depression had set in, there were plenty of takers. During the five years to 1624, when the Virginia Company was wound up, 4,500 settlers arrived, which was as many as had been shipped in throughout the previous twelve years. Between a third and a half were servants.[1]

The first known indentured servant was blacksmith Robert Coopy from the village of Nibley in the Cotswolds. Nibley had already etched its mark on history 300 years before when King Edward II was imprisoned in nearby Berkeley Castle and, according to legend, horribly murdered on the orders of his wife's lover.

We only know about Robert Coopy because his indenture document survives, the earliest still extant.[2] The agreement was between Coopy and a syndicate of local gentry who had just secured 8,000 acres in Virginia. They called this tract of untamed American forest after their corner of the Cotswolds, the Berkeley Hundred. Coopy indentured with them in the summer of 1619. In return for his passage to America, plus food and shelter, he was to be bound to the syndicate as a servant for three years. When that time was served, he would be offered a tenancy on thirty acres of syndicate land.

In the event, something stopped Robert Coopy going through with the indenture. He stayed in England, either too wise or too worried to try the New World. However, another of the Coopy clan,

Thomas Coopy, did go, presumably in Robert's stead. Like Robert, he was a skilled man, a carpenter and turner, and the evidence is that he had the same deal as Robert, plus the syndicate's agreement to pay his wife a few shillings while he was in America. That made it very generous compared to the deals other servants would get but Thomas Coopy would not live long enough to appreciate his relative good fortune.

In September 1619, Coopy embarked from Bristol on a 40-ton barque called the *Margaret*, one of the smaller ships on the Virginia run. She was chartered to take an advance party of thirty-three indentured servants plus three or four gentlemen to the Berkeley holdings in Virginia. Few of the servants were as multi-skilled as Thomas Coopy, and their indentures reflected it, most being far more onerous than his. Some of his fellow servants had to agree to be indentured for five years, some for seven, some for eight years to pay for their passage; some did not even have the promise of a yard of ground to rent on being freed.

All went well with them to begin with. The syndicate's advisers had wisely counselled against arriving in the heat of the Chesapeake summer – 'a most unfit season' when passengers arrived 'very weak and sick', there to fall under 'the great heat of weather'. As a consequence, considerable numbers died either at sea or soon after disembarkation before they could be 'seasoned' to the summer temperatures. The *Margaret*'s departure in September was designed to avoid these problems and seems to have succeeded. No lives appear to have been lost en route.

Nor were there any fatalities or attacks by the Algonquin after the party reached the Chesapeake and found their designated tract of forest. Today, the spot houses a national monument, marked by a grand Georgian mansion where America's ninth president, William Henry Harrison, was born. In 1619, it was a daunting chunk of wilderness. The advance party arrived on 4 December and celebrated with a 'thanksgiving' service that they vowed to repeat each year. It was these Gloucester men on the banks of the James River rather than the Pilgrim Fathers a year later in New England who first established a Thanksgiving Day in America.

The gentlemen of the syndicate certainly had reason to be

thankful. Thanks to the headright system, the party of men they brought on the *Margaret* entitled the syndicate partners to an extra 1,900 acres. Another fifty-three servants later recruited in the south-west of England would add a further 2,650 acres. On top of that, many more thousands of acres became due because of shares the syndicate bought in the Virginia Company. All told, the gentlemen from the Cotswolds more than doubled their American holdings in little more than a year.

Other syndicates did the same and rich individuals followed suit. Between 1619 and 1623, forty-four individuals or groups shipped more than 100 servants each to Virginia and claimed their land rewards.

We don't know how the Berkeley Hundred's indentured servants were treated after they were put to work. There is little more to go on than the records of mortality rates, which were dire across the colony. Of the 1,200 newcomers in 1619, more than 800 perished in the first year. Some were killed by Native Americans, some by disease and some by infections caught in the jam-packed ships bringing them. And judging by what we know of life in the tobacco fields in subsequent years, some were worked to death.

On the Berkeley Hundred, the death rate seems to have been lower than most. A list of settlers drawn up just nine months after Coopy's party arrived records four settlers as slain, presumably by Native Americans, one 'gent' killed by another 'gent', one drowning and nine unexplained deaths.[3]

Coopy survived those first months. He was made an 'assistant', an overseer, and was obviously a highly valued man – so much so that he felt able to press for his wife Joan and their children Elizabeth and Anthony to join him. The syndicate agreed – for a price. To compensate them for the room his little family would take on the next voyage of the *Margaret*, Coopy would have to indenture for an undetermined number of extra years in servitude or indenture his incoming family into bondage. The leading light of the syndicate instructed: 'Such conditions are to be made such that the husband retribute to us a competent satisfaction in the augmentation of the years of his, her and their son's and daughter's services.'[4]

In a period during which it was common for poverty-stricken families to farm out their children rather than see them go hungry, the syndicate's terms might not have seemed as alien as they do today. At all events, an agreement of some kind was reached and Thomas Coopy's family of three sailed to join him in America in 1620. Eighteen months later, all but one of the Coopy family were dead.

The first laws governing the treatment of servants like Coopy had been agreed four months before his arrival by a group of worthies gathered in the choir of Jamestown's little wooden church. This was the inaugural session of the House of Burgesses, the body created by the Virginia Company to give the colony a measure of self-government. One of their priorities was how to control the hundreds of Thomas Coopys arriving in the headrights rush and the tens of thousands of other servants who would follow.

The church was the only structure in the colony large enough to accommodate all twenty-two burgesses. The institution was modelled on the English House of Commons. Flanked by guards in flowing red robes, the burgesses attempted the same solemn pomp as in Westminster. They had a speaker and sergeant-at-arms, and, like the Commons, were dominated by landed interests. A new Governor, Sir George Yeardley, had succeeded the disgraced Samuel Argall and he presided.

High on the agenda was the competitive scramble for servants. Planters or their agents were stealing servants from under each other's noses even before they reached the colony. Back in England, servants who had just indentured for America were being 'enticed' to break the contract and indenture for the colony on better terms with someone else. Other servants were being enticed to jump ship on arrival and indent with a new master.

The burgesses decided 'most severely to punish the seducers and the seduced' but in the event targeted the servants alone. They were to be made to serve the full terms contracted with both masters, one after the other.[5]

Something of a precedent was thus established – extra time in servitude for 'desertion'. It would be used with growing ferocity in succeeding decades by Virginia and other colonies as increasing numbers of servants fled from their masters and the authorities attempted to deter them. In the 1630s, fleeing servants would face two days' extra service for every day away; in the 1640s, five days for every one away; and in the 1650s in Maryland, an extra ten days for every one away. A servant on the run for several weeks could face years of extra bondage. Needless to say, anyone helping them was punished, too.

At this first meeting, the burgesses underlined the masters' absolute rights over servants. They conferred on the master the right to use 'bodily punishment for not heeding the commands of the master'.[6] That would lead to a whipping post being installed in every locality. Masters would be given the option of bringing in servants to be punished there or administering the penalty themselves on their own plantations.[7]

The extra-time precedent applied to disobedience, too. In addition to a whipping, resistance to a master or an overseer was also to be punished by two years' additional servitude.[8] A taste of what servants might expect was given during the meeting, when the burgesses formed themselves into a court and sentenced an errant servant. The servant had allegedly slandered his master and indulged in an open display of 'wantonness' with a woman servant. The burgesses empowered the master 'to place this servant in the pillory for a period of four days, to nail his ears to the post, and to give him a public whipping on each day included in his sentence'.[9]

In later years, other, sometimes still harsher sentences, including the loss of an ear or both ears, would be handed out by the burgesses. Yet some of these were the same planters who had complained bitterly at how everyone was treated in the grim days of Sir Thomas Dale, calling it 'slavery'.

A first step in restricting servants' family rights was also taken at this inaugural meeting. It appears to have been prompted by the arrival of the first of the 'bridal boats', which were bringing marriageable 'maids' to the colony as part of Sir Edwin Sandys's scheme to boost family life. Prospective husbands were expected to buy their brides. But Sandys was fearful that the hearts of some of these maids might be captured by handsome servants and orders went out from London to prevent that happening: 'We would not have these maids married to servants,' the Virginia Company instructed.[10] The burgesses did their part by imposing a ban on any maid or woman servant in the colony marrying without 'the consent of her parents or masters or master'. Later, they would bring in laws banning all servants, male and female, of whatever age, from marrying without the master's sanction. They would also slap up to two years' extra service on any woman servant falling pregnant – even if her master was the father. Rules controlling human behaviour were to have the greatest impact on female servants.

This was just the start. Over the next century and a half, a good deal of the time of Virginia's House of Burgesses and of the assemblies of neighbouring colonies would be taken up with how to keep servants in check.

In London, the Virginia Company remained preoccupied with numbers. The frightening death toll of 1619 did not deter the messianic Sir Edwin Sandys. When news came through that nearly seventy per cent of those transported were dead, Sir Edwin and his assistant, John Ferrar, said they were sorry to hear it and advised planters to pray harder. They then looked for other sources of labour. Sir Edwin set up a committee to comb the whole kingdom for youths of fifteen years and over who were a 'burden' on their local parishes. Each parish was told that the company would take the youths to Virginia as apprentices for £5 per head. Meanwhile, the second and third batches of cockney children were sent.[11]

Sandys's biographer makes clear that he was generally too lofty to get into the grubby details of who was sent and how.[12] His deputy, John Ferrar, dealt with such matters. Whichever of them was responsible, they were not too fussy in their selection. Convicts from London continued to be transported while a number of girls picked up in London to be sent over as 'apprentices' appear to have been child prostitutes. One girl earmarked in the Bridewell records as destined for Virginia is listed as a 'lewd vagrant', another as leading 'an incontinent life' and being 'an old guest'.

Some of the maids dispatched on the bridal boats were probably prostitutes, too. A note from a company official complains that a few of the women were 'out of Bridewell' and 'of so bad choice as made the colony afraid to desire any others'.[13]

What should have been more disturbing for Sir Edwyn was a mounting tide of complaints from relatives of indentured servants. Company documents show there was uproar over indenture abuses. A company report asserted: 'Divers old planters and others did allure and beguile divers young persons and others (ignorant and unskillful in such matters) to serve them upon intolerable and unchristian like conditions.'[14] Another report lamented that 'the ungodly that have only respect for their own profit' were 'enticing young people into binding themselves as servants for years to pay for their transportation'.[15]

Sir Edwin Sandys was as much to blame as anyone. It was on his instructions that those first shipments of women and children were marketed and sold at set prices. One can safely assume that transported convicts who were not put to work on company lands were sold to planters as servants, probably for seven years. In this hungry market, it inevitably followed that some of these hapless individuals would be resold at a profit. It followed, too, that full-time dealers in people would soon emerge. According to Edmund S. Morgan: 'Men staked out claims to men, stole them, lured them, fought over them and bid up their price to four, five or six times the initial cost.'[16] As Ted Nace puts it, Virginians were moving toward 'a system of labor that treated men as things'.[17] Apart from anxious relatives and friends, few in England raised any objection to the traffic in servants that was developing in the colony. An exception was that ardent recorder of English America's history, and one-time leading actor in it, Captain John Smith. He was appalled. In 1624, he wrote from London:

> God forbid . . . that masters there should not have the same
> privilege over their servants as here, but to sell him or her
> for forty, fifty, or threescore pounds, whom the Company
> hath sent over for eight or ten pounds at the most, without

regard [to] how they shall be maintained with apparel, meat,
drink and lodging, is odious.

Smith warned that such a trade in people was 'sufficient to bring a
well settled Common-wealth to misery, much more Virginia'.[18]
 Smith was writing just as the Virginia Company was collapsing
and about to be wound up.

CHAPTER SIX

'THEY ARE NOT DOGS'

On Good Friday 1622, the English presence in Virginia came within an ace of being wiped out. It survived thanks to Chanco, an Algonquin youth who had converted to Christianity. The previous night, he warned settlers that an all-out attack was to be launched next day across the colony. The new paramount chief of the Powhatan Confederacy, Opechancanough, aimed to exterminate the invaders. Supposedly friendly tribesmen were to infiltrate settlements on the Friday morning and turn on the settlers.

News of the plan was spread to plantations along the James and Charles rivers, where devout men and women were preparing for the holiest day of the year, but it didn't spread quickly enough. The next morning, 347 out of a total settler population of 1,240 were killed, though the number was possibly higher since some plantations failed to record numbers of the dead.

Among the decimated plantations was the Berkeley Hundred, where Thomas Coopy's wife and children had been allowed to join him. That Friday, the official death toll on the Berkeley Hundred was eleven. The Coopys were not among those named but Thomas, his wife Joan and their son Anthony are listed as 'dead' in a report to England. Only the daughter Elizabeth was recorded as alive in 1624, working as a servant. If Opechancanough's warriors didn't make her an orphan, disease probably did. Back in Gloucestershire, when news of the fate of Thomas and his family percolated through to Robert Coopy, perhaps he blessed whatever or whoever had persuaded him to give up his place in America to his kinsman.

Terrible tales of bloodshed that Easter were followed by terrible tales of privation as everyone, especially the servants at the bottom of the heap, struggled to survive the effects of the massacre. The most quoted example of a wretched servant in these years was 22-year-old Richard Frethorne, who reached Virginia shortly before Christmas 1622.

Young Frethorne was a servant on Martin's Hundred, 20,000 acres of forest stretching around a bend in the James River nine or ten miles from Jamestown. This vast tract was granted to a syndicate of London merchants led by Sir Richard Martin, who we saw in an earlier chapter haranguing the House of Commons on Virginia's behalf. Somewhere between 100 and 150 settlers were on the plantation when Opechancanough's warriors struck. Eighty of them were killed. Twenty more, all of them women, were taken off as captives.

Richard Frethorne arrived about nine months later, when a war of attrition was being waged against the Native Americans. His letters show him to be sick, terrified and half-starved. Disease was raging all around and in his mind every cedar tree hid a waiting Indian.

He was working from dawn to midnight, carting supplies between the plantation and Jamestown, when he wrote the first of three letters describing his plight and begging his father to buy his freedom:

> I your child am in a most heavy case by reason of the nature of the country, is such that it causes much sickness, as the scurvy and the bloody flux and diverse other diseases . . . When we are sick there is nothing to comfort us . . . [We] must work hard both early and late for a mess of water gruel and a mouthful of bread and beef. A mouthful of bread for a penny loaf must serve for four men . . . If you did know as much as I, when people cry out day and night – Oh! that they were in England without their limbs – and would not care to lose any limb to be in England again . . . We live in fear of the enemy every hour, yet we have had a

combat with them on the Sunday before Shrovetide, and we took two alive and made slaves of them . . . and yet we are but thirty-two to fight against three thousand if they should come . . . Our plantation is very weak by reason of the death and sickness of our company . . . We came but twenty for the merchants and they are half dead just; and we look every hour when two more should go. There came four other men yet to live with us, of which there is but one alive; and our Lieutenant is dead, and his father and his brother.

. . . I have not a penny, nor a penny worth, to help me to either spice or sugar or strong waters, without the which one cannot live here . . . I am not half a quarter so strong as I was in England for I do protest to you that I have eaten more in a day at home than I have allowed me here for a week. You have given more than my day's allowance to a beggar at the door.[1]

A gunsmith, Goodman Jackson, took pity on Frethorne and offered him shelter after finding him at the end of a day's toil trying to sleep in an open boat in a rainstorm. Frethorne told his father what the gunsmith thought of his position: 'He much marvelled that you would send me a servant to the Company; he said I had been better knocked on the head.'

Frethorne pleaded, 'If you love me you will redeem me suddenly, for which I do entreat and beg.'

Like Thomas Coopy a year earlier, Frethorne vanishes from history at this point. It is commonly assumed that he was never redeemed by his father and died before he had been in Virginia a year.

Some leading settlers saw an opportunity being opened up by the Easter massacre. George Sandys, the brother of Sir Edwin Sandys, was one of them. He had secured the plum job of Treasurer of the colony which made him second only to the Governor. Sandys advocated mass enslavement of the native population. He argued that in the light of the massacre the tribes could 'now most justly be compelled to servitude and drudgery'. The planter John Martin said Native Americans would make ideal slaves. They were 'apter for work than yet our English are' and are able 'to work in the heat of the day'. They were even 'fit to row in galleys', he claimed.[2]

It was a widely held view and, as we have just seen from Frethorne's letter, settlers attempted to put it into practice. But mass enslavement of the native population on their own terrain was never realistic. In later years, large numbers of men and women from a range of tribes would indeed be enslaved and terribly used. But for the moment the settlers went instead for a war of extermination. Powhatan villages were put to the fire and hundreds of Native Americans killed in an effort to clear them all from the Chesapeake or kill them.

In fact, in 1622 it was the Native Americans not the settlers who had taken slaves – the twenty women captured at John Martin's plantation during the Good Friday attack. The pursuit and liberation of the women featured two of the most distasteful episodes of the Virginia Company period, with the colony's surgeon, Dr John Pott, playing the villain both times.

The first episode took place during a parley with tribal leaders in May 1623 at a neutral point by the Potomac River. Captain William Tucker and a delegation of settlers arrived to be met by Opechancanough, who was backed by a throng of warriors. The meeting had been called to discuss terms for releasing the white hostages but it didn't get that far. Tucker invited the Indians to drink from a flask of sack that Dr Pott had prepared. The Algonquin had learned not to trust the settlers and asked that the English interpreter take the first drink. He duly took a gulp but, by sleight of hand, from a different container. The Algonquin were right to be suspicious. Dr Pott had mixed a slow-acting poison in the sack.

One by one, the warriors drank. The settlers reported jubilantly that 200 later died. Opechancanough evidently did not drink, for he escaped. However, two of his chiefs were among fifty more shot down later that day in an English ambush.

The women remained hostages; freeing them was not the settlers' top priority. The settlers were pursuing their war of extermination and their womenfolk were secondary. They weren't finally ransomed till nine months later and once again Dr Pott played his unsavoury part. He paid two pounds' weight of coloured beads to ransom a young widow, Jane Dickenson, and then claimed her as his bound servant. It emerged that Mrs Dickenson's husband, whom she had seen killed in the attack, was indentured and still had three years left to serve on his contract. The good doctor insisted that the young widow serve out that time with him. In 1624, she appealed to the company for her freedom, describing the ten months she had so far served Pott as 'differ[ing] not from her slavery with the Indians'.[3]

The records do not say whether or not the company freed her. The doctor is reported to have been criticised for the mass poisoning but we can find no record of his peers blaming him for forcing Jane Dickenson into servitude – nor of them doing anything about it. In fact, a few years later, Dr Pott's standing was such that by popular acclaim he briefly served as de facto Governor of Virginia.

Fear of attack by the Algonquin was a constant on the plantations. As we shall see in the next chapter, a rain of arrows could cut a man down at any time. Yet, large numbers of servants would opt to take their chances with the Native Americans and seek refuge with them in future years rather than stick it out on the plantations. Life in the tobacco fields could be that bad.

A typical early plantation was an ever-expanding clearing on the Tidewater, the western shore of the Chesapeake where the James, Potomac, York and the Rappahannock rivers run into the bay. For servants on these holdings, life was one of unbroken labour. In the freeze of winter, they were out in the forest hacking down oak, pine and hickory to clear the ground for cultivation. For the rest of the year, they were into a relentless round of planting, nurturing, replanting, weeding and 'worming'. A servant was responsible for thousands of vulnerable tobacco plants, each with its own tiny hillock of earth, each requiring to be watched, nursed and coddled like a child for any slip could be ruinous. And when it was too dark to work in the fields, there were other tasks. The most hated was 'beating at the mortar' – pounding soaked corn with a pestle to make the daily bread for everyone, beginning with master and family.

> Sometimes when that a hard day's work we've done
> Away into the mill we must be gone

Till twelve or one o'clock a grinding corn
And must be up by daylight in the morn.[4]

Tobacco was 'a culture productive of infinite wretchedness', wrote Thomas Jefferson a century later. Those employed in it were 'in a continued state of exertion beyond the powers of nature to support. Little food of any kind is raised by them; so that the men and animals on these farms are badly fed, and the earth is rapidly impoverished.' Himself a hugely successful tobacco planter, the USA's third president concluded that it was a 'crop that wears out men and land'.[5]

In 1622, as the planters struggled to recover from the massacre, they were advised how best to man their fields for maximum financial return. Until then, although more and more indentured servants were being used, the Virginia Company itself relied heavily on sharecroppers – tenants – to work its plantations. So did some of the big syndicates. There were some waged labourers, too, usually skilled men. Then in 1622, the company engaged a Captain Thomas Nuce, evidently the Jacobean equivalent of our present-day management consultant, to compare labour costs on its plantations. Nuce advised that 'a more certain profit' would come from dropping the sharecroppers.[6] The Virginia Company was told to 'change the condition of tenants into servants', which it proceeded to do. Owners of large plantations followed the company lead and inside six years as many as ninety per cent of the labourers shipped in to the colony were indentured servants.

One group of 100 men contracted by the company as tenants found that their status and prospects had been changed mid-ocean. They'd been signed up as 'tenants by halves' – sharecroppers – only to be told on landing in the Chesapeake that fifty of them had been hired out, half of them to one of the richest planters in the colony who wanted more men to deter the Algonquin. Somehow, two of the fifty displaced tenants managed to get their cases heard in London and were given their freedom. But servants tended to be helpless and at the mercy of whoever held their indentures. One, who was supposedly a free man, wrote this of his master, a Virginia company official who was also a planter: 'He makes us serve him whether we will or no, and how to help it we do not know, for he has all the sway.'[7]

Within two years of the massacre, individual cases of abused servants began to attract attention. A Virginia Company official sounded alarm bells. He reported in June 1623 that 'divers masters in Virginia do much neglect and abuse their servants there with intolerable oppression and hard usage'.[8]

A year later, the first of a number of grim examples surfaced. Two young servants died after a catalogue of brutality at a tobacco plantation on the north bank of the James River called the Neck of Land. One of them was the cockney girl Elizabeth Abbott, who, it may be remembered, was among the first street urchins picked up in the London swoops of 1618. Elizabeth ended up as a field servant and was one of a minority of the children who did not succumb to Indian attack, malaria, cholera or the intolerable heat. She was beaten to death in October 1624.[9]

A spirited, wayward girl, whose morals scandalised her master and mistress, she had constantly taken time off from the toil of the tobacco fields, sometimes for days at a time, and was beaten regularly. One day, a fellow servant was ordered to punish her with a whipping for her latest absence. A witness claimed to have counted 500 strokes. Elizabeth staggered off the plantation and died on a neighbouring property. It says a lot about servitude in Virginia that even as she lay dying a neighbour who ministered to her offered to take her back so she could apologise to her master for her behaviour.

At an inquiry into her death, it emerged that another servant on the plantation, a youth called Elias Hinton, had perished the previous year after complaining that he had been hit on the head with a hoe by his master. The planter and his wife were both accused of cruelty. In their defence, it was claimed they were solicitous to their servants, that Elizabeth Abbott and Elias Hinton had to be 'corrected' because of their rebellious behaviour and they had ordered only 'moderate' punishments. From the scanty records that remain, the court appears to have backed the planters and they were exonerated.

Judging from the local court archives, similar instances of

the brutalising of white servants were taking place across the Chesapeake. There are libraries of batterings and whippings or careless inhumanity. As with the deaths of Elizabeth Abbott and Elias Hinton, the cruelty tended either to go unpunished or, if there was a successful prosecution, punishment was likely to be lenient. Two of Maryland's most sadistic brutes got off with being branded on the hand. Professor Edmund S. Morgan, whose research dipped deeper than most into the guts of American servitude, commented that the courts 'supported planters in severities that would not have been allowed in England'.[10]

An obvious explanation for the casual attitude of the courts to the excesses of planters was that the judges, or commissioners, were invariably planters themselves. Among Virginia commissioners in the 1660s was a planter whose mistreatment of his servants was a byword. Such men, sitting in judgment, had no interest in siding against their own kind and thereby fuelling the hopes of their own servants.

There is another explanation, too. This is the widespread perception that the typical indentured servant was the 'scum' of England – criminal, dangerous and lazy. It was a view dating from the days of Chief Justice Popham's notorious jailbird colonists and it stemmed from a prejudice that must have been reinforced every time a batch of convicts was shipped.

A jaundiced view of servants was taken by even the most enthusiastic of colonial supporters. In the 1660s, John Hammond, once a servant himself, published the pamphlet entitled *Leah and Rachel* that glowed with praise for the two Chesapeake colonies but described them as peopled by 'rogues, whores, dissolute and rooking persons'. Virginia and Maryland were the product of 'jails emptied, youth seduced, infamous women drilled in'.[11] In 1670, Governor William Berkeley described Virginia as 'an excellent school to make contumacious and disorderly wild youths hastily to repent of these wild and extravagant courses that brought them thither'.[12] Another contemporary called the colony 'the galleys of England'.

The servant whom planters saw as personifying evil was Thomas Hellier from Whitchurch in Dorset. At the age of twenty-eight,

Hellier signed up to go to Virginia as an indentured servant. He was wary, having heard stories of the brutality in the colony. But over some drinks in a tavern he was persuaded. He was assured that he would be given sedentary work and never be used as a labourer. When he landed at Newport News, he was sold to Cuthbert Williamson, who promised Hellier that he would be used to tutor his children 'unless necessity did compel'. Williamson's plantation was called appropriately Hard Labour Plantation and to the young servant's dismay he found that necessity continually compelled. There was no tutoring. Instead, Hellier was daily put to work in the tobacco fields. Initially, he didn't complain and vowed to stick it out. He had little option. The law bound him in absolute obedience to his master until his period of indenture was served. However, Hellier could not keep his promise to himself. Williamson's wife – Hellier's 'ill-tongued mistress' – kept goading and humiliating him, and this he couldn't stand. He tried running away but was caught after several weeks and returned to 'usage worse than before'. But then early one spring morning he donned his best clothes, picked up an axe and a knife and became a murderer. He killed Cuthbert Williamson, Williamson's wife and a servant.

His crime sent shivers down the spines of planters and their families across the English colonies. His account of the murder was given to a minister the night before his execution.[13] It was graphic. He struck the sleeping Williamson a fatal blow with an axe, which woke Mrs Williamson. She jumped out of bed screaming and grabbed a chair for protection. She pleaded for her life as the crazed servant came at her. 'But all in vain. Nothing would satisfy me but her life, she who I looked on as my greatest enemy.' A fellow servant called Martha Clark became Hellier's third victim when she tried to intervene.

Hellier delivered a long speech on the scaffold repenting his life and the killings but also directed at those who conducted the servant trade and at their clients. He talked bitterly of the 'baseness and knavery' of the merchants and traders who gulled the naive like himself into 'great misery and utter destruction' and then he addressed the masters:

> Also you that are masters of servants in this country, have
> respect to them, let them have that which is necessary for
> them with good words, not 'Down you dog' do such as this
> or such as that. They are not dogs.[14]

Of course there were villains and killers amongst the hordes of
servants coming into the Chesapeake, and not just amongst the
convicts. The free-willers crowding onto the 'pestered' migrant
ships included a share of society's sweepings. The great bulk
of them were in the fifteen-to-thirty-year age group and thus a
magnet for trouble. Hellier was undoubtedly one. In his confession
on the eve of his execution, he described a wastrel's life but not a
criminal one. In truth, probably like the majority of servants he
began his journey to America guilty of nothing more than poverty
and hope.

Another perception of indentured servants was far more
insidious. They came to be viewed as – and treated by colonial law
as – chattels, the property of their masters or mistresses. There is a
school of thought that will not accept that indenture meant chattel
status. It asserts that indenturing meant mortgaging one's labour
and nothing more: that fundamental rights were unchanged and one
remained essentially free. This is nonsense. In practice, autonomy
and freedom existed only at the discretion of the master.

What has been called the chattelisation of the servant began
when Virginia Company officials first sold children and convicts
prior to 1620. By 1623, servants were appearing in documents as
assets. Although legislation did not officially establish them as 'real
estate' – as would happen with Africans at the beginning of the
next century – that is what they effectively became.

Servants began to feature in planters' wills. A search through
genealogical material and other sources finds servants listed time
after time as portable assets, along with the cows and the silverware,
the flat irons and the bed linen:

Will of William White, linen-draper, London, 20 August 1622:

'I give and bequeath all my lands in Virginia, with all my servants, goods, debts, chattels and whatsoever else I have unto my beloved brother, John White.'

Will of Elizabeth Causley, Virginia, 26 November 1635:

'I Elizabeth Causley of Acchawmack being left and appointed sole and absolute executrix of my right dear and well beloved husband Henry Causley late deceased do hereby give bequeath and make over unto my children Agnes and Francis my plantation with all . . . my servants, goods and moneys whatsoever.'

Will of Abraham Coombs, St Mry'd County, Maryland, 26 December 1684:

'I give and bequeath to my dear & loving wife all my servants, being two boys and one woman servant together with all my stock of hogs.'

Inventory of the estate of Thomas Carter, 9 September 1673, Isle of Wight County:

'5 horses, 3 mares, 42 head of cattle, 22 head of hogs, tobacco in debts 5,500 lbs, 1 set of joiner's tools worth 400 lbs tobac, 1 bill of Christopher Hollyman – 800 lbs tob, 1 bill of Mr. Cobbs – 35 lbs tob, 2 feather beds and 2 flock beds, 4 servants – 2 whereof to serve 3 years apiece, one five years, and one four years. 102 ozs. of pewter, 2 pistols, 3 iron pots.'

As with the wills, so with the account books of merchants involved in the servant trade. If servants were lost at sea en route to Virginia, they were viewed as cargo and not as people to be lamented. When a Virginia-bound craft called the *Angel* was driven by storms into Barbados in 1655, many of her goods were lost and a statement reported: 'Amongst the goods saved were three servants valued at £30 who were disposed of in Barbados.' When three other servants tried to get ashore at a frozen Port St Mary in New England and vanished through the ice, the ship's captain was sued for the price they would have fetched.

Some wills put a value on servants – often not as high as that of other livestock. Abraham Moore of Virginia valued one boy 'having upward of three years to serve' at 1,200 pounds of tobacco. 'One grey mare' was valued at 2,000 pounds. Elias Edmond's estate in 1664 listed 'a maid servant to serve eight months' as worth 600 pounds of tobacco, half as much as the value put on a bed, blankets, some curtains and a few rugs.

The buying and selling of men appalled some of those who observed it. Virginia Company secretary John Pory and the explorer/historian Captain John Smith both condemned it. They were not alone. In 1626, an English sea captain called Thomas Weston refused to take a party of servants from Canada to America. He explained that servants were 'sold here up and down like horses' in Virginia and he held it therefore 'that it was not lawful to carry any'.[15] A Dutch sea captain reported seeing planters playing cards using their servants as gambling counters, and he rebuked them. He told them that not even the Turks treated their own in this way.[16]

By the end of the 1620s, three out of four people landed in the Chesapeake were indentured servants and that would continue to be the ratio. In several fundamental ways, these servants differed from the servant in England. In England, a servant contracted for a year and there was no power to force an extension. In England, he or she couldn't be sold. In England, the servant tended to be treated as a member of the household, not as livestock. In England, masters whipped servants but wouldn't easily get away with whipping them to death. Nevertheless, if you would believe some of the popular American histories published in the first half of the last century, there was little difference between the treatment and status of indentured servants who came to Virginia and the servant back home in England. Mary Johnston's take was typical of a widespread view: 'Servitude seemed to satisfy the needs of middling sorts of Englishmen who saw in the institution a marvellous opportunity to try one's luck in America at someone else's expense in return for a few years of service.' It was a temporary condition, she added, 'which neither stripped the servant of his humanity nor systematically degraded him'.[17]

A few decades later, in 1922, Thomas J. Wertenbaker was still more approving:

> Indenture . . . was in no sense a mark of servitude or slavery.
> It simply made it obligatory for the newcomer, under pain
> of severe penalties, to work out his passage for money and
> until that was accomplished to surrender a part of the liberty
> so dear to every Englishman.[18]

The arrangement, Wertenbaker concluded, 'proved satisfactory to all concerned'.

However, in the far-off wilds of Virginia, the estate owner with a whip and the legal right to demand unquestioning obedience could go much further than his equivalent in England. As Bernard Bailyn puts it in *Voyagers to the West*: 'The colonists lived in exceptional circumstances . . . They lived in the outback . . . where constraints were lowered and where one had to struggle to maintain the forms of civilized existence.'[19]

Of course, one day the indentured period would end and the servant would be free. That is one of the fundamental differences drawn between white indentured servitude and black slavery. One was a temporary condition; the other was perpetual. Except that huge numbers of white servants didn't live to see the day of freedom. In the early days, the majority of servants died still in bondage. Moreover, the bulk of those who did outlive their servitude ended up no better than when they'd arrived. They would emerge from bondage landless and poor.

As the buying and selling of people became the norm, the days of the Virginia Company were ending. The company had much to boast about but at least as much to lament. The death toll under Sir Thomas Smythe had been horrendous and under Sir Edwin Sandys it was even worse. In 1619, Sir Edwin Sandys took over a colony inhabited by 700 colonists. In the next three years a further 3,570 men, women and children joined them. That made a total of 4,270 people. In 1623, just 900 were still alive. Subtracting the 347 settlers who had been killed by Native Americans left more than 3,000 lives unaccounted for.

In the aftermath of the Good Friday massacre, the death rates came under scrutiny. James I set up an inquiry into how the colony had been run, commissioning an outsider, the Governor of the

Somers Isles, Nathaniel Butler, to conduct it. Virginia Company chiefs and their supporters in the colony heaped blame on the previous regime of Sir Thomas Smythe. The great merchant was accused of corruption, incompetence and subjecting the colony to slavery. Butler swept these claims aside. He reported that 'in government the colonists had wilfully strayed from the law and customs of England' and blamed the terrible mortality rates on the abuses, neglect and self-seeking of company officials. He warned that unless the evils were 'redressed with speed by some divine and supreme hand, instead of a plantation it will get the name of a slaughter-house, and so justly become both odious to ourselves and contemptible to all the world'.[20]

Virginia Company rule ended in 1624 when James I withdrew its charter and substituted royal government. The hard times were anything but over, however, for the successors of Thomas Coopy, Thomas Hellier and Elizabeth Abbott.

CHAPTER SEVEN

THE PEOPLE TRADE

The tobacco boom that lasted into the 1630s saved Virginia: new plantations appeared and the demand for labour intensified. Meanwhile, the indentured-servitude system spread as British colonisation thrust along the length of the eastern seaboard and new colonies emerged. To a greater or lesser degree, they were peopled both by men and women who had been forcibly transported and by free-willers who had voluntarily mortgaged their freedom. By the end of the century, some 200,000 men, women and children from the British Isles would have been transplanted to British America. The vast majority of these British colonists would be indentured servants.

The first of them to put down permanent roots beyond the Chesapeake were those seekers of religious liberty, the Pilgrim Fathers. Helped by an approving Sir Edwin Sandys, they were granted a charter to set up the Plymouth colony in New England in 1620. Eight years after their arrival, still more militant Puritans secured a charter for the Massachusetts Bay Company, also in New England. Almost simultaneously, the polar opposites in the Christian spectrum, Roman Catholics, were offered a refuge of their own in America. The Catholic Lord Baltimore was made Lord Proprietor of a vast territory encircling the north and east of Chesapeake Bay, which he was to call Maryland. His co-religionists among the English gentry were urged to relocate there.

The pace of expansion was set by the Puritans. In the 1630s, something over 20,000 of them would stream into New England and prove how wrong Sir John Popham's colonists had been three decades earlier to give up so quickly. One in five of this first influx was an indentured servant. By and large, these free-willers were never treated as badly as the plantation servants in Virginia but they were nevertheless very much a repressed underclass. The Puritan view of them was given by the Massachusetts Governor John Winthrop in 1630:

> God Almighty in His most holy and wise providence hath
> so disposed of the condition of mankind as in all times some
> must be rich, some poor; some high and eminent in power
> and dignity; others mean and in subjection.[1]

Two episodes in 1628 point to a mixture of self-righteousness and dour commercialism governing Puritan attitudes to servants. The first episode centred on a free spirit from London with a penchant for poetry, a lawyer called Thomas Morton. He took charge of a plantation and made the mistake of giving the servants there their freedom and promising to receive them as 'partners and consociates'.[2]

Morton was a senior partner in a trading venture led by one Thomas Wollaston. He and Wollaston had arrived in Massachusetts Bay with around thirty indentured servants in 1624. They began trading in furs from a plantation on a hill at the south-west corner of what is now Boston Harbour. Today, it is buried under a suburb of Quincy, known to locals as the City of Presidents. Four hundred years ago, the settlers, ignoring the Native American name, called this site Mount Wollaston.

New England entranced Thomas Morton: 'I do not think that in all the known world it could be paralleled,' he wrote. 'So many goodly groves of trees; dainty fine round rising hillocks . . . sweet crystal fountains, and clear running streams . . . 'twas Nature's Masterpiece . . . if this land be not rich, then is the whole world poor.'[3]

He was profoundly impressed by the Algonquin. They were so

compassionate 'that rather than one should starve . . . they would starve all'. There were no hungry beggars and no gallows 'furnished with poor wretches'. He concluded: 'Plato's commonwealth is much practised by these people.' Thomas Morton wanted to stay.

Two years after Morton's party landed, their principal, Captain Wollaston, decided that there might be much greener pastures down south in Virginia. The mother colony was booming, sucking in labour more eagerly than ever, so Wollaston took some of the indentured servants with him on a long and speculative trip to Jamestown. There he sold the servants, no doubt with little difficulty. It was so profitable a transaction that he sent back to Massachusetts for the remaining servants. Thomas Morton, who was set on making the plantation work, baulked at the instruction and mounted what was effectively a coup. He had Wollaston's lieutenant ejected from the plantation and gathered the remaining free-willers around him to offer alternatives. They could either go to Virginia to be sold into slavery or be his partners: 'We will converse, plant, trade and live together as equals and support and protect one another,' Morton promised.[4]

What followed outraged the Pilgrim Fathers. A free common-wealth was proclaimed on the plantation and it was re-named Ma-Re-Mount, the phonetic spelling of the original Algonquin name. It would be known – justifiably – as Merrymount during its short existence.

Morton was an Anglican and bon viveur. In that first burst of freedom for the servants, he or they organised the kind of celebrations for the next festival that had the Puritans muttering 'Satan'. The festival was May Day. Morton and his newly freed servants celebrated it on their plantation with a traditional 'old English festival'. The centrepiece was an eighty-foot maypole with a stag's antlers on its top. Morton composed an allegorical poem to the Greek goddess of spring, Maja, and he laid on 'a barrel of excellent beer' plus many bottles of alcohol. There was 'good cheer for all comers', especially Algonquin friends, who joined in as everyone held hands and danced in 'innocent mirth' around the maypole. It sounds to have been a loud affair of dancing, drinking and singing, a joyous V-sign to the grimly pious Pilgrims in the nearby Plymouth colony.

Among the Puritan settlers there was predictable outrage at this 'school of atheism'. They called the maypole an idol, the calf of Horeb. The Governor of the Plymouth colony, William Bradford, denounced it:

> They . . . set up a May-pole, drinking and dancing about it many days together, inviting the Indian women, for their consorts, dancing and frisking together, (like so many fairies, or furies rather) and worse practices. As if they had anew revived and celebrated the feasts of the Roman Goddess Flora, or the beastly practices of ye mad Bacchanalians.[5]

Morton was also said to be selling guns to his Algonquin friends, which understandably frightened settlers and added to their outrage. But there were other emotions, too. One was a fear among surrounding proprietors at the impact on their servants of Morton's free commonwealth. Numbers of servants were evidently fleeing their masters and finding refuge at Merrymount. We don't know how many but Governor Bradford accused Morton of entertaining 'discontents' and 'all the scum of the country'. Merrymount was a threat to every master. Morton was also probably doing too well commercially for their liking. His friendship with the Algonquin helped him to secure much of the fur trade and in its short existence it is estimated that Merrymount was six times more profitable than other plantations.

Puritan troopers stormed into Merrymount, seized Morton after a chase and hauled him in chains before Governor Bradford. Morton was too well connected to execute and so he was shipped back to England. The maypole was cut down and the houses were destroyed. There is no record of what happened to the servants. We assume they were thrust back into bondage, perhaps sent to Virginia and sold, as their original master first intended.

The second episode occurred within a year or so. A large group of indentured servants from East Anglia were among 180 souls sent by Puritan leaders into New England in 1628. The servants were landed at Salem and directed to settle a tract of land on the Merrimack River. They expected to be resupplied with food two years later when the famous Winthrop fleet arrived. However, when the fleet unloaded, the supplies earmarked for the Merrimack servants had vanished. The free-willers, who had been decimated by disease and had run out of provisions, appealed to the Puritan leadership in Salem for 'victuals to sustain' them but were turned down. A letter from the Puritan leader Thomas Dudley to the Countess of Lincoln written in 1631 explained why:

> We found ourselves wholly unable to feed them by reason that the provisions shipped for them were taken out of the ship they were put in, and they who were trusted to ship them in another, failed us, and left them behind; whereupon necessity enforced us to our extreme loss to give them all liberty.[6]

In other words, the free-willers were dumped, left to fend for themselves or to rely on the charity of the local Native Americans. Judging from Dudley's letter, that wasn't the worst of it. What upset these Puritans was the financial loss they had suffered in bringing all these souls over. Dudley lamented that the servants 'cost us about £16 or £20 a person furnishing and sending here'.[7]

Leaving servants to fend for themselves once they were of no more use would be one of the hard features of indentured servitude. Worn-out or dying servants would literally be dumped by their masters. It happened on a wide-enough scale for some colonies to legislate on the matter. Rhode Island, founded in 1636, would be the first to bring in an act to stop masters kicking out the sick and the lame under the pretence of freeing them. Virginia would follow, though not until more than a century later.

The Puritans in later years veered between treating indentured servants as children and treating them as potential delinquents. They imposed restrictions on all kinds of basic freedoms, legislated harsh punishments for runaways and approved the buying and selling of people. But more attention was given to the rights of servants and there was no stream of allegations about brutality and ill treatment. A crucial factor here was size. In New England, small farms predominated with only one or two servants apiece.

The situation in the Chesapeake, where a people business was in operation, was very different. The trade had developed to provide labour for the tobacco fields and would expand as colonialisation expanded. It featured most of the accoutrements of any trade – investors, agents, carriers, marketeers.

The investors were people of all kinds who spotted the chance of easy money through sending servants to the colonies and claiming the headright. In Virginia, as we have seen, they were entitled to fifty acres but the first investors in Maryland qualified for 2,000 acres for every five settlers they imported or 100 acres per person for fewer than five. The offer was later reduced but was so generous that Maryland would eventually have to drop headrights altogether for fear of running out of land.

Those keen to cash in on such a profitable opportunity ranged from the innkeeper with a relative or friend in the colony and a few pounds sterling to invest, to the great London and Bristol goldsmiths, cloth merchants and grocers with numerous contacts and large sums at their disposal. The Virginia historian Timothy Paul Grady investigated who was signing on servants for America from various parts of England and found nearly 3,000 different people in Bristol alone from 1654 to 1686.[8] Some signed up a party of servants and personally accompanied them to the New World, where they claimed headrights on themselves and on the servants. They then either sold the land and the servants, or had a go at tobacco planting on the land they had acquired with the manpower that had allowed them to acquire it.

Others used the network of agents and merchants who specialised in the trade to find and transport servants for them. One aristocratic investor was told that forty would-be servants could be delivered to her at a day's notice. These people brokers had printed indenture forms with blank spaces where the name of the servant and any extra obligations could be filled in. They had secure quayside buildings where servants were kept fed and happy till the ship was ready. And they no doubt regularly greased the palms of officials to turn a blind eye if servants changed their minds at the last minute and had to be stopped from slipping away.

Those already established in America indulged in a little servant trading on return trips to England. In *A Good Master Well Served*, Lawrence Towner quotes an entry made in the diary of Boston's mint master and leading goldsmith James Hull during the 1660s: 'Several children,' he wrote, 'I have brought over and all in good health and so disposed of them and providentially missed the having of one Sam Gaylor, who was after placed with Master Clark, and fell overboard and was lost on the way.'[9]

In America, ships from English ports carrying servants plied the Chesapeake's major rivers, stopping off to sell their cargoes wherever there was a demand. Their coming was advertised in advance. Posters and, later in the Chesapeake's history, newspapers announced the arrival of the latest cargo of servants. Potential buyers could read of the ages, gender and skills of those arriving and of when to clamber on board to inspect the human goods for themselves.

There were even sale-or-return clauses, conditions of barter requiring servants to be 'in perfect health' or 'able'. Those who weren't could be returned as 'refuse'. Some buyers became so indignant at discovering disease or infirmity that they went to court to get their money back. One forced a merchant who had sold him a young woman who turned out to have 'the pox' to pay for a cure and make a partial refund.

Like many high-paying ventures, the trade was risky. Ships and servants with them disappeared without trace. The year 1637 saw allegations by merchants that servants were being stolen en route to America. One merchant, Joseph Sanders, alleged that eighty-three of his servants were stolen by the captain of the ship transporting them after the man appointed as Sanders's factor died. Sanders petitioned the Privy Council to order their return. The very next month, another petitioner levelled the accusation against three ships' captains that they had 'embezzled . . . divers servants'.[10]

The journey from England continued to be unspeakably grim. In 1634, death rates on board and among those just landed were so high that John West, then acting Governor of Virginia, complained to the Commission for Plantations. He blamed the great numbers regularly squashed into most vessels. Merchants 'so pester their ships with passengers' that infection spread 'through throng and noiseomness,' he asserted.[11] Ill-conditioned, thin-blooded, town-bred servants were the most vulnerable. Eight of the servants on the *Mayflower* died within four months.

To the shipper, far and away the most profitable servants were those who postponed indenturing till they landed in America. The arrangement was for the captain to indenture and sell them on the basis of the cost of the fare. According to the Victorian historian Philip Bruce, shipowners took massive advantage of hapless migrants by hiking the 'fare money' enormously. There was 'an inclination on the part of [ship] owners to raise the rate extremely high in order to lengthen the terms of service and thus increase the profit of the voyage . . . not infrequently to four or five times the ordinary fee of the passage'.[12] The danger of putting oneself in the hands of a ship's master became notorious but it kept happening.

The main buyers of men and women were, of course, the big planters whose holdings automatically increased with every new servant they brought in. Men like William Tucker, who led the planters' reprisal attacks on the Powhatans after the 1622 massacre. In his will, drawn up two decades later, Tucker revealed that he had purchased at least 180 servants:

> I have transported divers servants thither which for every servant I am to have fifty acres of land, for my first dividend, which will amount unto 3000 acres for the first dividend, 3000 for the second dividend and 3000 acres for the third.

Tucker had a taste for understatement. His will ended: 'Such land may prove beneficial in time to my heir.'[13]

'Of hundreds of people who arrive in the colony yearly scarce any but are brought in as merchandise for sale,' the colony's secretary Richard Kemp reported to London in 1637.

All this was done in an atmosphere of fraud and rip-off. The Chesapeake in the 1630s was swimming with sharks feeding off

the headright system. It was easy. Even the dead could qualify
for a headright so long as they were on their way to the colony
when they died or had once visited. This invited deception and
corruption, and after Virginia became a Crown colony in 1624
the invitation continued to be proffered. One man who crossed
the Atlantic eight times was allowed to claim on himself for each
trip. Ships' captains allegedly registered entire crews as settlers and
claimed headrights on all of them, then sold the headrights, sailed
away and when the ship returned to the Chesapeake did it all again,
choosing a different settlement at which to land this time. In one
case, a servant was claimed on successively by the ship's master
who brought him, the merchant he was sold to and by the planter
to whom the merchant sold him.

Philip Bruce, who appears to have dug through every headright
ever claimed in Virginia, was outraged by the corruption and made
that clear in his *Economic History of Virginia*:

> The perversion was pushed so far that head rights were
> granted on the presentation of lists of names copied from old
> books of record, and it ended in the office of the secretary
> of the colony falling into the grossly illegal habit of selling
> these rights to all who would pay for one to five shillings
> for each right, without any pretension being made that the
> buyer had complied with the law.

The only settlers who didn't get their fifty acres were, of course,
the servants.

The headright scams were the tip of an iceberg of illegality.
As early as 1618, people began to vanish from around the ports
of England. They were kidnapped and sold on to the American
labour market. The first recorded instance was in Somerset, where
illicit warrants were used to arrest women victims who were
shipped out to Virginia. A second case saw a clerk called Robinson
use forged warrants to 'take up . . . yeoman's daughters or drive
them to compound to serve His Maj for breeders in Virginia'. He
was hanged, drawn and quartered. The punishment wasn't for
kidnapping but for forging the great seal. As we shall shortly see,

the kidnapping business became very big indeed in the following twenty years.

Officialdom, however, was more interested in controlling servants than worrying about how they were procured. Maryland not only matched the restrictions and punishments that Virginia had devised for her slave workforce but sometimes went further. In 1639, the Maryland Assembly made running away a capital offence. The next year, it changed the sentence. Death would only be the punishment if the servant refused to agree an extension of service at the expiration of the indenture. Initially, the formula was two extra days for every one away, then four days, and then ten days.

With one exception, none of the other colonies would be anything like as dependent on servants as the Chesapeake duo and so the same motive to repress wasn't there. Even in the Carolinas and Georgia there were relatively few white servants. The exception was Pennsylvania. In later decades, there would be as many English servants arriving in Pennsylvania as in Virginia and the servant laws there would be nearly as dehumanising as those in the Chesapeake. The only Virginian practice Pennsylvania curbed (and then only partially) was the selling of servants.

Of course, the years of bondage may well have been considered worth it had there been a rainbow at the end. But there seldom was. The typical indenture tied the servant tight – but not so the master. Sometimes the only requirements laid on the master were unspecified 'freedom dues' payable 'according to the custom of the country'. Many were led to believe that this meant land, only to find out on the day of liberty all those years later that it meant next to nothing. In a dingy Wapping tavern or in the bustling office of a Bristol merchant, it was not difficult, one imagines, to have fooled a starry-eyed young illiterate hoping for a new life. It is clear from the numbers of servants who tried for redress that this was a common experience.

Timothy Paul Grady sifted through years of court records from the two Chesapeake colonies and found them filled with numerous instances of masters cheating a servant of freedom dues or holding a servant longer than his or her original term and getting away with it. Grady judged that planter control of the legal system often nullified servants' rights.[14]

It would, however, be wrong to suggest that the courts were so loaded that the servants' cause was always doomed. There are numerous cases that went their way. Indeed, in Charles County Court, Maryland, advocates began representing servants around the 1640s and began winning. Who they were, or how many they helped, we don't know. But the archives reveal that the local justices decided to put a stop to it by blocking these Rumpoles. A tantalising paragraph in the archives reads:

> Whereas several attorneys have undertaken to manage servants' cases against their masters and mistresses to the mistresses and masters' great charge and damage, it is ordered that no person act as attorney for any servant hereafter except such as the court shall appoint.[15]

Planter-dominated courts made the following kinds of rulings:

- They backed the most successful planter of them all, Richard 'King' Carter and his brother Edward when they refused to free nine servants at the time specified on their indentures. The justification was that the indentures hadn't been made before the Lord Mayor or a justice of the peace. The nine were forced back to servitude on the Carter plantations.
- They deemed Richard Chapman's indentures valueless because they were 'only a certificate from some office in England not signed by any person'.
- They dismissed Thomas Damer's claim that he shouldn't have been sold 'according to the custom of the country' for seven years because he'd indentured for four years before leaving London. The court found he had no documentary proof and made him serve the seven years.
- They turned down the appeal for freedom by Francis and Thomas Brooke, who served an agreed term of four years only to be sold for another four. Inexplicably, they were ordered 'to return again' to their master and to 'serve him two years longer than . . . first covenanted for'.

Eventually, enough stink was caused in Maryland by 'custom of the country' rulings that the provincial assembly eventually laid down specifics. Adult servants arriving without indentures were to serve four years and get a suit of clothes, linen, socks and shoes, two hoes, one axe, three barrels of corn and that treasured fifty acres of land. Alas, this seems to have made little material difference. A study of the 5,000 indentured servants entering the colony from 1670–80 reveals that fewer than 1,300 proved their rights to freedom dues in land and just 241 ever became landowners. Of the 5,000, one in four is thought to have died still in bondage. Of the 1,300 who did prove their entitlement, some 900 sold their land immediately, many probably because they couldn't afford the fees for surveying it.[16]

Of course, humanity triumphed on occasion. It did for the sons of Thomas Allen of St Michaels, Maryland. Allen was among the first servants recruited for Maryland in the early 1630s. A decade and a half later, he was a free man again with some land, three young sons and a fear that something would happen to him, leaving his children impoverished orphans. Thomas's wife was evidently dead. In 1648, Allen wrote his will, which set out his fears. It tells how Allen, an outspoken Protestant, had fallen foul of a group of Catholic Irishmen and believed they planned to murder him. It pointed the finger at the Irishman responsible if he was killed and called on his friends to look after his two younger sons if he was murdered, as 'I would not have them sold for slaves.'[17]

Four months later, Thomas Allen was indeed murdered but not by Irishmen. His body was found on the seashore at Point Lookout, St Michaels, one early August morning in 1648. There were the entry marks of three arrows in his body and he had been scalped. His two youngest sons, Thomas and Robert, were missing.

The boys had been kidnapped by the Patuxent tribe, who had slain their father. News came that they could be ransomed. The tribe wanted 900 pounds of tobacco for Thomas, the older boy, and 600 pounds of tobacco for his younger brother Robert. A court of burgesses was convened and proceeded to order an audit of the dead man's estate. There wasn't much. Thomas Allen evidently didn't own land of any value, and the term of his indentured servant was nearly up. After sixteen years in the colony, his only assets of any worth were a small boat, a gun and fifteen pigs. After court costs were paid and Allen's debts discharged, there wouldn't be enough for the ransom. The worthy burgesses announced that the county wouldn't foot the bill. But they had a solution. If someone would pay the ransom, they would order that the boys be bound out to the ransomer as indentured servants till they were twenty-one – in their dead father's words, they would be 'sold for slaves'.

Happily, the dead man had genuinely good friends. Two of them paid the ransom and took the boys – but as sons not servants. As one declared when he committed himself to paying the 900 pounds of tobacco, it was done 'without any consideration of servitude or any other consideration whatsoever but his free love and affection'.[18]

How many did better than Thomas Allen and were able to build a good life and hand on a worthwhile stake in America to succeeding generations? In numerical terms, the answer must be 'many'. But in percentage terms, the answer is 'few'. Abbot Emerson Smith held that one in ten servants became a 'decently prosperous' landowner while another one became an artisan living 'a useful and comfortable life without owning any land'. The others 'died during their servitude, returned to England after it was over', or became 'poor whites' and 'occupied no substantial position in the colonies either as workers or as proprietors'.[19] In short, even those who outlived servitude were left in no better position for all those years of unpaid toil than when they first set foot on American soil.

CHAPTER EIGHT

SPIRITED AWAY

Economics dictates that when there is a demand for something, a market develops. The criminal mind dictates that where there is a market, there will be those willing to supply it by whatever means. And so the insistent demand for labour in the colonies gave rise to kidnapping. As related in the previous chapter, the first kidnapper was tried in England in 1618 (the year before the first shipload of children sailed from London), accused of abducting young women for the colonies. This was no flash in the pan. A criminal industry had been born.

By the middle of the seventeenth century, kidnapping was a flourishing business. In 1649, William Bullock, who settled in both Virginia and Barbados, wrote that 'the usual way of getting servants, hath been by a sort of men nick-named *Spirits*'.[1] In other words – despite all the other categories of people flowing into the colonial labour force, including free-willers, deported criminals, street children and the rest – men, women and children had to be inveigled or enticed into slavery to take up the slack in the colonial labour force. Spirits became the colonies' chief recruiting officers.

Bullock described how kidnappers spirited people away:

> All the idle, lazy simple people they can entice, such as have professed idleness and will rather beg than work; who are persuaded by these Spirits they shall go into a place where

food shall drop into their mouths; and being thus deluded,
they take courage and are transported.[2]

The numbers are unknown – crime statistics did not exist in the seventeenth century. According to the Virginian clergyman Morgan Godwin, 10,000 people were being spirited away every year by the late 1600s.[3] But this figure has been described as 'absurdly large', inflated for the purpose of propaganda.[4]

Walter Blumenthal suggests that it 'is not improbable' that the number of 'browbeaten indentured servants, transportees, convicts and kidnapped may have together exceeded ten thousand in certain years'.[5] This was especially likely during the middle years of the 1600s, when Cromwellian excesses were at their highest in Ireland.

We know of many cases of kidnapping through court records. Elizabeth Hamlyn became the first recorded spirit charged at Middlesex Assizes in London with 'taking diverse little children in the street and selling them to be carried to Virginia'. She was sentenced to be whipped and to appear again at the next session. Other spirits followed Hamlyn into the dock intermittently. Between 1625 and 1701, seventy-three cases of kidnapping came up at the Middlesex County Court.[6]

This small number of cases across so many years is not a measure of the size of the problem; it is, rather, an indication of the lackadaisical manner in which law-enforcement agencies dealt with it. Among those cases that did come to trial was that of Christian Chacrett, who stood trial in 1655. He was accused of being 'one that taketh up men and women and children and sells them on a ship to be conveyed beyond the sea'. According to witness Dorothy Perkins, Chacrett had inveigled the Furnifull family – husband, wife and infant – on board the *Planter*, bound for Virginia. In a trial of 1658, Anne Gray was accused of 'living idly and out of service' and of spiriting a sixteen-year-old maid onto a ship.

The scale of this shadowy trade is best estimated not by the number of cases but by the scale of criminal activity revealed through the evidence in the trials, for kidnappers often admitted to, or were accused of, very large numbers of offences. In 1671, a spirit called William Haverland was convicted of kidnapping and turned King's Evidence. He made accusations against a large number of other spirits, sixteen in all, including a haberdasher, a seaman, two victuallers and a waterman. Haverland claimed that a man named John Stewart had practised spiriting for twelve years, kidnapping people for Barbados, Virginia and other places – 'five hundred in a year, as he has confessed'.

If the evidence of Haverland is to be believed, Stewart accounted for 6,000 victims in just over a decade. While such a number cannot be verified, the evidence demonstrates that Stewart was considered by his peers to be admirably prolific and diligent in his trade. According to Haverland, Stewart paid twenty-five shillings to anyone who provided him with a victim. Stewart then sold them on for forty shillings apiece.

In another affidavit, Haverland accused William Thiene, a shoemaker of East Smithfield, of spiriting away 840 people, while Robert Bayley, who plied his trade from St Katherine's and St Giles, was described as 'an old spirit, who had no other way of livelihood'.

All these spirits required accomplices: strong-arm men and fences, or dealers in stolen goods; ships' captains or their agents; merchants both in Britain and in the colonies; through to corrupt officials and magistrates on both sides of the Atlantic. The usual operation involved luring the innocent, the gullible and the drunk into makeshift prisons where they could be held until a ship was found for them. If the spirit and a captain already had a business arrangement, the victims could be taken directly onto ships riding at anchor in the Thames. While victims once ensnared could be forcibly held against their will, violent tactics such as those used by the navy's pressgangs seem to have been a last resort.

Kidnapping developed to encompass several types of operative, each with a distinct role in the business. A key trade was that of 'office keeper'. As with 'spiriting', this was a euphemism. The office keeper provided a base from which to run operations, maybe a tap-room to entertain potential clients and possibly a secure cellar or attic to hold those awaiting a ship. The office keeper also provided a plausible front to the world. As with the spirit, the office keeper used deception or any other art to get the unwary or gullible on board a ship. The only difference seems to have been that while the kidnapper might not necessarily have worried about papers of indenture, the office keeper would by any devious means obtain a signature or, as most people were illiterate, a mark. The sly and shifty nature of the business is very well caught in this description of spirits in London:

> . . . three or four blades, well dressed but with hawks' countenances . . . those fine fellows who look like footmen upon a holiday crept into cast suits of their masters . . . are kidnappers who walk the Change in order to seduce people who want services and young fools crossed in love and under an uneasiness of mind to go beyond seas, getting so much a head of masters and ships and merchants who go over for every wretch they trepan into this misery.[7]

This was no honest business – it was a pernicious racket, as the writer made clear in his description of the spirits' victims:

> Half a dozen ragamuffinly fellows, shewing poverty in their rags and despair in their faces, mixed with a parcel of young wild striplings like runaway prentices . . . That house which they are entering is an Office where servants for the plantations bind themselves to be miserable as long as they live . . . Those young rakes and tatterdemalions you see so lovingly handled are drawn by their fair promises to sell themselves into slavery.[8]

The picture emerges of organised crime. Spirits targeted people across all sections of society. The unwary apprentice could just as easily fall prey to the kidnapper as the vagrant and unemployed. But the kidnapper did prefer the young to the old. This was no surprise, for the labour markets in America and Barbados favoured the young and healthy. Those most at risk were children over the age of ten, particularly teenagers, and young men and women aged up to their mid-twenties.

Spirits were active not only in London but all around the British Isles, in ports including Southampton, Aberdeen, Dublin and particularly Bristol. The illicit trade in Bristol was exposed by the unlikely figure of Judge Jeffreys, the drunken lawyer who was made Lord Chief Justice by Charles II. Today, Jeffreys is best remembered for conducting the Bloody Assizes of 1685, in which he sentenced around 330 of the Duke of Monmouth's rebels to death and 800 more to transportation. During the assizes, Jeffreys learned that a young boy had been taken from prison and illegally transported. It appears that the child was a victim of the sort of racket played out in many seaports. Petty thieves, rogues and vagabonds would be brought before the local justices and told the only way to save their necks was by agreeing to transportation. To this, most of the small-time villains, scared for their lives, would agree. The justices and their friends would then sell the rogues off to merchants or ships' captains for the slave marts of the New World.

In the case of this young boy, Jeffreys discovered the culprits. They included the city's Mayor, whom Jeffreys fined £1,000. The case of the child exposed the corruption of not only Bristol but of the age. It was to Judge Jeffreys' credit that he spotted this nasty little scheme and did his best to put a stop to it. Only three years later, when James II took flight, Jeffreys also tried to flee abroad but was recognised having a last drink in an inn and ended his days in the Tower of London, where he died of a stomach ulcer aggravated by alcohol.

Kidnapping was so prevalent that it became the subject of fiction, appearing in stories by writers including Daniel Defoe and Robert Louis Stevenson. One spirit was supposed to have made St Paul's Cathedral his headquarters. It is tempting to imagine the spirit practising his devious arts around and about the cathedral while the Dean, the poet John Donne, thundered from the pulpit about how deprived children might be given a second chance in a foreign land. The old St Paul's was swept away in the great fire of 1666 and maybe the spirit with it. It is hard to think of the wardens of Christopher Wren's neo-classical cathedral allowing such malign spirits to linger within.

By the middle of the 1600s, fear of kidnapping became so great that hysteria swept over the land, especially among families living in or near ports, and even causing occasional mass panics among young women and other potential victims. False accusations were made by citizen against citizen. In 1645, Margaret Robinson was called before a court to answer the accusation that she assaulted one Mary Hodges, 'saying she was a spirit'. William Gaunt and Thomas Faulkner were accused of attacking Margaret Emmerson and falsely claiming she was 'a spirit or an enticer or inveigler of children . . . there being no charge or accusation laid against her'. Some years later, Susan Jones was accused by Rebekah Allen of 'raising a tumult against her and calling of her spirit'.[9]

Kidnapping was the subject of sensationalist popular journalism of a style we would all recognise today. One undated broadsheet gives a typically vivid account of large-scale spiriting of children in London. The report was published by James Read of Fleet Street, London, and is preserved in the British Library. It begins with sensational headlines:

The Grand KIDNAPPER at last taken
Or, a full and true
ACCOUNT
OF THE
Taking and Apprehending
OF
Cap Azariah Daniel
For conveying away the bodies
OF
Jonathan Butler, and *Richard Blagrave,*
Also the confession he made before Justice *Richards*
In *Spittle-fields,* with his commitment to *New-gate*
With account of *Edward Harrison,* conveying away
The Children of *Thomas Vernon* Salesman, with the
Manner of his Confession how a Hundred and Fifty
Children more have been sent down the River in several
Ships; with his Commitment to *Newgate.*

The account contains so much detail of the scale of the spirit business that it is worth quoting further:

The noise which the detection of the former Kidnapper had made in the Town; occasioned such strict enquiries to be made after other children which have been lost, by their afflicted parents, that pursuant to their great care, all Houses near the Water Side, and all outward bound Ships now in the river, have been severly searched, and many Children rescued by those means from the dangers that threatened them, but though the theft was regained, the Thieves for the generality made their escape, and we have had but Three, and those not the Principal who have been taken in those abominable Practices, till Wednesday the 7th. Of this Instant September: When one Captain Azariah Daniel, Commander of a Ship now in the River, coming by the Stocks-Market, was met by two Gentlemen who having lost their children, pursuant to the information they had of him, were in search after him.

The two distraught parents had their wits about them, for they had already obtained a warrant from a magistrate for the arrest of Captain Daniel. While one of them went for a constable, the other followed the captain to a public house. The captain was arrested and taken before the magistrate, Justice Richards. The justice asked the suspect where he lived. The captain gave his true address, which was unfortunate for him because the magistrate immediately ordered his lodgings to be searched: 'And the rooms being searched, two Children were found in a garret.'

With the discovery of the children, both aged about twelve, Daniel was sent to Newgate to await trial. The same broadsheet contains a second case of a missing child:

Mr Vernon, a Salesman in the parish of Stepney, having but one Child and that some time since lost, was very Solicitous in enquiring after Him: And pursuant to his great care in looking after him, he received information that one Edward Harrison, a mariner who lived in the Neighbourhood, had been seen with a Boy about the Age of his son was described to be of, and who seemed very unwilling to go along with him.

Accordingly Mr Vernon went to Sir Robert Geffery's, and having gotten his Warrant, took a Constable with him and went to the House of Edward Harrison . . .

The prisoner seemed at first surprised at his unexpected apprehension, and seemed sensible of nothing of Guilt, protesting much for his innocency. But being brought before the Justice his courage failed him, and several convenient questions being put to Him by Sir Robert, he at last confessed he had conveyed the Child three weeks since aboard a Barbados Ship now in the River, and besides him there were above a hundred and fifty more aboard several other ships in the said River bound to his Majesty's Plantations. Having made his ingenious Confession his Mittimus [Daniel] was made for New-gate, and he was accordingly sent Prisoner thither.

And several Parents who have lost their children, have got the Lords of the Admiralty's Warrant in order to Search all outward bound ships for the recovery of them.[10]

Laws were passed to control spiriting. But they did little good. In 1645, Parliament ordered all officers of the law to keep a watch for those 'stealing, selling, buying, inveigling, purloining, conveying or receiving children . . .' Port officials were instructed to search all vessels 'in the river and at the Downs for such children'.[11] A year later, a further law required customs officers in England to keep records of those leaving, and for colonial governors to send returns of those arriving in their territories.

In 1654, Bristol council ordered that a book should be kept detailing the names of indentured passengers on board ships heading for the colonies. Merchants and other worthies petitioned Parliament in 1661 and 1662 to introduce official sanctions against spirits but it failed to act. In 1664, a plan was put forward to have every emigrant bound for the colonies interviewed and asked whether or not they were going of their own free will. In 1670, Parliament made kidnapping – 'any deceit or force to steal any person or persons with intent to sell or transport them into ports beyond the sea' – an offence punishable by death. None of it made much difference. The kidnappers continued to thrive.

Justice was very inadequately administered in London. As the great chronicler of immigration, Peter Coldham, notes in *Emigrants in Chains*: 'In the courts of the metropolis the theft of a horse merited much stiffer penalties than the theft of a person.'[12] In 1680, a spirit named Ann Servant was tried before Middlesex Assizes for assaulting a young woman called Alice Flax and putting her on board a ship that took her to Virginia, where she was sold. Ann Servant confessed to the crime and was fined thirteen shillings and sixpence. A horse thief would have been hanged.

In 1682, a government initiative to protect children from being spirited against their will laid out strict guidelines for indentures. How little effect all the government attempts to clamp down actually had can be judged from yet another case in the Middlesex court. In 1684, a male and a female spirit who had kidnapped a sixteen-year-old girl were fined the derisory sum of twelve pence. Such fines reflected both how the courts viewed kidnapping in general and also that magistrates and judges often allowed the accused to pay a sum in compensation to their victim. From the Middlesex records, it is obvious that many cases reported to the court never proceeded to trial.

At the end of the seventeenth century, spiriting continued to play as important a role in supplying labour to the British colonies as it had near the beginning. Kidnapping was allowed to flourish because it was respectable business's shady sibling. One authority has pointed out that 'instead of being deplorable outlaws in the servant trade [spirits] were the faithful and indispensable adjuncts of its most respected merchants'.[13] Newspapers continued to run stories about spirits, along with advertisements from those searching for lost relatives. In October 1700, the London *Post Boy* ran an advertisement from a father offering a reward for the return of his eleven-year-old son, who was feared kidnapped.

Spirits could continue to rely on authority turning a blind eye to their work and to their victims rarely living long enough to gain their freedom and return to confront them with their crimes. Yet, as we will see later on in Chapter Seventeen, in two celebrated instances kidnap victims did return to seek retribution and restitution.

But perhaps the most important reasons why kidnapping grew and thrived in the seventeenth century were that spiriting was a convenient way for society to rid itself of the unwanted poor and homeless, and that very often the government simply decided it had more urgent matters to deal with, such as those that unfold in the following chapter.

CHAPTER NINE

FOREIGNERS IN THEIR OWN LAND

In the Elizabethan period, young blades went to Ireland to prove themselves and get rich. As we saw in Chapter 1, Sir Walter Raleigh and his half-brother Sir Humphrey Gilbert went to make war. The poet Edmund Spenser settled there to lead the life of a gentleman on a confiscated estate near that occupied by Raleigh. There were risks, of course. Ireland was where court favourite the Earl of Essex ended his career in bloodshed and failure despite the assistance of the ruthless Francis Drake. What happened in Ireland over several centuries had a direct bearing on how the first English settlements in America were approached and developed. Many great English adventurers and soldiers learned their craft in Ireland before searching for greater – and easier – pickings farther west.

For the Elizabethan blue bloods and youthful gentry with fire in their bellies, Ireland became a land of adventure. By the late 1500s, all kinds of Englishmen were crossing the narrow stretch of water in search of their fortunes. Some fared well and others less so but in almost all instances their prosperity was bought at a heavy cost to the locals. We do not need to give a complete account of what happened in Ireland – for that has been told so often and so clearly by historians over the years – but attempt an impression of the forces, psychological as well as social and political, that propelled Ireland into the front line of the transatlantic adventure.

For any English ship putting out for the West Indies and America, Ireland was there to be sailed past or around. Ships stopped on the way for supplies and Ireland became an important point on the route to the west. It was natural that Irish men and women would get swept up in the great colonial adventure. Very early on, Irish servants were taken across the ocean under the indentured-servant scheme. No doubt many idle or curious people who ventured to the quaysides of ports such as Waterford in the south-east or Kinsale in the south-west were enticed aboard ships and became emigrants before they hardly knew it.

This adventure forged a firm link between England and Ireland, and then to the new colonies across the Atlantic. This triangular relationship grew throughout the seventeenth and eighteenth centuries and among the ties that held it were the chains of bondage.

The headright system that we have seen play such a key role in populating the American colonies was from early times used to promote emigration from Ireland. One seventeenth-century planter from Ireland managed to amass an estate of 32,000 acres in Maryland thanks to the numbers of servants he brought over. George Talbot from County Roscommon transported the astonishing number of 640 servants in the space of twelve years. He seems to have been determined to create an entire colony by his sole endeavours.

The emigrants from Ireland included the 'Scotch-Irish', Scots who had settled in Ulster. Many were moved to go because their particular nonconformist religion was officially discouraged at home. They found support and a welcome in colonies such as Delaware and Pennsylvania. This was particularly the case after the Restoration of the English Crown in 1660, when the official view on dissenting religions hardened. This impelled Irish Quakers to settle in Pennsylvania, the first Quaker state, and New Jersey. In the eighteenth century, Presbyterian ministers in Ireland began to lead their congregations to America, especially to Carolina, seeing themselves as leaders of flocks of 'lost' people in search of the promised land. Their zeal was no doubt sharpened by the official financial inducements offered for ministers to emigrate. The Test

Act of 1704 impelled more dissenters to make the journey from Ireland to America, for it not only barred them from high office but also ruled their marriages invalid.

The Irish Catholic experience was driven by a similar policy of exclusion. The Reformation under Henry VIII did not impinge all that much on Ireland but under Elizabeth I the desire to impose some uniformity of religion upon Ireland became much more strident. By the middle of the 1600s, Irish Catholics – the vast majority of the people – found themselves subject to an English scheme to eradicate them.

Of course, the English and the Normans had sparred with the Irish for centuries. The English thought of the Irish as uncivilised – despite their uncanny ability to entice colonists into taking on their culture and way of life. Vikings, Normans, Welsh, Scots and English had gone to Ireland over the centuries and many had been swallowed up by it, like a lost goblet taken slowly down into the bog. The eminent social and economic historian Fernand Braudel has pointed out that the Irish were seen by the English as different in quality from the Scots or the Welsh:

> The Irish were the enemy, savages simultaneously despised and feared. The consequences were mutual incomprehension, high-handedness by the invaders, and horrors whose sinister catalogue needs no elaboration: the story has been told with lucidity and honesty by English historians themselves.[1]

The English in America thought it reasonable to settle in a land already inhabited by others. They viewed the indigenous population as one to conquer, eradicate or enslave. This view of the world was undoubtedly learned, and it was probably learned in Ireland. By viewing the Irish as barbarians, the English could have no qualms about invading their land.

The Anglo-Norman invasion of Ireland prepared the mindset that was to propel the English farther west four centuries later. Just as 1066 is a date to be remembered by every school child in England, 1166 should be remembered by every child in Ireland. It was the date when the deposed King of Leinster, Diarmait Mac

Murchada, invited Henry II of England into Ireland to help him regain his crown. Henry stayed and by 1171 had firmly established a bridgehead reaching from Dublin to Drogheda. It was to be called the Pale, after the Latin *palus* or stake. What happened to the Irish after that was to have interesting parallels with what happened in the American colonies.

A few years after Henry established his bridgehead, a Welsh cleric named Giraldus Cambrensis wrote a lasting work of collective character assassination. *The History and Topography of Ireland* listed all the Irish vices: blasphemy, laziness, treachery, incest and cannibalism among them. Cambrensis's fiction provided the basis for English views of Ireland for several hundred years and rankled with the Irish for just as long. Such beliefs helped to justify the deeds of ruthless military leaders such as Sir Humphrey Gilbert, of whom we have already heard so much. His policy in Ireland was to slaughter even non-combatants on the grounds that terror among the population 'made short wars'.

The Anglo-Norman expeditions into Ireland marked the start of a sorry and drawn-out history of enmity and struggle. The Irish would be cut off from their own laws and at the same time not allowed recourse to the laws of the colonisers. A group of Irish noblemen complained to the Pope that under the English laws no Englishman could be punished for killing an Irishman. The Irish were made into second-class citizens without the rights accorded to others. The 'compelling parallels' between this and in the way in which the slave-labour system in America accorded rights to some but not to others has been highlighted by Theodore Allen in *The Invention of the White Race*.[2]

As Allen relates, under Anglo-American slavery, 'the rape of a female slave was not a crime, but a mere trespass on the master's property'. It is interesting to compare this with Ireland in 1278, when two Anglo-Normans were brought into court and charged with raping one Margaret O'Rorke. They were found not guilty because 'the said Margaret is an Irishwoman'. We can see that from the twelfth until the sixteenth century, Ireland was a laboratory in which social ideas and legal conventions would be forged and which found their echo in the labour systems of the American colonies.

A law enacted in Virginia in 1723 provided that 'manslaughter of a [black] slave is not punishable'. Under Anglo-Norman law in Ireland, for someone standing accused of manslaughter to be acquitted he had only to show that the slain victim was Irish. Anglo-Norman priests granted absolution on the grounds that it was 'no more sin to kill an Irishman than a dog or any other brute'.

The first serious rebellion in Ireland began in 1594 and became known as the Nine Years' War. Hugh O'Neill, Earl of Tyrone (a title given to him by Henry VIII), was Ulster's most powerful leader and he was alarmed at the increasing pace of plantation. After starting well, Tyrone threw in the towel in 1603 and submitted to James I, who had just succeeded Queen Elizabeth.

Hugh O'Neill's rebellion sparked other uprisings around the country, especially in Munster, in the south-west. There were high-profile casualties, including Sir Walter Raleigh and Edmund Spenser. Raleigh bounced back from this reversal; for Spenser, it was the end of his fortunes. The creator of the pastoral ideals of *The Faerie Queene* was buried in Westminster Abbey at Chaucer's feet at the age of forty-six but not before he had made a helpful suggestion of what to do with the Irish: they should be starved from the landscape. Spenser's proposition would prove to be prophetic.

Four years after his rebellion ended, Hugh O'Neill, along with several other Irish nobles and their families, sailed out of Lough Swilly and into exile in Europe. The 'flight of the earls' was the signal the English had been waiting for. Ulster had long been a thorn in England's side, with home-grown opposition providing a possible platform for Spanish designs. As O'Neill sailed over the horizon, all chance of organised resistance receded with him. Now the coast was clear for the plantation of Ulster. It was September 1607, just five months after the English settlers had founded Jamestown.

The colonisation of Ireland led to a large proportion of the indigenous population becoming rootless. The English colonists found they faced problems quite similar to those they had at home. Wandering vagabonds and vagrant villains roamed the land, though more freely than in England, where the Poor Laws kept the homeless tied to their native parishes. Some saw transportation as the obvious answer to the problem of what to do with the native Irish in general. There was even a proposal as early as 1607 to transport seven or eight thousand of the most obdurate rebels and vagrants. These imaginative schemes proved to be before their time. It was not until Cromwell came to Ireland with his more robust attitudes that they would be taken up, and then with some vigour.

In London, there were those who felt strongly that the plantation of Ireland was a better bet than the plantation of North America: for a start, it was much closer. The Solicitor General, Sir Francis Bacon, thought the Irish project scored strongly on religious, political and investment criteria. The financial arrangements for the two ventures were remarkably similar; in fact, the organisation of the Ulster venture followed the lines established for North America. Just as the money for America was raised in the City of London through newly created joint stock companies such as the Virginia Company, the Ulster venture was also funded by City investment. One important difference was that while the American companies were promoted by private enterprise, the Irish Society was forced on largely unwilling City merchants by the King.[3]

While struggling to make a go of planting Ireland, the English continued with their transatlantic endeavours. They would carry some Irish with them. The first English toehold in the West Indies was on St Christopher (now St Kitts), where some French had already settled. Captain Thomas Warner, a dogged Suffolk Puritan, together with his wife, son and a small number of men, claimed the island for James I. Warner had already travelled widely in the New World and had seen the Amazonian basin. Now he wanted a place that he could settle and make something of.

St Christopher already had its local inhabitants, the Kalinago people. They had arrived many years before, drawn by the island's good soil and had displaced the previous inhabitants, the Arawak, by being better at warfare. They were not to be trifled with. After the Kalinago had come the Spanish, then a handful of French Jesuits, followed by the Spanish again, and then by the first Englishman, John Smith, passing through on his way to Virginia. Thomas Warner came next. He developed a wary relationship with the Kalinago chief, Ouboutou Tegremante, and within two years had established his little colony sufficiently well, he felt, to sail to England for more colonists. While he was there, he picked up a warrant from Charles I giving him control over a sizeable part of the West Indies. The new colonists that returned with Warner in 1626 were mainly Irish indentured servants who slashed and burned the vegetation to make room for the arable crops they would live on and the crop they would sell, tobacco.

And so the Irish came in numbers to the Caribbean. In the 1640s, a fanciful report claimed some 20,000 Irish were living on St Christopher. Although this number seems improbable, we can take it that a good number of Irish did arrive on the island. In whatever manner they arrived, as voluntary indentured servants or as transportees, they became, in their multitudes, slaves in the plantations. St Christopher prospered through tobacco. Those Irish who survived their indenture could start up their own smallholdings on the island's fertile land. But when the Virginian tobacco trade picked up, the smaller producers began to suffer. Some Irish in the Caribbean went on to become major planters and slave owners themselves.

Into this stark new world sailed a trading ship called the *Abraham* in 1636. The reports of its dealings between Ireland and Barbados are contained in a unique series of letters preserved at the Admiralty in London and these give an excellent insight into the recruitment process for servants in the mid-1600s.[4] The ship was owned by a merchant named Mathew Cradock, a Puritan and the first governor of the Massachusetts Bay Company. His agent or supercargo, Thomas Anthony, had the job of drumming up a human cargo in Ireland before the ship arrived. The men and women Anthony persuaded to sign up would be indentured for four years and sold in the colonial labour markets.

Anthony was a punctilious employee and his letters provide a record of a man who wished his boss to know that his slow progress was not for want of trying. Though he laboured for months, Anthony had difficulty raising the necessary numbers to make up his cargo. Cradock had hoped for a hundred servants but Anthony faced competition from a local ship and from a Flemish ship out of Amsterdam.

When he arrived in Kinsale on 28 April, four months before the *Abraham*, Anthony vigorously put the word out for people wishing to start a new life, writing on 13 September (the spelling and grammar are so idiosyncratic that we have changed quotations into modern usage for the sake of comprehensibility): 'And now it may please you to be informed that upon the first days of market after the ship's arrival, both here at Bandon, Cork, and at Youghal, we caused the drum to be beaten . . .'

After many recruiting trips around the country, Anthony still had not got his complement of 100 servants:

> And hither unto we have entertained and forthcoming the number of 61 persons, whereof there is 41 men servants, the rest women kind, from 17 to 35 years and very lusty and strong bodied which will I hope be means to set them off to the best advantage . . .

To obtain his complement of sixty-one, Anthony seems to have had to resort to some knavery, probably involving kidnapping, as the mayor of Kinsale put him in the town gaol until he had released two of the servants recruited locally. Anthony spent only a few days in prison, indicating either a quick bribe or the release of those he had not recruited legally. Finally, in November, the *Abraham* set sail for Barbados.

We know the level of profits that Anthony made for his boss, for he wrote to him on 13 February 1637, nearly a year after he had arrived in Cork. By then his cargo had diminished to fifty-six, three having probably died on the journey (a very low rate of mortality as rates of death on board ship could sometimes reach twenty or even thirty per cent) and two having absconded in Cowes on the Isle of Wight. 'From Cowes we brought 56 servants for your accounts which were disposed of to sale; ten of them to the governor of this place in 450 weight (pounds of tobacco) apiece and all the rest in 500 . . .' In total, Anthony's cargo made a profit of 27,500 pounds of tobacco – a nice sum, even without the thwarted bonus of the kidnapped inhabitants of Kinsale.

Back in Ireland, fifty years after Spenser's death, his radical proposals were about to be put into play. A new and more strident plantation policy paved the way for the large-scale movement of the Irish across the Atlantic. The political events that led up to this mass migration of people began in England but quickly spread to Ireland. As relations between Charles I and Parliament worsened in the 1640s, the Irish Catholics saw a chance of making capital. The centre of the rebellion was in Ulster, where the plantation of large numbers of Protestants had made the situation very volatile. The rebels killed some 4,000 Protestant settlers and up to another 8,000 are thought to have perished through starvation and want. Exaggerated reports circulated in London that up to 100,000 Protestants had been killed. The Irish uprising spread throughout the country. A confederacy was formed to fight the English, with even the Old English reluctantly joining in, but it was riven with disagreements and militarily flawed.

The English Parliamentarians decided to take firm action. An act was passed in 1642 to raise the finance for an army to crush the Irish. The act offered 2,500,000 acres of confiscated Irish land at knock-down prices to merchant adventurers – those who would invest in the army that was to be raised to suppress the insurrection. The Irish, their religion and their propensity for siding with England's enemies would be crushed once and for all, and the adventurers would be rewarded with the land confiscated to enable Protestants to resettle the island. The Irish would become outlaws in their own land and their former property would be sold off at below-market prices to pay for the military operation that would have taken it from them. It was as brilliant as it was brutal – one of those elegant pieces of synergism that must make the difficult task of ruling occasionally satisfying.

A contemporary though not impartial observer, the Papal Nuncio, Giovanni Battista Rinuccini, said that the Irish transported to the Indies were 'held like slaves under a cruel lash'.[5]

Among many sad stories, Rinuccini reported the case of the wife of a Catholic man being deported because of his faith pleading to be allowed to accompany her husband into exile. The woman was refused on the grounds that she was not strong enough to work in the Indian Islands (the West Indies). She was thrown into prison, while her husband was sent to his fate.

Sir Phelim O'Neill, one of the key leaders of the rebellion, carefully made clear that the argument was not with the King but with Parliament. To begin with, this was a good move but it ceased to be so when Charles I was beheaded in 1649. On 20 June that year, Oliver Cromwell was appointed Lord-Lieutenant and commander-in-chief of the army in Ireland. Macaulay, in his *History of England*, describes vividly what Cromwell achieved:

> Everything yielded to the vigour and ability of Cromwell. In a few months he subjugated Ireland, as Ireland had never been subjugated during the five centuries of slaughter which had elapsed since the landing of the first Norman settlers. He resolved to put an end to that conflict of races and religions which had so long distracted the island, by making the English and Protestant population decidedly predominant. For this end he gave the rein to the fierce enthusiasm of his followers, waged war resembling that which Israel waged on the Canaanites, smote the idolaters with the edge of the sword, so that great cities were left without inhabitants, drove many thousands to the Continent, shipped off many thousands to the West Indies, and supplied the void thus made by pouring in numerous colonists, of Saxon blood, and of Calvinistic faith.[6]

Cromwell began his war in Ireland in August 1649 by marching against Drogheda, a prosperous town thirty miles north of Dublin and a key strategic position from which to advance into Ulster. On the evening of 11 September, the Parliamentarians overwhelmed the town, slaughtering officers and soldiers. Catholic priests and friars were treated as combatants and killed on sight. A moment of gruesome farce came when the commander of the defending forces, Sir Arthur Aston, was bludgeoned to death with his wooden leg, in which Parliamentarian soldiers believed he had hidden gold coins. Some 3,500 people died in the storming of Drogheda. Parliamentarian losses were around 150. Many of the surviving defenders were transported to Barbados.

An interesting two-way trade in people was developing in which something beneficial emerged for both those wanting to colonise Ireland and those backing America: native Irish could be deported to feed the voracious labour market in America while making room in Ireland for planters from England. This does not seem to have been an orchestrated movement but it was a nice piece of serendipity for nascent imperial capitalism.

In the ensuing turmoil, famine followed war on a terrible scale. Proposals for deportation came quickly to the fore. It is difficult to know how many people were banished during this period, for no records exist. However, there are clues to what was going on. The Puritans who now ruled Ireland had only one goal: the total subjugation of Ireland by the method of destroying its people and planting in their stead Protestant stock from England and Scotland. The destruction of the Irish was to be carried out by three methods: by starvation, by banishment to the West or to Continental Europe and by transportation across the Atlantic. Priests, defeated soldiers, men, women and children were all shipped off at various times from various locations. The transportation of the Irish began in the late 1640s and certainly reached a high level in 1652–3, the years that mark the partial obliteration of the Catholic people of Ireland.

On 1 April 1653, Cromwell's Council of State issued a licence to one Sir John Clotworthy to transport to America 500 Irishmen. The licence was careful to point out that these unfortunates should be 'natural Irishmen' in case the assiduous Sir John made the mistake of sending off some descendants of the 'Old English' or Anglo-Norman settlers. Such a mistake was made when young women descended from the early Anglo-Norman settlers were abducted and sold by traders to the sugar plantations in the West Indies.[7] Licences were granted to English merchants throughout the year. In June, the Council of State in England ordered that 'the governors of the precincts be authorised to transport 8,000 Irish'.

Later that year, the Council of State granted a licence for 400 Irish children to be taken to New England and Virginia. Around the same time, a contract was signed with Boston merchants to carry off 250 women and 300 men from ports along Ireland's southern and south-eastern coast. The contracted merchants, Leader and

Selleck (the latter a merchant who was particularly prominent among those importing Irish labour), were to be allowed to search for their slaves within twenty miles of Wexford, Waterford, Kinsale, Youghal and Cork. The onerous task of having to search along such a long stretch of coastline was mercifully mitigated when the English grandee with control over Cork, Lord Broghill, said he would allow the merchants to pick their slaves from among the people of Cork alone.

In the 1650s, Ireland was a desolate place. The land became dreadfully depopulated due to war, famine and disease. Hundreds of thousands of Irish people vanished over a mere decade or so. Charles Walpole described the situation:

> The English government had a grim excuse for re-peopling Ireland. The desolation of the island was complete: one third of the people had perished or been driven into exile; famine and plague had finished the work of the sword; the fields lay uncultivated; and the miserable remnants of the flying population were driven to live on carrion and human corpses. The wolves so increased in numbers, even round the city of Dublin itself, that the counties were taxed for their extermination, and rewards of £5 were paid for the head of a full grown wolf and £2 for that of a cub.[8]

Wolves were not the only troublesome creatures with a price on their heads – there were also the priests and the tories. Tories were guerrilla fighters, who lived in the forests, mountains and bogs and operated mainly at night, launching raiding parties against those who had usurped their lands.[9] Some degenerated into banditry. Freedom fighters or rogues, they all had a price. One way of dealing with them was to hold four people hostage against the capture of any tory committing a crime. If within twenty-eight days the crime went unsolved and the tory had not given himself up, the four would be shipped off to the colonies. As for the priestly classes, the ordinary holy man's head was priced the same as that of a wolf but a bishop's head would fetch twice that, namely £10. Keeping or hiding a priest would merit banishment and the confiscation of all property. A Franciscan who had to flee Ireland told of one such case:

> Anno 1657, I myself saw this iniquitous law carried out into iniquitous execution in the City of Limerick, in Ireland by Henry Ingoldsby, Governor of the same City. A certain noble gentleman of Thomond, named Daniel Connery, was accused of harbouring a priest in his house, and convicted on his own confession (although the priest had safe-conduct from the Governor himself), and declared guilty of death. And then, as he said, out of mercy, the sentence was changed, commuted, and he was despoiled of all his goods, and bound in prison, and finally condemned to perpetual exile. This gentleman had a wife and twelve children. His wife was of a very noble family of Thomond, and she fell sick and died in extreme want of necessities. Three of the children, very beautiful and virtuous virgins, were sent off to the East [*sic*] Indies, to an island they call Barbados, where, if they are still alive, they spend their days in miserable slavery.[10]

Catholics who refused to attend a Protestant church could be fined. If they could not raise the money to pay – as was no doubt the case for the majority – they would be transported to Barbados and 'sold as a slave'. In Galway, merchants procured numbers of the population for sale to the slave markets of the Indies. Invasion and occupation turned people against one another. Corrupt officials engaged in the trade.

During this time, those Irish who had been banished or transported were dismayed to discover that the suppression of their language and religion was replicated in the transatlantic colonies. The Puritans were determined people but so were the Irish Catholics. Priests disguised themselves and went secretly about their work in both Ireland and the West Indies to keep their religion alive. Even on islands that had already had French or Spanish (and therefore Catholic) settlements, Irish Catholics were forbidden to attend religious services, except in Protestant churches, as was the case at home.

With the end of the Confederate War in 1653, transportation continued. The war had created large numbers of widows and orphans, and many of these were shipped to the West Indies. According to Walpole, women and orphans were rounded up from workhouses and prisons. They were, he said, 'boys who were of an age to labour and women who were marriageable, or not past breeding'.[11] The children were put to work in the fields, while the women were married off to planters.

The creation of a colonial Ireland cost the native Irish dearly – they lost not only their lands but what remained of their reputation. The Irish character, already blackened by Cambrensis and by a tendency to stage occasional uprisings, was reputed to be so bad that when American colonies got to hear of it they began to fear even the impoverished and emaciated souls who migrated to their shores. As a result, acts were passed prohibiting the landing of Irish in Massachusetts. One such act, in 1654, was formulated by a committee appointed by the General Court of Massachusetts to consider proposals for the public benefit:

> This Court, considering the cruel and malignant spirit that has from time to time been manifest in the Irish nation against the English nation, do hereby declare their prohibition of bringing any Irish, men, women, or children, into this jurisdiction, on the penalty of £50 sterling to each inhabitant who shall buy of any merchant, shipmaster, or other agent any such person or persons so transported by them; which fine shall be by the country's marshal levied on conviction of some magistrate or court, one third to be to the use of the informer, and two-thirds to the country. This act to be in force six months after the publication of this order.

For those Irish already in the colonies, they continued to be singled out for particularly harsh treatment. In 1658, the authorities decided that English bonded servants in the American colonies should have their minimum bond period extended from four to five years. It was already five years for Irish servants, and so to keep the differential intact, the length of servitude for Irish servants was increased from five to six years. Following the Restoration of the monarchy two years later, this extra year of servitude was withdrawn for servants from both England and Ireland 'in the interest of peopling the country'. The extra year had proved to be a disincentive to those who wished to relocate to the New World voluntarily.

In 1688 in Massachusetts, a remarkable event occurred that opened a strange window into the world endured by enslaved Irish men and women – and provided more than a little insight into the minds of their masters. It involved allegations of demonic possession involving an old washerwoman and a family of Puritans. The case was a precursor to the witchcraft trials in Salem in 1692.

The old Irish servant at the core of our tale is thought to have arrived in Massachusetts in the 1650s, when, despite the official ban on emigrants from Ireland, many Irish continued to be sent. An account of the case was written by Cotton Mather, the famous minister of the North Church in Boston. It begins as follows:

> Memorable Providences, Relating to Witchcrafts and Possessions. A Faithful Account of many Wonderful and Surprising Things, that have befallen several Bewitched and Possessed Persons in New-England. Particularly, A Narrative of the marvellous Trouble and Releef Experienced by a pious Family in Boston, very lately and sadly molested with Evil Spirits.[12]

Mather had a questing mind and a vivid imagination, and he was quick to spot the Devil's work among his flock. The Devil could be discovered anywhere, even in the inexplicable illnesses of a Boston stonemason's children:

> There dwells at this time, in the south part of Boston, a sober and pious man, whose Name is John Goodwin, whose Trade is that of a Mason, and whose Wife (to which a Good Report gives a share with him in all the Characters of Virtue) has made him the Father of six (now living) Children. Of

these Children, all but the Eldest, who works with his Father at his Calling, and the Youngest, who lives yet upon the Breast of its mother, have laboured under the direful effects of a (no less palpable than) stupendous Witchcraft. Indeed that exempted Son had also, as was thought, some lighter touches of it, in unaccountable stabs and pains now and then upon him; as indeed every person in the Family at some time or other had, except the godly Father, and the suckling Infant, who never felt any impressions of it.

Mather's tale is one of demonic attacks upon the children in which they suffered assaults by unseen hands. When one Goodwin child suffered pains in the neck, another did and so on. Physicians of great repute were called but could only agree that it must be witchcraft. As luck would have it, a likely suspect was close to hand – a non-believer in the earthy form of an old Irish woman called Anne Glover, known as 'Goody', whose daughter was the Goodwins' washerwoman. Anne had victim written all over her: she was beached in a foreign land run by English Puritans, whose idea of a good time was to hunt out demons and Catholics. Massachusetts must have been a dull place in the late seventeenth century but Goody was soon to liven things up. Among her powers, she could make children fly and ride on invisible horses.

About Midsummer, in the year 1688, the Eldest of these Children, who is a Daughter, saw cause to examine their Washerwoman, upon their missing of some Linen which t'was feared she had stolen from them; and of what use this linen might be to serve the Witchcraft intended, the Thief's Tempter knows! This Laundress was the Daughter of an ignorant and a scandalous old Woman in the Neighbourhood; whose miserable Husband before he died, had sometimes complained of her, that she was undoubtedly a Witch, and that whenever his Head was laid, she would quickly arrive unto the punishments due to such an one. This Woman in her daughters Defence bestow'd very bad Language upon the Girl that put her to the Question; immediately upon which, the poor child became variously indisposed in her health, and visited with strange Fits, beyond those that attend an Epilepsy or a Catalepsy, or those that they call The Diseases of Astonishment.

At her trial, Anne Glover failed an elementary test for possession – she could not recite the Lord's Prayer in English. This was hardly surprising, for she spoke not a word of the language. It has been said she could recite the prayer in Irish and in Latin but that this cut no ice with the court. The knitted dolls found in her house proved she was obviously up to no good. Foreigner, Roman Catholic and devil worshipper, Anne scored a hat-trick. She was hanged. As Mather himself said at the end of his account: 'This is the Story of [the] Goodwins Children, a Story all made up of Wonders!' Never a truer word has been written.

The days were numbered for Irish servants like Goody Glover and her daughter in Massachusetts, though other American colonies remained open to the importation of Irish labour. The same was true for island colonies such as Jamaica and Barbados. To this day in Jamaica, Irish surnames abound. The first Irish imported to the island arrived shortly after the British captured it from the Spanish. When the Cromwellian generals William Penn (the father of the founder of Pennsylvania) and Robert Venables failed to take Hispaniola from the Spanish in 1655, they took Jamaica, not wishing to return home and face Oliver Cromwell empty-handed. The island's economy required extra labour and so they turned to islands already stocked with strong young Irishmen: Barbados, St Lucia, St Christopher and Montserrat. Barbados in particular seems to have had plenty of labourers to choose from. In 1660, half of the white people in Barbados were said to be Irish. They were rarely the planters but unquestionably the servants.

After the wars and social upheavals of the middle of the century, one might have expected that transportation of Irish to serve as slaves in the English colonies might have died out. It did not, but it did tail off. In the hills and bogs, bandits and rebels continued to be rounded up occasionally and shipped off to cool their heels in the colonies. And even in the farthest outposts of the colonies,

Irish continued to be indentured. In Newfoundland in the 1680s, fishermen, many of them Irish or Scottish, accumulated debts they could not pay off. They were then forced to give themselves up as indentured servants.

But the flow of Irish labourers to the colonies was not yet staunched, nor would it be for some time yet. In the following century, Ireland and its people became subject to new laws that made transportation a key part of its penal system. Meanwhile, dissent was brewing in another part of the nation.

CHAPTER TEN

DISSENT IN THE NORTH

On a bleak headland in the Orkney Isles off the north of Scotland stands a roughly made stone pillar, forty feet tall. It is a thin, tapering four-sided pillar in the form of an obelisk but, instead of the usual pyramidal top, it is finished with a rounded cap, giving it the look of a giant chess piece. This is the monument to a tragedy that occurred on 10 December 1679, a few days before the winter solstice.

Orkney lies at fifty-nine degrees north, almost the latitude of Greenland, and in mid-December the sun barely edges into the sky. Reaching its zenith at ten degrees above the horizon, the sun hangs in the sky for barely six hours a day, providing a glimmering light from about nine-thirty in the morning until just three-thirty in the afternoon. Into this eerie world sailed the *Crown of London*, commanded by Captain Thomas Teddico and carrying a cargo of 257 prisoners locked below deck. The prisoners were the remains of a defeated army of religious dissenters, Covenanters, who denied the right of either king or bishops to rule over their church. For their dissenting views, they had been prepared to fight and, if necessary, to die. Now, at sea off the largest Orkney island of Mainland, fate was ready to deal them a further blow.

The ship was supposed to be on its way to the West Indies, though Teddico's true intentions have been questioned. By sailing into such northerly latitudes in the dead of winter he was risking his ship, the crew and the prisoners locked below. The *Crown* had begun its journey at the port of Leith, outside Edinburgh, in November. A better route would have been to strike a southerly course down the east coast of Scotland and around the south coast of England. To have headed north to the Orkneys might seem to imply that the captain had some dark mission to accomplish.

A gale blew up and Captain Teddico decided to see the storm out at anchor off the headland of Scarvataing at the entrance to Deerness Bay. At ten o'clock in the evening, the ship dragged its anchor and was driven onto the rocks. According to one account, the crew made it to safety by cutting a mast and using it as a bridge to dry land. One of the crew is said to have taken an axe to the deck to cut an exit for the prisoners. Some forty to fifty made it to land. The rest perished with the ship.

The shipwreck of the *Crown* could well have been the catalyst for Robert Louis Stevenson's famous scene in *Kidnapped* in which the brig carrying the abducted hero to the colonies founders in heavy seas. David Balfour clings to a yardarm and makes it ashore to freedom.

In the case of the Orkney wreck, many of those who survived were subsequently rounded up and transported to become slaves in the plantations. In the troubled history of Scotland during the seventeenth century, these rebellious men were only a small sample of those who found themselves suffering a drastic penalty for their religious beliefs. As one twentieth-century historian has remarked, 'The troubles of these times cast many an unfortunate Scot ashore in the New World in a condition differing little, if at all, from that of the negro slaves who toiled in the tobacco and sugar plantations.'[1] It was the era when the concept of the colonial penal colony was being turned into fact and the policy of political banishment, long used in Ireland, was introduced to Scotland.

The circumstances leading up to the deaths off Scarvataing had their origins many years before, at the beginning of one of the most important and turbulent periods in British history. For many centuries, Scotland and England had had a border dispute. The disputed areas were known as the 'debatable lands'. Traditionally, these areas were lawless havens for robbers, army deserters and villains. In 1617, the English court of law, the Star Chamber, sent a copy of a new code for establishing peace in the border area to Scotland's ruling body, the Privy Council, for its consideration. Of course, the King expected the Scots would bow to his will but they did nothing of the sort. The sticking point for the Scots was Section Thirteen. This provided for a survey of all villains and layabouts in the territory so they could be rounded up and shipped off to Virginia, which would become in effect a gulag for the troublesome and the unwanted.

The Privy Council would have been as concerned about law and order as the Star Chamber, so this provision appeared at first sight to be one to which no exception could be taken. However, the Scottish lawmakers declined to accept the wisdom of Section Thirteen. They had spotted a snag: Virginia and all other colonies were controlled by England and so any deported Scots would come under the control of English masters. Those worthy of transportation might be scum – but they were Scottish scum and as such deserved better. The traditional Scottish sentence of banishment allowed the banished one to decide upon the country of his or her exile. Transportation in this case meant serving under English rule. Unfortunately for the delicate sensibilities of the Scots, London insisted. The Privy Council gave way, while continuing to express its reservations.

The following year, 1618, yet greater Scottish reservations were expressed regarding interference from London. In his attempt to bring the Presbyterian, democratically minded elders of the Church of Scotland to heel, James I had new rules drawn up, imposing rites and ceremonies that were thought to have more than a whiff of Catholicism about them. The Five Articles of Perth included kneeling to take communion and confirmation of church membership conducted by bishops. To encourage recalcitrant Church of Scotland ministers, it was suggested that those who did not wish to conduct their church services by the articles might find themselves deported. During the half-century or so of struggle between state and Covenanters that was to follow, this threat became real.

In 1625, James I died. His son Charles inherited the crown

and with it all the unresolved political and religious tensions that had bedevilled the state during his father's reign. Mutual distrust continued between Scotland and England. A key part of this was the continuing animosity between the reformist, Calvinist, Presbyterian strain of Christianity and the more traditional, ceremonial strain preferred both by James and Charles. Both father and son failed to address these factors, just as they had done little to ease the tensions between the Crown and various political factions; when combined, these elements provided the impulse that led to Scotland and England being convulsed by war.

One of the catalysts for what was to come took place in the ancient churchyard of Greyfriars Kirk in Edinburgh. Today, tourists visit to stare at the bronze statue of a small dog, Greyfriars' Bobby, famous for having lain on his owner's grave for fourteen years during the nineteenth century, before himself being carried off by time. But Greyfriars and its churchyard are famous for more significant events than the story of the relationship between a dog and its owner.

In 1638, a large group of well-established citizens met in the kirk to sign a covenant by which they affirmed their Calvinist views and their opposition to the Catholic Church. Even though Catholicism had ceased to be the official faith of England after the Reformation, many Protestants harboured worries about the new King. He was married to the devoutly Catholic princess Henrietta Maria, the daughter of Henry IV of France. The Scottish dissenters believed the Church could be led by no man, only God himself. They were determined to resist all innovations by Charles, including the introduction of a new uniform book of liturgy.

The resistance within Scotland did not rest solely on religious differences but also on political grounds. Charles packed the Scottish Privy Council – the ruling arm of government in Scotland – with bishops of his own choosing, so excluding many of the most powerful figures in the land. The common cause between Presbyterians and the nobility was a potent mix.

After the first copy of the National Covenant was signed before the altar of Greyfriars Kirk, further copies were distributed to parishes around Scotland. Soon, many thousands had put their name to a document that set itself forcefully against the will of the King, a monarch who still adhered to the doctrine of the divine right of kings. Eight months after the first signing of the Covenant, the General Assembly of the Church of Scotland voted to expel all bishops from the church. This was the starting point for what became known as the Bishops' Wars.

Charles I's early life indicated he was not cut out to deal with these complicated times. He was frail and had a bad stammer. When he acceded to the throne, he took steps to change his image into that of an omnipotent ruler. He commissioned portraits by the painter from Antwerp, Anthony van Dyck. In his acclaimed triple portrait, van Dyck portrayed the King from several angles, in effect, giving him three heads. In the event, Charles was unable to hold on to one.

Although Scottish, Charles hardly visited the country, where the political atmosphere had darkened. Miscalculations within his court, together with the increasingly implacable nature of the Parliamentary and religious dissent arraigned against him, were to spark a catastrophic civil war involving England, Scotland and Ireland, culminating in 1649 with Charles's divine body being parted from his all-too-fallible head on a scaffold outside his glorious banqueting hall in Whitehall.

It may be unfair to blame Charles alone – or anyone else, for that matter – for the violent mêlée that overtook the kingdom during the Civil War. It was as if the country had reached a point where matters of power and personal conscience had to be determined one way or the other. But even the execution of the King and the foundation of a republic did not resolve matters.

The Scots were suspicious of the forces at work in Parliament in London and of the increasingly radical forms of religion in England. Sentiment swung behind the Crown in the shape of the executed King's son, named Charles after his father. Although there were many who were wary of a member of the Stuart family, which had been no friend to the Presbyterians, Charles was declared King of Scotland and in June 1650 arrived hopefully from exile in France. Charles publicly and cynically agreed to a new covenant renouncing Anglicanism. In England, this gave his potential support base a pummelling. Politics in the seventeenth century was a difficult game, especially if one wanted to be king. Parliament suspected that Charles would now soon raise an army and advance on England.

On a September day in 1650, Cromwell led an army of 16,000 men over the Scottish border. Cromwell's genius resided in being well prepared. But the self-taught general was not only sensible in preparation, he was also flexible in battle. Perhaps his greatest quality as a commander was that he could inspire his men. At Dunbar, he faced a much stronger Scottish force of 23,000. According to reports, before going into battle Cromwell appealed to the enemy commander to consider his position. After all, Cromwell did not see that he had a quarrel so much with the Presbyterian troops as with Charles himself. 'I beseech you in the bowels of Christ think it possible you may be mistaken,' he said. The Scots took no heed. Maybe one group of zealots knew better than to trust another. Three thousand Scottish soldiers died in the battle and many broke ranks and fled.[2] Cromwell's smaller army won the day.

Cromwell took 9,000 to 10,000 prisoners. About half of them were quickly freed as being too badly injured to remain a threat. Plans were drawn up to disperse the remaining prisoners among the colonies in Ireland, Virginia and Barbados. How many were in fact sent is unknown, for a series of calamities were to overwhelm both plans and the prisoners.

The remaining 5,000 prisoners were force-marched to Durham. Along the way, 2,000 or more died of illness, exhaustion and starvation. Others simply drifted away. On 11 September, the survivors were herded into various makeshift prisons in Durham, including the castle and the Norman cathedral, one of the most beautiful hymns to the miraculous in northern Europe. For many, the cathedral became their place of death. Army commanders siphoned off the money allocated to feed them. Malnutrition led to disease and the cold sapped the prisoners' strength. The desperate soldiers ripped up pews and wooden panelling to burn in dwindling efforts to keep warm. Starvation was their chief enemy. By the end of October, 1,600 had died. Of the remaining 1,400, many were deported to the West Indies as slave labour. How many

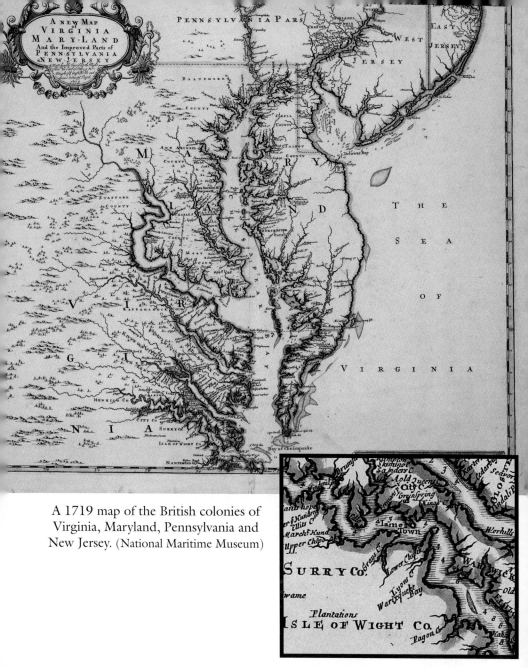

A 1719 map of the British colonies of Virginia, Maryland, Pennsylvania and New Jersey. (National Maritime Museum)

The James River running into Chesapeake Bay at its southern end, with the first successful English settlement, Jamestown, located just above the wording 'Surry Co.' (National Maritime Museum)

Sir Humphrey Gilbert, the blood-thirsty pioneer who first claimed Virginia for England and became a national hero after dying a romantic death. (National Portrait Gallery, London)

Sir John Popham, the highwayman who became Lord Chief Justice and tried to colonise New England with convicts. (National Portrait Gallery, London)

A replica of the brigantine *Godspeed*, one of the fleet of three ships that brought the settlers to the first successful English colony in America at Jamestown in 1607. One of the passengers described his companions as 'unruly, lascivious sons and bad servants'. (NASA)

Early settlers sought religious freedom in the colonies, like these Catholics depicted attending the first mass in Maryland in 1634. But for the majority of settlers, freedom was an illusion. They would spend years in bondage.

England's first merchant prince, Sir Thomas Smythe, who effectively controlled Virginia from England and set white slavery in motion. (National Portrait Gallery, London)

No wonder the Earl of Carlisle raises an eyebrow: he was given Barbados by Charles I, even though others had paid to develop it. (Photographic Survey, Courtauld Insitute of Art)

The Hanging Judge, George Jeffreys, of whom it was said, 'Would sooner hang a man than eat his mutton', became an unexpected hero when he broke up a transportation racket in Bristol. (National Portrait Gallery, London)

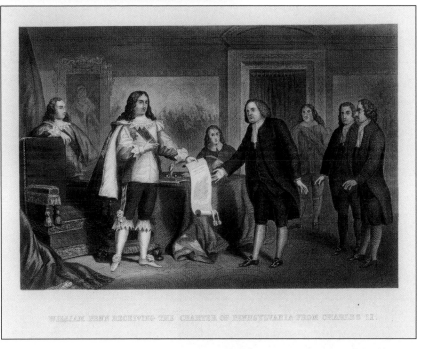

WILLIAM PENN RECEIVING THE CHARTER OF PENNSYLVANIA FROM CHARLES II.

The Quaker William Penn receives the warrant from Charles II for Pennsylvania, the land of freedom, in which white slavery was to become widespread.

The angelic-looking Mary of Modena, second wife of James II, made money selling rebel prisoners into bondage in the American colonies. (National Portrait Gallery, London)

Queen Anne: her portrait was used in propaganda to entice tens of thousands of Germans to America, where some had to sell their children. (National Portrait Gallery, London)

The Centaur, one of the disease-ridden hulks on the Thames used to house
hundreds of prisoners when America closed its doors to British convicts.
(Greenwich Heritage Centre)

Convicts, including two
children, sentenced to
transportation and chained by
the neck, en route to a prison
hulk on the Thames.
(Greenwich Heritage Centre)

George Washington, the upholder of liberty – but not for slaves, either black or white.

G. Washington.

BENJAMIN FRANKLIN. (*From the Portrait by Chevillet.*)

Benjamin Franklin told the British Parliament that for every convict they sent over, a rattlesnake should be sent back, though 'the rattlesnake gives warning before he attempts his mischief; which the convict does not.'

is not known but it is safe to assume that not nearly as many were deported as originally planned for.

This was not the only example of Parliament using transportation as a solution to political dissent. The decisive battle of Worcester was fought in 1651 between a combined Scots-Royalist army under the direct command of Charles II, and the Parliamentarian army under the command of Oliver Cromwell. It was to be the final battle for both commanders and a 'crowning mercy' according to the victorious Cromwell. Eight thousand Scots soldiers were taken prisoner. While Charles went into hiding, pending his escape to France, the Parliamentarian Council of State charged the Committee for Prisoners to grant a licence for the transportation of the Scots to the West Indies. In 1656, Scottish prisoners who had fought at Worcester and been transported complained that their sentences of servitude were being illegally extended to seven years. A committee of inquiry back in London investigated the matter and upheld their sentences.

Four years later, the Council of State was issuing directives for Scots, Irish, English and other seamen imprisoned in Plymouth Castle to be sent to Barbados, and a further 1,200 men imprisoned in Portpatrick in Scotland and Knockfergus in Ireland were to be sent to Jamaica.

Not all fared badly. Many years later, one of the Scots who settled in New Jersey from around 1680 onwards wrote home that he had had a drink with one of the 'old buckskin planters', a Scot who 'was sent away by Cromwell to New England as a slave from Dumbar [sic]. Living now in Woodbridge like a Scottish Laird, wishes his countrymen and his Native Soyle very well tho' he never intends to see it.'[3]

Following Cromwell's death in 1658 and the Restoration of the monarchy in 1660, the threat of transportation might have lifted over Scottish dissenters. It was not to be. Charles II, who had only a few years earlier signed a covenant supporting Presbyterianism, quickly moved to re-establish episcopacy, rule of the church by a hierarchy of bishops. For twenty years, the Church in Scotland had been run along Presbyterian lines. Now it seemed that the Scottish wish for the liberty to worship in their own manner was again to be thwarted.

From the year of the Restoration of the monarchy, concerted efforts were made to enforce Anglican disciplines upon the Church of Scotland. Serious disruption followed. In 1670, a law was passed making it mandatory that anyone with knowledge of conventicles, or religious gatherings, should divulge such information to the authorities. This was widely disobeyed. Soon prisons and tollbooths were overflowing with prisoners. Threats of deportation were widely issued, though just how many people were actually transported is hard to estimate.

One case highlights differences between the Anglican authorities and Presbyterian population. The friends of sixty or more men about to be transported interceded upon their behalf to two of the archbishops. These being 'good merciful' men, they reaffirmed the sentence.[4] A London merchant, Ralph Williamson, petitioned for the right to sell the sentenced men off for the best price. His request was granted and the Virginia Governor was instructed to waive his colony's prohibition on criminals so that the Covenanters might be imported. Williamson carried his human cargo to London for sale, only to discover that no ship's captain on the North Atlantic run would take the Covenanters, for feeling ran high in favour of the dissenters. Money was raised at church services and they were finally returned to Scotland. Williamson also returned, the poorer and wiser for his pains.

Williamson's experiences might help to explain the mystery with which we began this chapter: Captain Teddico's decision to take the *Crown* on a perilous voyage to the Orkneys rather than plot a southerly course to London. For what if Teddico had not intended to take his cargo all the way to the Indies but rather to sell it to American agents in England? Perhaps he had heard about the hostile reception that Williamson had received the previous year and decided to take his human cargo around the north of Scotland and down the west coast to sell in Liverpool or Bristol. Perhaps he felt the perils of the sea were preferable to the perfidy of London traders.

As the royal will began to be felt, dissent quickly spread, particularly in south-west Scotland, where congregations gathered to hear sermons given by banned preachers. Some of these religious protestors were of an extreme form of Covenanter and the army was deployed to track down and break up these illegal assemblies. In Lanarkshire, Ayrshire and Galloway, the King's policy led to an atmosphere of suspicion, to informers and the threat of imprisonment or deportation. Some skirmishes exploded into armed rebellion.

In 1679, a troop of dragoons was dispatched to disperse a large conventicle reported to be mustering outside Kilmarnock in Ayrshire. When the dragoons reached the spot that intelligence had indicated, a boggy moor called Drumclog, they were met by a large religious congregation protected by 250 armed men. The Covenanters were ready for trouble. Armed with an array of weapons ranging from muskets to pitchforks, they managed to see off the dragoons, who found themselves mired in the boggy ground. The victory was not much more than a brief skirmish, with few casualties, but it acted as the catalyst by which many more took to arms. Within a week, several thousand had gathered at Bothwell Bridge, by the Clyde in Lanarkshire.

Instead of forging themselves into an army, however, the rebels turned themselves into a religious debating society. As the government forces gathered, the rebels became increasingly fragmented, bickering over the role of more moderate Presbyterians in their midst – all in the drive to create a spiritually pure 'God's Army'. The numbers of combined rebel forces reached at one point perhaps 7,000 or more. But by the time the battle commenced, they were down to 4,000, with many having simply drifted away. In the event, the divine spark was not with the dissenters during the battle. The government forces, commanded by the Duke of Monmouth, the illegitimate son of Charles II, now outnumbered them. Numbers hardly mattered, though, for the rebel force was badly commanded and lacked discipline on the field of battle as much as it had beforehand. With the rebel infantry quickly abandoned by its cavalry, the fight was soon over. Four hundred foot were killed and the army broke into disarray, many fleeing with their commanders. Monmouth issued orders to prevent more bloodshed and 1,200 rebels were taken prisoner.

The fate of the prisoners was not dissimilar to that of those imprisoned in Durham Cathedral. They were marched east to Edinburgh, where, as the city's prisons could not take so many, they were imprisoned in a makeshift gaol at the southern end of Greyfriars Kirkyard. Several Covenanters who were already wanted for crimes against the state were hanged in the city's Grassmarket. For the remainder, imprisonment soon became a trial of endurance. Their prison amounted to little more than a walled pen, open to the sky, so that the inmates were at the mercy of the elements. Some townsfolk took pity on them and threw scraps of food over the prison walls. But as summer turned to autumn and on to winter, the future looked bleak for the prisoners.

Several hundred of the Covenanters agreed to sign a bond to relinquish their dissenting ways and were set free. Of the remainder, some died. The survivors who still refused to denounce the covenant were sentenced to transportation and slavery in the colonies. These were the men who were shipwrecked in Orkney.

According to *A Cloud of Witnesses*, a compilation of names and stories of numbers of those who were punished for their part in the Covenanting rebellion in 1712, from 1678 onwards 'there were banished to be sold for slaves, for the same cause for which others suffered death at home, of men and women about 1,700'.[5] Of these, many survived their servitude and went on to settle in America. Some of those transported even made it home to Scotland. Among them was the Covenanter farmer John Mathieson, transported for 'converse with rebels'. Mathieson was one of thirty who were transported to Carolina. He was deported in a ship owned or chartered by a notorious Glasgow merchant, Walter Gibson, in the summer of 1684. Some time before he died around 1709, Mathieson wrote his story, which was published a century later in a collection of dying testimonies.[6] 'I became acquainted with some of these who were declared rebels, and then I was to understand matters better, and be as they were in judgment and practice . . .'

Mathieson's journey to Carolina took, by his account, nineteen weeks. If this was so, then everyone on board must have suffered terribly. Since voyages were expected to last eight or ten weeks, severe shortages of food and water must have caused real hardship. Sickness would have become a major problem and many on board could have died. When the voyage ended, Mathieson's afflictions were not at an end, as, together with his fellow deportees, he rebelled against being sold as an indentured servant.

> Their cruelty to us was because we would not consent to our own selling or slavery; for then we were miserably beaten, and I especially received nine great blows upon my back very sore, by one of his sea-fellows, so that for some days I could not lift my head higher nor my breast; which strokes or blows I looked upon to be the beginning of all my bodily pains and diseases that have been upon me since that time until now.

By some chance (he does not tell us how), Mathieson and some of his colleagues escaped from the plantations in Carolina and sailed to Virginia, encountering a storm en route. From there, he and his companions travelled on. How they survived, we are not told but the options would not have gone beyond living from hand to mouth and taking labouring jobs when and where possible. After some period of time, Mathieson was forced to become indentured to keep body and soul together:

> . . . whereafter soon I fell sick; and during which sickness I was kindly entertained and taken care of by the man and his wife in whose house I lay, and with whom I had bound myself. For, albeit we had escaped from them that had brought us over, and could not work to them, yet we behoved to work for something to bring us back again. From thence I came to New York on my journey homeward, where I agreed with a shipmaster to bring me to London.

When he finally returned to Scotland, Mathieson had an unusual and poignant homecoming at his farm at harvest time:

When he entered the house, his wife was busy preparing dinner for the reapers. She did not recognise him, but took him for a traveller, who had come in to rest himself. She pressed him to take some refreshment, which he did, when she went out to the field with a portion for the reapers. As she went out, he rose, and followed her at a respectful distance. She turned round, and fancying he had not been satisfied with her hospitality, said to the bystanders, 'The man wants a second dinner.' The words drew the eyes of the reapers on him, when one of his sons whispers to his mother, 'If my father be alive, it is him.' She turned round, looked into the stranger's face for a moment, and then ran to his embrace, crying out, 'My husband!'[7]

As elsewhere, transportation of undesirables of any and every sort became good business in Scotland. The impetus for the founding of Scottish settlements in America came from a proposal from the Provost of Linlithgow to the Scottish Privy Council in 1681, urging that the advantage of such colonies was that they would 'void the country of very many both idle and dissenting persons'.[8] The good Provost was acting for a group of merchants who stood to make a profit from the transportation of human cargo to the colonies. A few months later, one of those merchants, Walter Gibson – the same man who had expedited the transportation of William Mathieson – wrote to the Privy Council that he was willing to carry to the colonies 'thieves or robbers sentenced by the Lords of Judiciary or other judges, to be banished thither, and all sorners [vagabonds], lusty beggars or gypsies'.[9]

Gibson got his warrant. Magistrates were ordered to give into his tender care those who had been convicted of minor crimes and thus would normally clutter up the prisons and be a burden on the parishes:

> strong and idle beggars, gypsies, or other vagabond persons who live by stouth [probably here meaning strong-arm tactics] and robbery and have no visible means to support themselves . . . to the effect that they be transported to the

petitioner's ships to the plantations and the country freed
of them.

As in Ireland and England, Scotland was fortunate to find that
its social and colonial policies could fit so comfortably with the
needs of its merchants and even of those lawyers and worthies
holding senior official positions.

CHAPTER ELEVEN

THE PLANTER FROM ANGOLA

All through these middle years of the seventeenth century, a vast trade in black slaves was developing but it largely passed by the English colonies on the mainland. The 'twenty and odd Negroes sold' in Point Comfort in 1619 were no more or less enslaved than the free-willers or convicts they would have encountered on the shore. It took decades more for the plantation owners of the Chesapeake to begin to buy people in any numbers from the black slave market and much longer for the legal edifice of black bondage to evolve. The story of an African who is believed to have been among those arriving in 1619 shows that the onset of racial slavery in America had the most unlikely twists and turns.

Anthony Johnson, as the African came to be known, not only secured his freedom but also became a successful planter himself and went on to buy servants of his own, white as well as black. Thirty years after Johnson first touched American soil, he got into a dispute with a servant, a fellow African who was demanding his freedom. Johnson resolved it by persuading a court to enslave the man for life. This was one of the first cases of lifetime slavery being imposed in North America – a black man playing one of the villains in the ghastly tragedy that was beginning to unfold.

The Africans from the *White Lion* are thought to have been bought originally by the two wealthiest planters in Virginia. One was Sir George Yeardley, Governor of the colony, a venal man who seems to have acquired more white servants than anyone else in those early days of the colony.[1] The other was Abraham Piersey, the Virginia Company's trading agent. It is widely claimed that this transaction marked the beginning of slavery: that almost from the start the men and women from the *White Lion* were a separated class, lower in status than all those around them. The picture is of Johnson and the other Africans suffering greater debilities, subject to more degradation than the white servants: one colour chained and kicked; the other merely chained. English racism was supposedly at work, dividing black and white from the moment the Angolans trooped ashore.

In reality, however, the Africans appear to have been treated as indentured servants, no different from the English servants. Racism may well have existed, but in the rush to profit, the colour of a field labourer was a secondary consideration. Having enough hands to hoe the next 10,000 tobacco hills was paramount. Black mixed with white in the tobacco labour gang and would continue do so into the next century in some places.

As the African-American writer Lerone Bennett Jr puts it:

> Not only in Virginia but also in New England and New York, the first Blacks were integrated into a forced labor system that had little or nothing to do with skin color. That came later. But in the interim, a fateful 40-year period of primary importance in the history of America, Black men and women worked side by side with the first generation of Whites, cultivating tobacco, clearing the land, and building roads and houses.[2]

Between the servants themselves, there appears to have been little if any racism. According to the African-American historian Audrey Smedley: 'Early references to blacks reveal little clear evidence of general or widespread social antipathy on account of their colour.' Professor Smedley writes: 'Records show a fairly high incidence of co-operation among black and white servants and unified resistance to harsh masters.'[3] The earlier historian of servitude Edmund S. Morgan found hints 'that the two despised groups initially saw each other as sharing the same predicament'.[4]

Perhaps the story would have been different had the sale of the *White Lion*'s cargo triggered an overpowering influx of Africans. It had no such impact. No one's eyes in London or in Jamestown seem to have been opened at this point to the possibilities of using African labour in any major way and for some time only limited numbers of Africans were shipped in. Over the next ten years, several English privateers reportedly did arrive in the Chesapeake with Africans for sale, and men and women were brought in from Dutch territory and from the West Indies, but Virginia continued to rely on the white servant trade. By the mid-seventeenth century, Africans numbered only 300 out of a total settler population of 11,000.

From these small numbers there emerged some stories of individual success. After their indentured period expired, a handful of Africans went on to secure land of their own and to prosper. They 'apparently had no difficulty in acquiring property of their own and engaged in business and commercial activities on the basis of equality with whites,' writes Professor Smedley. 'Some black men of substance even acquired slaves of their own.'

Anthony Johnson became one such man of substance. His first Jamestown master appears to have sold him to another very wealthy man, Edward Bennett, a merchant ship owner. In 1622, Bennett sent Johnson and fifty or more servants to clear the woods for a plantation on the James River at a point now known as Fort Boykin. The merchant called the plantation Bennett's Welcome. His party arrived at the site in February 1622. The following month, before a palisade could be built, the Powhatan Confederacy launched its Good Friday massacre. Anthony Johnson was one of only twelve survivors of the attack at Bennett's Welcome.

Johnson spent up to another dozen years as a servant before being freed and allotted a tract of land to farm on the Pungoteague River. Over the next three decades, he built a sizeable land-holding and imported more than a dozen servants, some English, some African. The headrights claimed on these people helped Johnson accumulate 1,000 acres. Perhaps the only marked difference between Johnson and the white planters around him was the name that he gave his Northampton County plantation. He called it Angola.

The American dream was also coming true for several other Africans imported as indentured servants. But after 1640, the prospects for Africans overall were worsening right across the eastern seaboard of America. English colonies on the mainland had begun edging in different ways towards racial slavery and at a different pace, with the men in power quite possibly having little idea of where they were heading. Massachusetts, for instance, goes down in history as the first colony to legalise slavery – but no race was targeted when it did so. Indeed, at first glance the Massachusetts declaration on slavery reads more as a trumpet blast for freedom than the reverse. It announces: 'There shall never be any bond slavery, villinage or captivity amongst us' and then lists the exceptions – everyone from prisoners of war to 'such strangers as willingly sell themselves or are sold to us' and anyone else 'judged thereto by authority'.[5]

The worsening position of the Africans manifested itself first in the lifetime enslavement of isolated individuals. Who this first happened to isn't known. But the earliest recorded cases are of men who were being punished for running away, and, what is more, for running away together with white servants. The whites they ran with received especially vicious punishment, too, though short of enslavement for life. This would be reserved for blacks.

The runaway is one of the constants throughout the history of American servitude. From the dreaded days of Sir Thomas Dale, men and women were slipping away into the forests or taking to the water in the hope of finding refuge with Native Americans or losing themselves in another colony. They would continue to do so long after the English period and up to the American Civil War. To run was the only resort of the desperate servant/slave. Judging from the increasingly harsh deterrents adopted from the 1630s, more and more were running as the seventeenth century advanced.

As with virtually every servant crime, the first stage of punishment was a whipping. In Virginia, constables apprehending runaways were instructed to administer an immediate whipping and every constable who escorted them on the journey back to the plantation was told to follow suit: 'Every constable into whose hands the captive shall be committed shall . . . whip him severely.'[6]

Maryland flirted briefly with making 'desertion' a capital offence but instead adopted the Virginia way – slapping an extra stretch of time on the servants' indenture period. At first, the formula was two days' extra servitude for every day on the run but in Virginia that escalated to five days for every day absent and in Maryland to ten days. Other colonies followed the Chesapeake lead but were generally content with the two-for-one ratio. But all added something else to the extra time a runaway faced – compensation for the cost of hunting him or her down. Some planters' expense claims were staggering, including such items as the planter hiring his own horse to himself. At the end of it, someone who had tasted perhaps a few months of freedom faced years of extra slavery.

This harshness reflected the planters' determination to stamp on all signs of dissent at a time when the whiff of insurrection was beginning to spread. Discontent could be scented across the Chesapeake in a series of mini-rebellions and plots and acts of violence on the plantations in which black and white servants acted together. In this atmosphere, escape attempts were viewed as part of the same movement.

In 1640, the Virginia planter Hugh Gwyn raised a hue and cry over three servants who had escaped into Maryland. One was a Scot, one a Dutchman and one, John Punch, was an African. On hearing the news that they had been caught and detained in Maryland, their master Gwyn decided to have the three sold where they had been picked up. That would save him the extra expense of bringing them back in chains and produce enough cash to purchase more tractable servants. However, the idea of runaway servants possibly going unpunished mortified the Virginia court. It ruled against such a 'pernicious precedent' and in June 1640 asked the Governor of Maryland to have the three returned to Virginia for 'such exemplary and condign punishment as the nature of their offence shall justly deserve'.[7]

The next month, the escapees were arraigned in a Virginian court. All were given thirty strokes of the whip. In addition, the two whites were ordered to serve their full terms with Gwyn, plus an extra year on top. Moreover, after that was served they were to be bound for a further three years as servants of the colony. For John Punch, the African, the news was even worse. After his whipping, he was to 'serve his said master or his assigns for the time of his natural life here or elsewhere'. John Punch is thus the first recorded case of the lifetime enslavement of an African American.

Two weeks later, another mixed-race group of servant escapees appeared in the same court. They consisted of an African, four Englishmen and two men described as Dutch, though they bore English names. They had taken part in a well-organised attempt to reach Dutch territory by river. They stole a skiff plus 'shot and guns' and took off on a Saturday night. When they reached the Elizabeth River, their skiff was spotted and they were caught. The alleged ringleader, one of the 'Dutchmen' named as Christopher Miller, was punished with venomous severity. He was to be given thirty strokes of the whip, have the letter R branded on the cheek and spend at least one year wearing a leg iron ('longer if said master shall see cause'). When he had served out the full contracted period with his master, Miller was to become the property of the colony as its servant for a further seven years. The second Dutchman was to serve those seven extra years, too.

The 'Englishmen' were punished slightly less severely. After whipping and branding and serving out their contracted time, one was to serve the colony for three years, and two others for two and a half years. The other Englishman among them was merely put on probation. Perhaps he gave his companions away.

As for the African, who was named as Emanuel, he was to be whipped, branded and shackled. There is no mention in the records of him serving extra time, so it can be assumed that he, like John Punch a few months earlier, was enslaved for life.

Over the next decade, perpetual slavery of Africans evidently became common enough for the extraordinary story of John Casor to be played out. This was something of a test case, in which a black servant claimed his indentured period had expired years before and his master counter-claimed that he was his servant for life. The

174

twist in the story is that the master seeking this lifetime sentence was Anthony Johnson.

The case was fought out in the early 1650s. Casor had fled Anthony Johnson's Angola Plantation and sought refuge with a neighbouring planter. The runaway insisted that he had been held for seven years beyond his indentured term. The neighbour, Robert Parker, believed Casor and kept him on his own plantation. Johnson was determined to get his property back and went to court. The ensuing legal battle saw Robert Parker representing the runaway Casor in court. The case dragged on for two years, presenting the bewildering sight of a white planter fighting a black planter to save a black servant from perpetual slavery.

At one juncture, Johnson was persuaded by his sons to free Casor but then reneged on the settlement. In the end, Johnson triumphed. The Northampton County Court ruled that Casor had indeed been a slave all along and instructed that he be returned immediately to Johnson, who was to be compensated for the two years Casor had been free. Robert Parker was ordered to pay him damages for sheltering the runaway. Twenty years later, Casor was still owned by Mary Johnson, Anthony Johnson's widow.[8]

By then, lifetime black slaves were becoming the norm and all the colonies had passed laws either recognising slavery in principle or specifically legalising it. Massachusetts led the way in 1641, followed by Connecticut in 1650, Virginia in 1661, Maryland in 1663, and New York and New Jersey in 1664. Others followed later.

These laws left black freedmen like the Johnsons still free, but they were no longer treated like other planters. They could still buy black servants but they were barred from buying white servants. In 1671, another measure made all 'non-Christian servants' newly shipped into Virginia slaves for life. Non-Christian meant African. Two years later, the colonial assembly passed another act validating the enslavement of Indian captives.

Legally, servitude and slavery had been divided and a further move underlined this. Virginia enacted legislation making black slavery hereditary. The relevant act read:

> Whereas some doubts have arisen whether children got by any Englishman upon a negro woman shall be slave or free, Be it therefore enacted and declared by this present grand Assembly, that all children borne in this country shall be held, bond or free only according to the condition of the mother.

That utterly reversed the basic principle in English common law that a child's status followed that of the father.[9]

Although there was no abrupt surge of Africans, the racial balance in the tobacco fields was changing. In the first quarter of the seventeenth century, white outnumbered black in the Chesapeake by more than twenty to one. By the last quarter of the century, the ratio had narrowed to three to one, with 2,000 black slaves in Virginia and 6,000 white servants. By the end of the century, the gap was closing fast. Estimates put the numbers landing in neighbouring Maryland in 1698 at between 600 and 700 whites and about 450 Africans.

The shift from the time-limited servitude of Englishmen to the lifetime slavery of Africans was prompted by economics as much as racism. The Caribbean plantations were demonstrating the much larger profits that an openly enslaved workforce could produce and the Chesapeake planters took note. More and more, black slavery appeared the better long-term investment. This was especially so when mortality rates began to fall. In the decades when half the workforce died inside five years, it wasn't good business to purchase men for a life term at twice the price of a time-limited white servant. When mortality rates improved, that calculation changed and lifetime slaves became more worth buying. One might have expected this to be the beginning of the end for the white slave business but there was still much money to be made out of the trade in white labour.

CHAPTER TWELVE

'BARBADOSED'

The earliest known reference to sugar cane is in a Hindu love charm from the ancient hymns of the Atharva Veda:

> I am sweeter than honey, fuller of sweetness than liquorice.
>   Mayest thou without fail long for me alone (as a bee) for
>   a branch full of honey.
> I have surrounded thee with a clinging sugarcane to remove
>   aversion, so that those shalt not be averse to me.[1]

The thought of being entwined with sugar cane would have been greeted with hollow laughter by those slaving under the tropical sun in order that sweet palates in England might have their moments of delight with the sugared cakes and tea in vogue in the seventeenth century. Although sugar has been associated with love through the ages, the men and women who cut and refined sugar in the Caribbean in the seventeenth century must have cursed the day the fibrous cane's sweet heart was ever discovered.

In 1493, Columbus stopped off at La Gomera in the Canary Islands and began a romantic liaison with Beatrice de Bobadilla, the island's governor. After a month, he remembered his destiny and decided to move on. He carried with him a present of sugar-cane cuttings, which he brought to Hispaniola. The Portuguese introduced sugar cane to Brazil, the Dutch brought it to Guyana and the French to Martinique. Sugar was widely planted as a cash crop in Cuba, Jamaica, Puerto Rico and other smaller islands. The English brought it to Barbados – along with servants to grow it.

In this chapter, we shall concentrate on the island of Barbados, so as to avoid countless comparisons. Besides, Barbados rapidly became the most important economic entity in Britain's new colonies, outstripping the settlements in America in terms of economic importance. It did this by concentrating on the development of a viable cash crop with a constantly replaceable labour force to work it. Any considerations about building a new society were cast aside. Such ideas could be left to those developing the colonies 2,000 miles to the north in America. Barbados was about commerce and the island became a vast agricultural factory with an enslaved workforce working under a tropical sun. Barbados was different in another way, too. Any hope that labourers might have of setting up their own little farm upon the expiry of their indenture was largely in vain. Economies of scale came into play and small tenant farmers were squeezed out by large plantation owners. In Barbados, people worked for the plantation owners or starved; or they left.

A love of good eating sucked Barbados out of obscurity. Humanity's sweet tooth owes its desire to a simple biological need: sugar runs in our blood, darting through our veins. The human chemical plant directs glucose straight into the bloodstream, providing energy like a drug rush. After such a high, blood-sugar levels inevitably dip. A lucky rule of commerce dictates that for every craving there is an equal and opposite rush to supply. Caribbean islands like Barbados were there to prevent sugar lovers going into withdrawal.

Barbados took its time to reach its pre-eminent position. In the 1620s, Captain John Powell took possession of the island in the name of King James and reported its existence to his employer, the wealthy London merchant Sir William Courteen, who headed a syndicate that established a little colony of eighty or so in 1627.

At the beginning, the English settlement of Barbados nearly faltered due to the problems of finding a workable cash crop. Captain Powell knew the Dutch governor of Guyana, from whom he purchased cotton and tobacco, along with various edible vegetables and sugar cane. The cane was to make 'kill-devil', or rum. The early planters were optimistic that they could follow where Virginia led and form an economy based on tobacco and cotton. To help them establish such an agrarian economy, Powell brought a group of forty Arawak tribesmen from Guyana as agricultural instructors. The Arawaks were soon betrayed and enslaved. Shortly afterwards, the enterprising planters kidnapped more Arawaks to work their fields for them. They were simply among the first of many to be betrayed and debased on the island of Barbados.

The English settlers and their backers also squabbled over ownership of the colony. Sir William Courteen's syndicate, which had borne the initial risk and costs, was shouldered aside by a syndicate headed by the Earl of Carlisle. Influence mattered as much then as it does today, resulting in Carlisle being granted a patent by the King and taking control.

Among the more forceful planters who shortly arrived to make their fortune was James Drax, a larger-than-life figure who later told the memoirist Richard Ligon that he had arrived with £300 in the 1620s and planned not to leave until he could buy a £10,000 estate in England.

As things worked out, Drax, his brother William and their fellow farmers had a ditch or two to cross before they would attain solid economic ground. The decision to grow tobacco was a bad move. A better-quality leaf was being grown in Virginia and so Barbados switched to cotton and indigo. Even then the island was in competition with more established industries and with other nascent English colonies, such as St Christopher and Montserrat.

Right from the very beginning, conditions for indentured servants in Barbados were atrocious. The man appointed by the Earl of Carlisle as governor in 1629, Sir William Tufton, tried to ameliorate the lot of the servants but the planters rebelled. In a placatory gesture, the planters were allotted an extra 10,000 acres to be shared among them. Carlisle sacked Tufton and appointed another governor in his place, one Henry Hawley, who appears to have been a bad lot. Tufton rebelled, and he and his supporters were tried for mutiny and hanged.[2] Sir William may have been a compassionate man but perhaps not a wise one.

In the 1640s, something happened that turned the plantation of the Caribbean into a goal more important for England than even the colonies on mainland America. European sugar prices shot up. The new Barbadians saw their chance. According to some accounts, the suggestion to move into sugar cane came from Dutch Jewish traders who had been sailing the region long before the British arrived, and who imported the sugar business from Guyana. Others say that James Drax was the hero of the hour, not only bringing sugar cane from Brazil but also setting up the first efficient sugar mills.

In 1640, St Christopher changed over to the cultivation of sugar cane and Barbados quickly followed. By 1642, sugar-cane farming was up and running in Barbados. By 1644, roller mills were in use that could squeeze a piece of cane so hard it could turn fifty per cent of its weight into liquid. The romance was wrung out of sugar; it became an industrial commodity.

Both the crop and the technology were now in place for a revolution that would make men rich at a speed impossible in England. True, there were side effects. Such quantities of high-octane rum became available that in a few years in Connecticut a General Court Order allowed the confiscation of 'whatsoever Barbados liquors, commonly called rum, Kill Devil or the like'.

One other ingredient was necessary for success: a large, cheap workforce, sugar farming being even more labour intensive than the cultivation of tobacco. In 1630, there were only some 1,800 people in Barbados. This was soon to change rapidly. In 1634, the total number of servants shipped from Britain was 790 males and forty-six females, of whom 246 were aged between ten and nineteen years old.

The first cargo of English convicts arrived in 1642 to work on the new sugar crop. Barbados was on its way to becoming a penal colony in all but name. The transportation of convicts has been described as a 'deferred death sentence'.[3]

Prior to the Restoration of the monarchy in the 1660s, even more people from the British Isles arrived in the West Indies than in America, perhaps three-quarters of the total who emigrated.[4] Of these, half were Irish. In the period leading up to the American

Revolution, half of all Scots, English and Irish crossing the Atlantic went to the West Indies.

As in America, the servants were slaves in all but name and were treated as chattels. On 12 June 1640, estate agents valued the estate of one George Bulkley. They noted livestock worth 42,000 pounds' weight of cotton, household stuffs worth 1,125 pounds of cotton and nine servants worth 3,120 pounds of cotton. Barbadian servants could be sold to pay a debt or inherited upon death of a planter.

Fortunes were made. The enterprising James Drax became the richest planter on the island. He was one of those who had benefited from the share-out of the 10,000 acres after the fall of Sir William Tufton. Drax's monument stands today, a large grey block of a house built in the 1650s. From the exterior, Drax Hall is no tropical pleasure dome designed to titillate and delight the viewer. It was built as a stolid, fortified house of power; the unyielding shape of his home said something about its owner. Drax had influential friends in England and the organisational abilities to make a success of his new enterprise. He established an estate that became the envy of all. Architecture might not have been Drax's forte but with his business based on food he certainly knew how to entertain. The following is an example of the sumptuous fare on offer at one of his *regalios*.

For the first course, the theme was beef, the most expensive item on a tropical island menu. Drax served rump boiled, cheeks baked, chine roasted, breast likewise roasted, tongue and tripe minced and baked in pies seasoned with sweet herbs, spice and currants: in all, fourteen varieties of beef.

The plates were cleared away. After the glory of the steer, more humble beasts had an opportunity to show their worth: Scots collops (escalope of pork), a fricassee of pork, a dish of boiled chickens, shoulder of young goat dressed in thyme, a kid with a pudding in its belly, suckling pig – and on and on.

Finally, there were custards and creams, preserves of fruit, cheesecakes, puffs and more. To drink, there was the ubiquitous kill-devil, plus brandy, claret wine, white wine and Rheinish wine, sherry, Canary red sack, spirits from England, and 'with all this you shall find as cheerful a look and as hearty a welcome as any man give his best friend', reported a satisfied guest.

While the planters feasted, out on the island's farms the African slave settled down to sleep on a plank in a dormitory, having feasted royally on a portion of his weekly allowance of a bunch of plantain. In his hovel, the European bond slave dined on potatoes and Indian corn, and perhaps some beans. No fine wines to sluice down this meal, though a spirit distilled from sugar was used as a medicine to revive those who developed a fever – a recurring hazard on the island. We don't know how Drax treated his European and African workers. Perhaps he was better than some, or worse. Some indentured slaves were treated kindly. In 1657, a planter bequeathed to his servant Desmond O'Doyle 'my best suit of clothes and my best hat', plus six months off if he proved a dutiful servant to the departed one's wife. However, plantation workers were generally dealt with in a more perfunctory manner.

Ireland, with its ready supply of young men with little adequate employment, became a labour exchange for the Barbados sugar industry, although Scottish youths were in even more demand. The need for labour on Barbados outstripped supply from the British Isles. In 1646, the government published a memorandum to encourage the trade in servants and in 1652 an act was passed allowing two or more justices to issue a warrant for vagrants and beggars to be shipped to the colonies, whether to island colonies or America.

Due to the political turmoil of the seventeenth century, many Irish and Scots were banished to Barbados for political or religious reasons. If they could only get through their seven years or so of labour, they hoped, then *arbeilt macht frei* – work might set them free. If only. For them, Barbados was a penal colony. Those who worked their indentured years here were not part of a plan to create an empire through settlement. No, they were simply part of a mercantile plan to develop capitalism on the island. Their role was purely that: to work and, through their labour, create profit. In some colonies in America, the headright system placed the bonded workforce at the centre of a settlement plan. In Barbados, it made the worker a unit of production that had a monetary value. A new term entered the English language – to be transported to the West Indies was to be 'Barbadosed'.

For much of our knowledge of the lifestyle of planters and their workforce in Barbados, we are indebted to the aforementioned Richard Ligon, who sailed from London on the *Achilles* on 16 June 1647. He wrote of his experiences in *A True and Exact History of the Island of Barbados*. Ligon is an engaging travelling companion, who tells us he was forced to make the journey because he lost all his money in some 'barbarous riot' and is now compelled in middle age to try his luck again. In fact, Ligon was a Royalist supporter who seems to have lost his money and property in the Second English Civil War. Destitution staring him in the face, he found himself in the position of the character in the proverb for whom 'need makes the old wife trot' and he headed to Barbados to try his luck.

Ligon's work is part traveller's tale and part manual for those who would wish to start a sugar plantation. He describes how sugar was refined and details the economics of buying and running a plantation. To buy a 500-acre estate at the beginning of the 1650s, he explained, would cost £14,000. For this outlay, one could expect an annual gross profit, after operating costs, of £8,849. This return was estimated on good-quality sugar fetching three pence a pound in London and was only possible because the workforce costs were next to nothing. Thirty white indentured servants and 100 Africans would run the estate free of charge after an initial fee to buy them for a set number of years.

The cost of feeding the workforce was minimal since almost all their food was grown on the estate. Ligon carefully took note of the smallest details:

> The servants built their own shacks and, as for their clothes, these are as rudimentary as decency and the climate will allow. The male servants receive shirts at four shillings each and drawers at 3 shillings. Their caps, if provided, cost 4s and shoes, if they are given any, 3s. The women are given petticoats at 5s a piece and smocks at 4s.[5]

If they served in the farmer's house, the women were provided with a waistcoat and a nice cap. The African workforce was even more simply provided for, with drawers for the men and petticoats for the women. Their upkeep was subsidised by their children, who were sold from planter to planter 'like hogs'. Ligon estimated the total cost of the workforce per year was £1,349, leaving a net profit of £7,500.

Of course, there were risks. Ligon points out that health was an issue: 'Sicknesses are there more grievous, and mortality greater by far than in England, and these diseases many times contagious.' An English mercenary soldier passing through Barbados in the seventeenth century wrote:

> This is the dunghill where our England doth cast forth its rubbish. Rogues and whores and such like people are those that are generally brought here; a rogue in England will hardly make a cheater here; a whore if handsome makes a wife for some rich planter.

Those who first made a go of the frontier life must have been made of stern and determined stuff to withstand the rigours of climate and the unknown. When the small holdings of the pioneers gave way to the large sugar plantations, life for the few became agreeable and the rough and tough men without capital drifted to other colonies such as Virginia or Rhode Island in search of a living and a dream. For those with capital and a hunger to make quick money, Barbados became the Mecca of the west:

> A man that will settle here must look to procure servants, which if you could get out of England for 6 or 8 or 9 years time only paying their passages, or at the most but some small above it, it would do very well.[6]

And so it would. By doing our own sums, we can cast new light on just how well the indentured-labour system benefited the sugar manufacturers. From his notional labour force and total annual profit, we can work out that Ligon's labourers contributed £57.69 of annual profit each to the planter.

From this, we can extrapolate that, thanks to the low one-off cost of buying a labourer, a planter would expect a profit of around £230 over four years or £288 over five years. All this profit could be gained because of the servant's want of £6 or so for a ticket. By Ligon's figures, the servant earned that for his master in thirty-eight days. If we consider the price the planter might have paid for a servant – to err very much on the high side, say £20 – we can work out that a servant would earn that for his master in 126 days. And remember, overheads were low: a servant's clothing cost only a few shillings, they built their own huts and their simple food was grown on the estate.

How different it all could have been if the plantation owner had paid a wage to his workers. If so, it might have been at the typical seventeenth-century English farm labourer's rate of ten pence to a shilling a day – or about £15 a year.[7] This would mean that over a four- or five-year period of indenture, total wages would amount to no more than £60 to £75. In such a case, the four-year profit margin from the labourer's work would drop from £230 to £170, and over a five-year period from £288 to £218. From these figures we can see that the economy of the sugar industry on Barbados in the mid-1600s did not rely upon the indentured-servant system – it used it to create a class of slave labourer whose efforts boosted profits rather than merely making the colonial enterprise possible.

Let us consider if there might have been another way in which migration of the impoverished masses might have been managed. What if the penniless migrant had been advanced credit with which to buy his or her own ticket? This is not such a fanciful idea for its time as might at first appear, for in the eighteenth century a form of credit system did evolve. If an equitable form of credit had been available, it is reasonable to suppose that a labourer might have been able to pay off the price of an Atlantic voyage sooner than the periods of indenture then operating. On a wage of £15 or so per annum, a thrifty labourer could perhaps have paid back the lender over time. For a skilled man such as a carpenter, in 1642 earning up to £25 or even more, the task would have been proportionately easier. Given the levels of profit made from the exertions of each labourer, it is perhaps also worth considering whether or not a notional level of pay for an agricultural labourer in Barbados might not have been considerably higher than the current rate in England.

The servant was made to work for anything from four to seven years, or even more. The fact is that the indentured-labour market was a crude racket and the servants were coerced and conned into unnecessarily lengthy periods of slavery just as in Maryland or Virginia. The indentured servant did not simply sell his or her labour for a period of time to pay off the cost of a sea crossing; the circumstances they encountered in the labour market forced them into giving a substantial period of their productive life to another for free. In his ground-breaking book on slavery, Eric Williams pointed to the many differing types of servitude and bondage, being careful to make distinctions between them and what he saw as the true slavery suffered by Africans – a life term that was inherited by their children.[8] While this was definitely the worst situation of all, it was worse by degree rather than by intrinsic nature. It has been argued that since the indentured servant was not born a slave, this was sufficient to differentiate him from one.[9] The lengths to which some previous writers on this subject have gone to separate out servitude from slavery seems to us to miss the point that there were, and are, different types of slavery.

In Barbados, the illegitimate children of servants were forced to work for nothing but their food until they were twenty-one. Other methods were used in the attempt to keep servants for longer than the period of their indenture, including adding years on for infractions of the endless rules that governed their lives. Many of these rules can be seen as being deliberately irksome, so that servants were likely to break them at some point.

At the conclusion of a servant's indentured term, his master was usually obliged to give freedom dues comprising a sum of money, some implements and clothing, a piece of land, or even some configuration of all three; in practice, this hardly happened. By the 1640s, the plantation owners had taken over most of the good land on the island. It became difficult for newly freed servants to set up a farm. The former servant would find that he or she had to work for a plantation owner for a subsistence wage. In this way, the labour force was effectively kept in thrall to the plantation owners for life. In 1676, the island's Governor wrote: 'As for the lands in Barbados, I am confident there is not one foot that is not employed down to the very seaside.'[10]

Ligon describes the position of each person in the social strata of Barbados:

> The island is divided into three sorts of men, viz. Masters, servants and slaves. The slaves and their posterity being subject to their masters for ever, are kept and preserved with greater care than the servants, who are theirs but for five years, according to the law of the island. So that for the time the servants have the worst lives, for they are put to very hard labour, ill lodging, and their diet very slight.

This is a crucial first-hand account, for Ligon observed that the white Europeans were being treated differently from the Africans – they were being dealt with more harshly. The African's lot was a terrible one, for to be wrenched from homeland to toil for another without the comfort of even a family life is as dreadful a fate as could be imagined. However, for a period of time, it appears that the European was more likely to die an early death in the fields than the African. The climate of Barbados made it particularly unsuitable for unremitting hard manual labour. Ligon tells us that indentured servants were bought on board the ships that brought them and taken straight to the plantations, where they were immediately ordered to make their own cabins. After that, they were put to work in the fields without any time to acclimatise.

> If they be not strong men, this ill lodging will put them into a sickness; if they complain, they are beaten by the overseer; if they resist, their time is doubled. I have seen an overseer beat a servant with a cane about the head until the blood has followed, for a fault that was not worth the speaking of, and yet he must have patience or worse will follow. Truly, I have seen such cruelties there done to servants as I did not think one Christian would have done to another.[11]

The plantation owners ranged from the merciful to the cruel, 'but if the masters be cruel, the servants have very wearisome and miserable lives', noted Ligon. Food was very basic: potatoes for dinner and loblolly (a kind of gruel or porridge) or bonivist beans or potatoes for lunch. Very occasionally, there might be meat, and that only if a steer had died. It could get cold at night. With no bedclothes to keep the chill from a servant's hammock, and having to sleep in the shirts and drawers in which they worked, 'a cold taken there is harder to be recovered than in England by how much the body is enfeebled by the great toil and the sun's heat . . .'

This, then, was the island home to many thousands of displaced English, Irish and Scots. Long lines of labourers would clear the tropical forest, then plant the cane. Harvesting was particularly back-breaking work, for the best part of the cane was near the root and so the plant had to be cut close to the ground. Overseers ensured regimented efficiency. It was unrelenting work in an unyielding climate. Under the tropical sun, it must have been a most terrible place in which to labour day after day with little respite and with frequent applications of the lash. For the Irish, it must have been especially unpleasant to find themselves under a regime that was designed and administered by Puritans and Cromwellians, who would have seen their Irish Catholic workers as the enemy not only of their country but also of their religion. The reasons for cruelty therefore existed on three levels: identity, religion and commerce.

The treatment of white bonded-slaves in the Caribbean caused concern to some of those in authority. In 1651, Barbados passed a law saying that no merchant should send a servant under fourteen years of age without the written permission of a guardian or person in authority. This was ignored. A few years later, a Colonel William Brayne wrote a letter to Oliver Cromwell from Jamaica saying that the planters should employ Africans. The reasoning was that 'the planters would have to pay for them and would have an interest in preserving their lives, which was wanting in the case of bond servants'. Such observations by the colonel and others led to tens of thousands of Africans being shipped into Barbados in the middle of the century.

The civil wars in England had far-reaching effects on the tiny island of Barbados. It is estimated that between 1648 and 1655, 12,000 political prisoners arrived as a result of the conflict. Deported Royalist prisoners were sold as bonded slaves. Rank was no safeguard. In 1656, two Royalist officers named Rivers and Foyle wrote: 'The Master of the ship sold your miserable petitioners and the others . . . for 155lb weight of sugar apiece (more or less according to their working facilities).' In a petition to Parliament, they described:

> this insupportable captivity . . . grinding at the mills, attending furnaces, or digging in this scorching island, having nothing to feed on . . . but potato roots . . . being bought and sold from one planter to another, or attached as horses and beasts for the debts of their masters . . . [12]

In 1659, an impassioned debate erupted in Parliament over the plight of Rivers and Foyle. Sir Arthur Haslerigge, one of the five MPs whose attempted arrest by Charles I had hastened the onset of the English Civil War, confessed that when he heard the petition read out, he had almost wept: 'Our ancestors left us free men. If we have fought our sons into slavery, we are of all men most miserable.'[13] Despite such sentiments, Rivers and Foyle received no redress.

Apart from the Royalist prisoners, wealthy Royalist refugees also turned up on the island. They saw it as a bolt-hole in which to escape the revolution being forced along by Cromwell and the Parliamentarians. This tipped the political scales in Barbados significantly towards the Crown. However, the pragmatism shown by the merchants and planters enabled them to continue their trade without significant political strife.

This happy state of affairs could not last. When Charles I was beheaded, the island declared itself for Charles II. Parliament was quick to respond. All trade with the island was suspended. Likewise, all trade between Barbados or any other English colonies or Dutch ships was forbidden. By this manner, England got a stranglehold on Atlantic trade and held the tiny rebellious isle of Barbados to book. A military force was sent to ensure that the island toed the line. After some skirmishes, the island continued to hold out against the forces of the Commonwealth. Sir George Ayscue, who commanded the Parliamentary forces, wisely decided that the policy of divide and rule was the way forward. It worked: after several prominent Barbados citizens and their troops went over to the Cromwellian side, the game was up for the mouse that roared. In January 1652, Barbados surrendered.

The planters of Barbados had one important piece of work still to do so that their labour system would run smoothly and without hindrance. They required a code to set down the exact nature of the relationship between master and servant. The assembly set about its essential task, saying it was 'much feared that some persons within this island have exercised violence and great oppression to and upon their servants through which some of them have been murdered and destroyed'. This last statement was no doubt true, for as in Virginia there were tales of servants buried in shallow graves. The Act for the Ordaining of Rights between Masters and Servants came into being in 1661. As with so many drear documents throughout history, it had pretensions to be something other than what it was. Yet it was an ordinance of such stringency that one might be forgiven in not understanding that those to whom it applied already existed in conditions of forced labour.

Article One of the new act began well by banning the importation of children – but only if they were English. Irish and Scots children could still be imported. Article Two laid down that for those under eighteen years of age, indentures should not exceed seven years; for those over that age, five years. Article Three logically stipulated that servants could not trade – for how could a chattel run a business?

After these 'reasonable' conditions, the act laid down some sanctions, taking its cue from Virginia and Maryland. In some respects, the new laws were harsher than those in America, in others less so; but all were draconian. Laying a hand on a master or mistress: one extra year. Stealing so much as a loaf of bread: two extra years. Marrying without the consent of one's master: four extra years. A pass system was encoded – absence without consent from the plantation at any time inside or outside work hours: one year for every two hours. Trying to escape: three extra years. A servant becoming a father: three more years.

This document became the blueprint for the Slave Code of 1688, enacted to control the lives of forced labourers from Africa. This should surprise no one, for what was the 1661 act other than a slave code in itself?

By the mid-1660s, a high proportion of the working population in Barbados was Irish. Some of what we know of the population of the Irish in the Indies and their condition comes from the priests who travelled to minister to them. According to Father John Grace, 12,000 Irish lived in Barbados and surrounding islands. He also reported 600 Irish slaves in a small island off St Christopher. An official observer, whose report is preserved in state papers, reported that in 1667 Barbados had no more than 760 'proprietors' and 8,000 effective men, of which 'a very great part Irish, derided by the negroes as white slaves . . .'

The same observer noted that on plantations he had seen at any one time 'thirty or forty English, Scotch and Irish at work in the parching sun, without shirt, shoe, or stocking; and negroes at their trades in good condition . . .'[14] How long these so-called servants would have survived in such conditions is anyone's guess.

There were recurring rebellions. In 1649, a major slave uprising was put down only because an African slave girl informed upon the mutineers. On the island of St Christopher, Irish deportees rebelled in 1666. The following year, the Irish on Montserrat rebelled. The English authorities hanged up to 400 rebels.

In 1675, after a series of conspiracies and disturbances in Jamaica, martial law was declared. In the same year in Barbados, a major rebellion by Africans was planned across a large number of plantations. The plot was foiled and 110 slaves were charged with conspiracy. The conspirators knew what awaited them if found guilty. Five took their own lives before they were brought to trial. Fifty-two slaves were executed in the most brutal fashion, six being burned alive and eleven beheaded.

A later plot involving both Irish and African slaves in Barbados was also quashed. Twenty Africans were executed but the Irish were allowed to go free. A further conspiracy by Africans to take over the entire island was uncovered and foiled. Uprisings continued in Jamaica and other colonies, including New York, for a hundred years and more.

In Barbados, the landowners' perennial fear of mass rebellion by Irish and Africans combined was to lead to the exclusive use of African labour. By the middle of the 1600s, the European bonded slave labourer was beginning to play a diminishing role in West Indian agriculture. They were moved on to other tasks, becoming agricultural overseers and factory workers. African labour cost less and was generally less troublesome. In 1684, a census showed the population of Barbados consisted of 20,000 whites and 46,000 blacks. When slavery was abolished in 1834, there were 15,000 whites and 88,000 blacks. But European labourers continued to arrive.

To this day, there are people in Barbados with Irish names known as 'Red-legs' because of their blistering skin: not much to be remembered by for so unhappy a history. Even though the role of the European labourer both grew and began to decline within the seventeenth century, as we shall later recount, early in the next century the Irish legal system would develop to ensure a continued source of almost free Irish labour for the plantations.

In the meantime, increasing wealth brought consolidation of political power for a planter elite. Drax Hall and one or two other Jacobean mansions stand as monuments to the sugar industry and the beginnings of industrial capitalism. Though slaves continually resisted their bondage, and indentured servants rebelled from time to time, the control of the powerful planters remained effectively unrivalled until the nineteenth century.

There was one final twist in the status of white and black slaves in Barbados. By the last decade of the seventeenth century, the Irish had become so rebellious and mistrusted by the authorities that African slaves were recruited into the very militia that had the task of putting down slave rebellions. Africans carried arms to police both other Africans and their European colleagues in servitude. It would appear that the white indentured labourer had by now outlived his usefulness in the West Indies or elsewhere – but it was not so. A well-paying racket is hard to kill off.

CHAPTER THIRTEEN

THE GRANDEES

In Virginia, more than 2,000 miles away from Barbados, most of the indigenous population had been cleared from the Tidewater, on the eastern shores of the Chesapeake, and the world of the Virginia grandee was being constructed. In the middle decades of the seventeenth century, roots were laid down for an aristocracy that would dominate Virginia for 200 years. Men whose descendants would include some of America's most revered leaders were busy building their fortunes – the first Washington, the first Maddison, the first Lee.

These big planters were concentrated along the necks of land between the four rivers of the Tidewater, where tens of thousands of acres had become personal fiefdoms. Each was a self-sufficient mini-colony with its own wharf, tobacco warehouse, forge and a village of wood-framed dormitories and dwellings where one man's word was law.

The centrepiece of the mini-colony was the 'big house', the planter's mansion. One of the first mansions, built in 1665, still stands. Known as Bacon's Castle, after a man who would shake Virginia to the core, it is a brick Jacobean manor house with all the baroque trimmings you might find in England. As the years passed, such mansions would be replaced by still grander Georgian edifices, as the planter elite consciously projected itself as a natural aristocracy.

It was not just their wealth that endowed them with superior pretensions. Many could claim an aristocratic lineage back in England. The typical grandee was the younger son of English gentry who arrived in the Chesapeake a wealthy, well-connected man already. Some historians argue that their attitudes to white servants and, later, to black slaves reflected the English aristocracy's disdain for the servile classes.

This new brand of planter arrived after 1630 and displaced the old pioneers – the 'ancient planters' – as the driving force of the Virginian economy. In parallel with their arrival in Virginia, other ambitious men were opening up the colony of Maryland on the eastern and northern shores of Chesapeake Bay.

Their use of labour was ruthless. This is evident from the truly staggering increases in productivity achieved in Virginia. After 1624, output per tobacco worker more than doubled, and then it doubled again, and doubled again. In the 1620s, the yield averaged 400 pounds of tobacco per worker. By the end of the century, it averaged 1,900 pounds. This does not appear to have been the result of the introduction of new technology or new equipment. In the 1660s, there were some 7,000 workers on Virginia's plantations but only 150 ploughs between them.[1] One is driven to the conclusion that workers achieved this fivefold increase in productivity due to the brutal pressure that was exerted upon them, day in day out, for decades. Edmund S. Morgan refers to the principal significance of indentured servitude being that it taught planters how to use violence to compel workers to work, thus setting a precedent for the violence of African slavery.[2]

Authority was not much interested in the welfare of servants. The long-serving Governor of the colony Sir William Berkeley was among those who regarded them as scum. Sir William, who served from 1642 to 1652 and from 1660 to 1676, was an archetypal Cavalier. His bearing, attire, his language and his attitudes all reflected the court of Charles I. His ideal society was rooted in an older England, where rule was channelled through an aristocratic elite and there was no room for notions of universal liberty. A notorious statement he made in 1671 about education laid bare the kind of man he was:

> I thank God there are no free schools [in Virginia], nor
> printing, and I hope we shall not have [them] these hundred
> years; for learning has brought disobedience and heresy and
> sects into the world, and printing has divulged them and
> libels against the best of government. God keep us from
> both.[3]

He was a planter himself, with two sizeable plantations. On one
he built a splendid mansion called Green Springs, which his wife
Lady Frances described as 'the finest seat in America and the only
tolerable place for a Governor'. Green Springs was the focal point
of the Tidewater aristocracy. From here, Sir William and his lady
presided over a social and political nexus in which rich planters'
families intermarried and the menfolk automatically secured the
posts of power in the administration and the militia. Crucially,
they packed the Governor's council, the topmost body in the
province. Members of this council had many privileges, including
exemption from taxes. Another privilege, an absurdity to our eyes
but presumably a mark of greatness then, was the right to gold
braid on their clothes. The historian Theodore Allen dubbed this
elite 'the plantocracy'.[4]

Among notable figures whose family fortunes were founded
in the Chesapeake during the time of Governor Berkeley was
General Robert E. Lee, the revered Confederate leader in the
American Civil War. His ancestor Richard Lee was one of the
early Tidewater grandees. He was among a number of the English
gentry connected to Governor Berkeley who were encouraged to
try their luck in the colony. The Governor, it seems, brought Lee
over to the colony and claimed a fifty-acre headright for importing
him. Later, during the English Civil War, young Lee was sent on a
mission to Europe. He returned with a shipload of provisions and
took the opportunity to add to the cargo thirty-eight men and
women whom he indentured to himself as servants. On arrival in
the province, he claimed their headrights, 1,900 acres, and never
looked back. He rose to be magistrate, burgess, member of the
Governor's council, colonel of militia and Secretary of State.

Future generations would be told that Colonel Lee was a

benefactor of the poor who gave land away. A description of him in a book written by the Lee family after his death reads:

> He was a man of good stature, comely visage, and enterprising genius, a sound head, vigorous spirit and generous nature. When he got to Virginia, which was at that time not much cultivated, he was so pleased with the country that he made large settlements there with the servants he had carried over; after some years, he returned to England, and gave away all the lands he had taken up, and settled at his own expense, to those servants he had fixed on them; some of whose descendants are now possessed of very considerable estates in that colony. After staying some time in England, he returned again to Virginia, with a fresh band of adventurers, all of whom he settled there.[5]

Judging from his will, if the Colonel did give anything away, he kept a lot more. When he died, Lee left one plantation in Virginia plus ten English servants and five negroes to his wife; a second plantation plus ten English servants, ten negroes and three islands in Chesapeake Bay to his eldest son; a third plantation with ten English servants and five negroes to a second son; and a fourth plantation – 'Paradise plantation' – plus an unspecified number of servants to another son; and two other plantations to other children.

The Lee empire was overshadowed by that founded by Colonel John Carter, who created the most successful dynasty on the Tidewater. The Carters, too, came from the ranks of England's gentry. John Carter arrived in the province in the 1630s, reportedly with 'considerable wealth' and good connections. He acquired land on a peninsula between the Rappahannock and Potomac rivers. There, he carved out the Corotoman Plantation, enthusiastically using the headright system to expand his holdings. In one shipment, he landed eighty servants at Corotoman and headrights increased his holdings by 4,000 acres. With money went power. Carter became a member of the Governor's council and a colonel of the militia. Such men made the system their own. When one

Carter servant was convicted of killing three hogs, a court ordered him to serve six extra years. When another Carter servant ran away for twenty-two days, the court accepted Carter's claim that he had spent more than 1,300 pounds of tobacco finding the escaper. The court slapped on an extra term of fifteen months – almost twenty-two days for every one day away.

His son Robert, who was born at Corotoman in 1663, would outdo everyone, earning for himself the title 'King' Carter after accumulating 300,000 acres, branching out into heavy industry and textiles and becoming one of the most powerful men in England's colonies. His status can be gleaned from the manner in which servants addressed him. One of his former servants, a Mary Harrison, wrote to him in what appears to be an attempt to buy her children's freedom from the planter. She must have borne the children during her service with Carter, which meant that by law the boys automatically became the planter's servants till they were twenty-one and any girls till they were eighteen. It is a begging letter that begins with clumsy audacity and then becomes servile. She writes:

> I was speaking to you concerning my two boys and your answer that you would consider about it. I should be glad to have an answer to it for I want to move this Fall nearer to my husband, and at the same time I should be glad to have my small children with me if your Highness pleases.

Mrs Harrison went on to ask about her 'big children', too:

> I should be glad to have them from your honour and to set your price on them what I am to pay a year, hoping your honour will not be too hard on me as I shall have rent to pay and then all to find in clothes, for it will always be my study to keep my payments good to you.[6]

What happened to Mary Harrison and her family is not known. The Carters were not benevolent masters, however, and hung on to their servants as long as possible. One day, they would stun fellow planters by voluntarily freeing hundreds of slaves . . . but that was far into the future.

In the 1660s, the treatment of servants in some plantations was so notoriously harsh that planters in Virginia's colonial assembly warned their fellow planters that fresh settlers would soon stop coming:

> [The] barbarous usage of some servants by cruel masters is causing so much scandal and infamy to the country in general that people who would willingly adventure themselves hither are . . . thereof diverted and by that means the supplies of particular men and the well-being of His Majesty's country very much obstructed.[7]

Two of the plantation scandals of the time, one in Maryland and one in Virginia, illustrate what the burgesses meant. The two planters involved could hardly have been more different. One was a hot-tempered illiterate, a drunkard who had somehow become a commissioner or magistrate as well as a substantial planter; the other was a well-heeled English gentleman, cool and calculating. Both got away with murder.

The site of the first murder was the Crayford plantation on Love Island, Maryland. The owner was a militia captain called Thomas Bradnox, a successful planter since the 1650s but a man with a violent past. The Maryland state archive records that in his younger days Thomas Bradnox stood accused of 'rebellion, sedition, rapine, thefts, robbery and other like felonious practices' and was pardoned on three separate occasions.[8] Why he got off, we don't know. Bradnox was a drunkard yet he acquired 2,000 acres of land on Love Island, was made captain of the militia and became first a sheriff then a commissioner.

One morning in 1660, a young servant on the Crayford plantation, Thomas Jones, was found dead, apparently beaten to death. At the subsequent inquest, servant witnesses from the plantation described the dead youth as sickly and ill and continually abused by Captain Bradnox. It seems that Jones had been hit, starved and humiliated as Bradnox tried to force more work out of him. Among other things, the servant had been forced to drink his own urine. The last beating was administered by the planter just before Jones's death. Examined today, the evidence seems overwhelming but Bradnox was exonerated of any wrongdoing. The jury – which would have been made up mainly of landowners – decided that the 'stripes' given to the boy before he died were 'not material' and he had died of a fever brought on by dropsy or scurvy.

During the inquest, another of Bradnox's servants, Sarah Taylor, gave evidence against her master. Taylor had run away several times after suffering Bradnox's violence. After the inquest, Bradnox made her pay for speaking out.

He beat and abused Sarah endlessly. Once more, she fled the plantation. It was difficult enough for a man to travel on land through the Tidewater, let alone a woman, and Sarah didn't get far. She was given shelter in a neighbouring plantation where a search party sent out by Bradnox tracked her down. They found her hiding under a bed. Hauled into court by Bradnox and found guilty of 'desertion', she was ordered to apologise on her knees to him. The kindly neighbour who had helped her also had to apologise to Bradnox. A cycle now developed of more beatings, more futile attempts to get away, followed by more beatings. It was finally brought to a close after someone persuaded magistrates to see the girl and examine her. A panel of three commissioners inspected the scars left on Sarah by the beatings she had suffered. Having seen the evidence, the three commissioners freed her and cancelled her servitude.

Bradnox wasn't finished. He complained that there had been a conspiracy to deprive him of his 'property', Sarah, and he appealed to the Governor of the colony to order her to be returned. Before the appeal was heard, Bradnox died but his wife carried on the fight to regain Sarah. Mistress Bradnox failed in this and in the end Sarah Taylor stayed free. However, the Governor decided that the planter's widow should be compensated for the loss of the servant. He ruled that the three commissioners who had freed Sarah should pay the widow the going price of a woman servant with several years to serve.

Shortly after the Bradnox case, the tide of abuse cases in

neighbouring Virginia finally shamed the Virginia elite and it issued its warning about the 'scandal and infamy' cruel masters were causing the colony. The assembly followed that up by banning the private burial of servants on the grounds that on a number of occasions those burying them were thought 'sometimes not undeservedly [as] being guilty of their deaths'.[9]

It must have been about this time that the body of the white youth described in our introduction was dumped in the cellar of a house in Annapolis under a pile of household rubbish. The manner of his burial and his sorry physical condition prompted anthropologists to suggest that he was a servant who had been thrown away with the rubbish to lie undiscovered for four centuries.

Measures were finally taken to improve the lot of servants in March 1662. The House of Burgesses ordered masters to provide all servants with 'competent diet, clothing and lodging' and not to 'exceed the bounds of moderation in correcting them beyond the merit of their offences'. More striking still, servants were reminded that they had the right to complain. However, the cruelty continued.

Our second plantation scandal was one of the most notorious of the entire colonial period. The Henry Smith affair began in 1666 on the Oak Hall plantation in Accomack County, Virginia. The local Virginian historian, Jill Nock Jeffery, describes the case as having 'all the elements of a modern-day crime thriller – kidnapping, adultery, rape and murder'.[10] Beyond the salacious detail, there is no better illustration of the different ways servants could be degraded and abused.

Henry Smith's origins are obscure. He appears to have been from the English gentry and to have arrived in Virginia with numerous servants in the early 1660s. Going by the experience of one skilled man whom Smith recruited, he made generous promises about allowing time off and other perks, all of which were forgotten on arrival. Smith emerged as a presence in Virginia in 1664, when, aged about thirty, he secured the first of a succession of headrights. Between 1665 and 1666, Smith paid for the transportation of at least 160 people, earning certificates for 8,000 acres of land in the Chesapeake.

Smith owned two plantations, Oak Hall and Occohannock. Jill Nock Jeffery has compiled a grim story of the nature of the regimes there and how the man himself was exposed. The disclosures started in June 1668, when two of his servants spoke out in the Accomack County Court against him. Jean Powell complained that Smith had physically abused her. In evidence, she displayed in court the marks of bruising and lashes on her back. Then Ann Cooper, another of Smith's indentured servants, charged him with fathering her illegitimate child. It was the beginning of an avalanche of revelations.

Three months later, a child was born to another of his indentured servants, Elizabeth Carter, who was also Smith's mistress. The baby was secretly delivered at the home of one of Carter's friends, Jane Hill, without a midwife or anyone else being called. The two women declared it to have been stillborn and called neighbours to witness the tiny body. However, the neighbours spotted blood and bruises around the head and reported this. Carter and Hill were arrested and charged with murder.

Infanticide by unmarried mothers was common enough on both sides of the Atlantic at this time, as women always bore the brunt of the ferocious laws penalising 'fornication'. No one had more to fear than an indentured servant in America. The mother of an illegitimate child faced a whipping and a fine to compensate her master for the time off she would spend caring for the infant. Since few servants had any money to pay fines, the mother had to compensate by serving extra time – usually two years. Her child became a slave before it could walk. The law initially specified that girls born to a servant would themselves become a servant and remain so until they were twenty-four years of age (later reduced to eighteen) and boys until twenty-one. While these children did not face a lifetime in bondage like the offspring of black slaves, given the short life expectancy of those days, they faced almost half a lifetime as chattels.

The law was no kinder to the woman if her master was the father of her child. True, she would be removed from his service but only to be placed with another master. She would still have to pay the penalty for fornication and serve the extra years if she had no money. As for the master who might have raped her, if he was classed as a gentleman he could not be whipped. All he faced was a fine and the loss of a servant.

Elizabeth Carter was acquitted of murdering her baby but was ordered to pay 500 pounds of tobacco or receive twenty lashes for bearing an illegitimate child. She was also ordered to receive thirty lashes for taking 'physic' during her pregnancy. During her trial, Carter named Smith as the child's father and claimed he had lured her into his bed with promises of marriage. She said that she participated in a *ménage à trois* with Smith and his first wife's sister. Smith denied all of Carter's charges but was judged to have fathered the dead child and fined 500 pounds of tobacco. He was recognised as a gentleman and so was spared the whip.

More of Smith's servants began to come forward pleading for protection against him. A picture of violence and deprivation, and then of rape and murder, emerged. Servants wore rags on their feet and dared not ask for shoes. Their diet consisted of hominy and salt, and sometimes nothing at all. Almost all had been beaten savagely and repeatedly. Some had been kept in bondage long after the expiration of their indentured period. Others had vanished after being taken for punishment to an island owned by Smith and still known today as Smith's Island.

One set of rape allegations came from a former servant called Mary Jones. She claimed that when her indentured period expired, Smith refused to free her. She was held for fourteen months on his island, tied 'neck and heel' and suffering many whippings. Smith raped her several times. As in England at this time, rape was rarely punished or even prosecuted in the Americas. The least likely rapes to be punished were those of indentured servants. Women servants were widely seen as loose and corrupt, like servants in general.

This time, however, the servant was believed and Smith was ordered to be taken into custody. Emboldened by this, other servants came forward with allegations. They included another alleged rape and two murders. Smith was said to have beaten two male servants to death: John Butts (known as 'Old John') and Richard Webb. The record does not reveal details of Webb's death, or whether the allegation led anywhere, but it does include damning evidence on the fate of Old John. He was evidently about sixty years old and exhibited all the fragilities of a body worked beyond design. According to other servants, his inability to work like a younger man made him a target for Smith's cruelty.

In 1666, Old John was beaten for stealing a piece of bread. He ran away but returned to the plantation. Citing the sixty year old as a runaway, Smith took him to the constable, Captain Bowman, for the statutory punishment for runaways: up to thirty strokes of the whip. Bowman saw bruising on Old John's arm and remarked that the man looked more in need of a nurse than a whipping. He refused to administer the punishment.

An infuriated Smith took Butts home, where he cut off one side of the servant's hair to mark him as a runaway, stripped him and began to whip him. Two other servants watched and counted forty or fifty lashes before their master stopped. Smith then put a 'plough chain' around Old John's ankle and forced him 'to work by day and grind [corn] by night'. He continued to thrash him. About three weeks after the visit to Captain Bowman, Old John died while sleeping in an open tobacco house.

The local justices found that Smith had beaten Butts in 'contempt of justice' but, because the relevant records did not survive the American Civil War, we don't know if Smith was ever tried for murder. What we do know is that, despite all the evidence and all the outrage caused by the various allegations, Smith was acquitted of rape and freed. Not only that, two of his alleged rape victims, Mary Jones and Mary Hues, were judged to have lied and were ordered to serve double the time specified on their indentures for making false accusations. The one blessing – if a relative one – was that they were sold to new masters and not returned to Henry Smith, an indication that the court knew very well that they told the truth.

It has been suggested that political influence with Governor Berkeley may have led to Smith being let off the hook, for it seems that he was neither jailed nor even fined. He was able to sell his lands and move to Somerset County in Maryland. However, in Governor Berkeley's defence, he may have had other things on his mind. Virginia was edging towards rebellion – or rather her servants were.

CHAPTER FOURTEEN

BACON'S REBELLION

To this day, Nathaniel Bacon remains a paradox. He was an aristocrat from one of England's most illustrious families yet he almost sent Britain packing from America a hundred years before George Washington. Some see him as a self-serving adventurer who tapped into the grievances of thousands in a bid for personal power. Others see Bacon as a true revolutionary, a crypto-Cromwellian, and his rebellion as the first stirrings of American independence.

There were numerous uprisings and small-scale rebellions in England's American colonies before the final break with Britain but none as serious as that led by Bacon in 1676. The danger he posed was reflected in the venomous description of him by a royal commission that was appointed to investigate the rebellion a year later. He was:

> ominous, pensive, [with a] melancholy aspect, of a pestilent and prevalent logical discourse tending to atheism . . . of a most imperious and dangerous hidden pride of heart . . . and very ambitious and arrogant. But all these things lay hid in him till after . . . he became powerful and popular.[1]

This man sent the Governor, Sir William Berkeley, scurrying for safety across the Chesapeake, saw Jamestown burnt to the ground and the mansions of the Tidewater estates ravaged, and roused all the servile classes – white and black – in revolt.

Bacon was twenty-nine – 'indifferent tall but slender, black-haired' – when he arrived in the province two years earlier. He came from the same family as James I's Lord Chancellor, Sir Francis Bacon, and he was married to a cousin of Governor Berkeley. Needless to say, the well-connected young man was immediately inducted into the planter elite. He acquired two plantations and was appointed to the Governor's ruling council.

He arrived in a province that was in a state of increasing unrest. After the end of the English Civil War, Virginia had been viewed by Cromwell as a dumping ground not just for the Irish but for English undesirables, too. Cromwell's military commanders swept up hundreds of prostitutes, beggars and vagrants with a view to transportation. After filling gaols in the Midlands with them, one of Cromwell's generals boasted: 'I may truly say that you will ride all over Nottinghamshire and not see a beggar or a wandering rogue.'[2]

It is unclear how many of England's cast-offs and rogues Virginia now had to accommodate but there was a rising tide of protest at the 'Newgateers' being shipped over. With the Restoration, it got worse. As well as the sweepings of the prisons, the province was forced to accept as servants veterans of Cromwell's New Model Army. A number of mini-insurrections by servants followed and former Roundheads were said to be involved in every one.[3] The most serious, in 1663, became known as the Servants' Plot. It was a localised uprising that was contained in Gloucester County. But it was considered grave enough to be put down with a studied show of ferocity and the ringleaders' severed heads were displayed on chimney pots. To prevent more outbreaks, servants' movements were restricted across the colony. Planters were warned especially to keep their men on the plantation on the day of rest, Sunday.

Action was also taken to stem the flow of convicts. In 1670, Virginia's General Court warned that 'the great number of felons and other desperate villains sent over from the prisons of England' were a 'danger' to the colony.[4] Urgent protestations were made to the King and he agreed to suspend convict shipments.

But Virginia's tensions went much deeper and wider. In

1672, the assembly reported that a 'Negro rebellion' was in the making and expressed fears that white servants would join it. The assembly stated that 'many negroes are now out in rebellion in sundry parts of this country' and warned that 'very dangerous consequence may arise to the country if either other negroes, Indians or servants should happen to fly forth and join with them'.[5]

In fact, there was discontent throughout Virginia, from servants and slaves, to ex-servants and middle-ranking planters. Land was the constant grievance. Most ex-servants had none. Either they weren't allocated any on attaining liberty or, if they were, they couldn't afford the very expensive business of having it surveyed. The minority who managed to acquire a plot didn't feel that much better off. These were bad times for the tobacco business and many small men were going to the wall.

The focus for the discontent was Governor Berkeley, who was so obviously the grandees' man. On everything – land patents, taxes, appointments, even the siting of protective forts – Berkeley appeared to favour the grandees. The tax system was especially resented. Berkeley and his council insisted on a poll tax, which meant that an ex-servant with fifty acres was taxed as heavily as the grandee who once owned him and had 10,000 acres.

Virginia ignited in 1675 when a war broke out with one of the few native American tribes still with a toehold in the Chesapeake. Like so many conflicts between settler and Native American, this originated in a tiny incident – the theft of a few hogs from a plantation – and escalated into widespread butchery. Hundreds died on both sides.[6]

Nathaniel Bacon joined the Indian war after a servant on his plantation was killed. Within weeks, he emerged as leader of the most violent settlers who favoured total extermination of the indigenous population. This set them at loggerheads with the Governor, who counselled conciliation, distinguishing between 'bad' tribes who should be destroyed and 'good' tribes who behaved. Sir William's motives were probably mixed. On the one hand, he was trying to serve imperial ends by sustaining Native American allies in case of further wars against the French. On the other hand, he and his grandee friends had a lucrative fur trade with those tribes he dubbed as 'good'.

Bacon and the wild men wouldn't be reined in. They continued to defy the Governor by harrying the tribes. In one surprise attack, 120 Native Americans were slaughtered in what became known as the Battle of Bloody Run. Bacon boasted how his war party 'fell upon the men, women and children . . . disarmed and destroyed them all'.[7] Only three of Bacon's men were killed. He became a hero.

Over several months, Bacon and Berkeley duelled: the Governor ordered the younger man's arrest and then pardoned him; Bacon had the Governor in his hands but released him.[8] As the contest ebbed and flowed, it became an argument over more than the tribes. Bacon, the aristocrat, raised a class banner against those who ruled the colony. He painted them as parvenus and corrupt bloodsuckers who took a soft line with the Native Americans because of the money being made from trade.

Bacon was forceful when in full flow:

> Let us trace these men in authority and favour to whose hands the dispensation of the Country's wealth has been committed; let us observe the sudden Rise of their Estates compared with the Quality in which they first entered this Country . . . let us consider their sudden advancement and let us also consider whither any Public work for our safety and defence or for the Advancement and propagation of Trade, liberal Arts or sciences is here . . . adequate to our vast charge . . . and see what sponges have sucked up the Public Treasure and . . . juggling Parasites whose tottering Fortunes have been repaired and supported at the Public charge.[9]

In June 1676, during a stalemate in the struggle between the rival factions, the Governor called a new election for the House of Burgesses. Bacon and other critics of the Governor romped home in the seats they contested. Most were freemen: 'men that had but lately crept out of the condition of servant', as one upper-crust observer from England later sneered.

Reforms were pushed through the new assembly, reducing the power of patronage. The contest became a rebellion. Bacon insisted on raising a force under his own control to wage war on the Native Americans, at which the Governor once more ordered his arrest. Bacon's class rhetoric increased. He published a Declaration of the People, indicting Berkeley for unjust taxes, favouritism and not protecting the small planters in the border territories. Twenty of Berkeley's leading supporters, most of them grandees, were named as 'wicked and pernicious counsellors aides and assistors' who had violated His Majesty's interest in Virginia while 'acting against the commonality'.

At this point, Bacon offered freedom to every slave and servant who deserted their masters and joined him.[10] As far as is known, he did not, however, free his own servants and slaves, nor those of his adherents.

Hundreds of runaways, both black and white, rallied to his support, along with landless freemen, poor farmers and owners of smaller estates. The women amongst them were described as 'great encouragers'. Sir William Berkeley dismissed them as 'rude, dissolute and tumultuous felons'.[11] The grandee Nicholas Spenser labelled them 'trash of which sort this country chiefly consists, we serving but [as] a sink to drain England of her filth and scum'.[12] In fact, Bacon's supporters included men and women from every level below the grandees. Lists of those who actively backed the rebellion included scores of fairly substantial planters, plus magistrates and burgesses.

By August, Bacon had sufficient men to hold Jamestown and the western shore. More than that, he believed that he could defeat an army being sent from England.[13] Sir William sailed to the eastern shore, where he bided his time till that help from England arrived. Under the initials T.M., a burgess and supporter of Bacon wrote an account of the rebellion including the spectacular incident that now took place in Jamestown. It featured two more of Bacon's supporters among the burgesses: Richard Lawrence and William Drummond. Lawrence was supposed to have been motivated to join the rebels by love. It was said that he was 'in the dark embraces of a blackamoor, his slave, and thought Venus was . . .

to be worshipped with the image of a negro'. T.M. described how Lawrence and Drummond set an example to the crowds in the captured capital:

> Here resting a few days they concerted the burning of the town, wherein Mr Lawrence and Mr Drummond owning the two best houses save one set fire each to his own house which example the soldiers following laid the whole town with church and statehouse in ashes, saying, 'the rogues should harbour no more'.[14]

The rebellion came to an abrupt end with Bacon's sudden death. In October 1676, he fell ill and before the month ended he was dead of the 'bloody flux'. Though the rebellion disintegrated, numbers of supporters, black and white, remained at large. In November 1676, Thomas Grantham, a naval captain delegated to help the Governor, caught up with one of the last bands of rebels. He inveigled most of them into surrendering by promising them their freedom:

> I . . . met about 400 English and Negroes in arms . . . some were for shooting me and others were for cutting me in pieces. I . . . did engage to the Negroes and servants, that they were all pardoned and freed from their slavery: And with fair promises and rounds of Brandy, I pacified them, giving them several notes under my hand that what I did was by the order of his Majesty and the Governor . . . Most of them I persuaded to go to their homes, which accordingly they did, except about eighty Negroes and twenty English which would not deliver their arms.

Grantham outfoxed this remaining group by persuading them he would take them to a rebel-held fort. Instead, he took them to within range of a man-of-war. 'They yielded with a great deal of discontent,' reported Grantham, 'saying had they known my purpose they would have destroyed me.'[15] Grantham was later knighted.

It is doubtful that any of those who surrendered were given their freedom – an iron collar and a whipping was their likely fate. Governor Berkeley was in no mood to give anything to the rebels. When William Drummond was captured and brought before him, Berkeley said, 'I am more glad to see you, Mr Drummond, than any man in this colony! You shall be hanged in half an hour!'

'What your Honour pleases,' replied Drummond.[16] Twenty-three others followed Drummond to the gallows, all without trial. Richard Lawrence was among them. The fate of Lawrence's lover is unrecorded.

The Governor's vengeance took Charles II aback. 'The old fool has taken more lives in his naked country than I have taken for my father's murder,' the King remarked.[17] Berkeley had in fact hoped to copy the King, who had ordered Oliver Cromwell's corpse to be disinterred from its impressive tomb in Westminster Abbey, dragged to Tyburn, hanged, beheaded and quartered. Berkeley planned the same for Bacon's corpse but when the coffin was opened it was full of stones. The Governor was left with only a ditty to express his loathing for his dead adversary: 'Bacon is dead I am sorry at my heart / That lice and flux should take the hangman's part.'

Substantial numbers did find freedom after the rebellion. Between 880 and 890 bond labourers of every race fled Virginia. Most were soon recaptured and returned in chains. Others succeeded in getting away and created the maroon communities of the Cumberland Plateau.

The Royal Commission set up to investigate the rebellion ladled out bromides about the 'credulous silly people' whom Bacon had misled. Two-thirds of the colony were 'vulgar and most ignorant people who had been seduced', said the commission. One of the Tidewater elite, Richard Lee, was more honest and acknowledged that the rebellion was about inequality. 'Hopes of levelling,' he said, lay behind the 'zealous inclination of the multitude' to support Nathaniel Bacon.[18]

Lee and his fellow grandees were left to worry about the implications of the revolt. From Maryland, where an attempted uprising was suppressed, the Governor warned that unless a method of rule was adopted that would 'agree with the common people . . . the Commons of Virginia would mire themselves as deep in rebellion as ever'.[19]

A nightmare vision was conjured up of armed blacks and whites rising in unity against the planters. The support Bacon inspired brought home to the elite their basic vulnerability. They had no sizeable yeoman class as a barrier to servile revolt. European colonies in parts of the Caribbean had created a yeoman class by encouraging planters to parent children with slave or servant women. The Chesapeake colonies had not done this; in fact, they had positively discouraged inter-racial coupling. The task facing Virginia's rulers now was to fashion a class that gave them 'as many Virginians with a stake in suppressing servile insurrection as there were in fomenting it'.[20]

They played the race card. The status of the European servile class was upgraded and a sense of racial superiority instilled. Meanwhile, the process of degrading non-whites was accelerated. Law after law deprived Africans and Native Americans of rights, while bolstering the legal position of European servants. In the space of twenty years, non-whites lost their judicial rights, property rights, electoral rights and family rights. They even lost the right to be freed if their master wanted to free them. In parallel, whites gained rights and privileges. Masters were forbidden from whipping their white servants 'naked without an order from a justice'. They were told to provide real freedom dues: corn, money, a gun, clothing and fifty acres of land. And the notion of a 'white race' was promoted. Hitherto, the English had never applied colour to distinguish race. Now white servants, whose daily condition was little different from that of Africans, were taught that they belonged to a superior people.

On the big plantations, white and black began to be given different clothing. Living quarters were segregated. Sometimes the races ate separately. But whites remained chattels and when they ran away they were pursued as ferociously as ever. White slavery went on. Not only that, as the eighteenth century advanced, a vast new pool of potential white slaves materialised as the peoples of central Europe began to share the American dream. But they wouldn't prove easy to handle.

CHAPTER FIFTEEN

QUEEN ANNE'S GOLDEN BOOK

In February 1709, when the ice was hardly broken on the Rhine, a stream of boats sailed through the chilly waters carrying thousands of peasants. They sang hymns and folk songs and were generally in high spirits. Bound together by expectation and buoyed up by hope, the passengers had left their homes in Germany to float downstream toward the Netherlands and into the unknown. The travellers became known as the 'Poor Palatines' but, like almost everything about the episode, this description was not the whole story. It is true that among the migrants were many villagers from the Palatinate region, but others came from the duchies of Württemberg and Baden and the innumerable other small duchies and princely states in the area that today comprises part of western Germany.

Although most were illiterate, the catalyst for their strange odyssey was a book. One work alone, a volume that few of the many thousands floating down the Rhine could possibly have read, propelled 30,000 peasants from their homelands and towards the promise of a new life in America.[1]

The volume was commonly known as 'Queen Anne's Golden Book', but it had nothing to do with Queen Anne, the British queen, and it certainly wasn't made of gold.[2] However, those who clapped eyes on it would certainly have noticed the picture of Queen Anne on the cover and the elaborate gold lettering on the title page. The book was an anonymous propaganda piece written to extol the virtues of emigration to America. It first appeared in the Rhineland in 1706. Even the best advertising campaign is unlikely to have the spectacular effect of making multitudes sell up, risk all and change their lives. There has to be something more. In the case of the 'Golden Book', that extra ingredient was the message that not only could a new life be had but, better still, someone else would pay. As the emigrants would soon find out, the promise was pie in the sky. The German migrants would become ensnared in the British indentured-servant system, facing seven years' labour in a colonial industrial enterprise. Uniquely, the Germans would defy the British authorities through collective passive resistance.

The 'Golden Book' had such an effect because of a religious connection between Germany and America. One of the earliest links was forged by the English Quaker, William Penn, who travelled through the Palatinate in the 1670s preaching a form of religious observance that chimed with local German feelings. A few years later, Penn became the proprietor of a new American colony that he modestly named Pennsylvania. It was designed as a land of religious tolerance but it was also a land from which Penn stood to make a fortune – if he could people it. In 1681, Penn wrote a pamphlet translated into German, explaining the virtues of his territory. He followed this up a year later with a *Brief Account of the Province of Pennsylvania*, published in both English and German. Another similar pamphlet followed two years after that. Penn was nothing if not persistent.

Persuasive though advertisements by Penn and his allies undoubtedly were, none could account for the phenomenon of 1709, when masses set sail. For one thing, the Palatines and their neighbours were almost unanimous in their desire to go not to Pennsylvania but Carolina. They had 'Queen Anne's Golden Book' to thank for that. The work's real title, engraved in gold, was *A Complete and Detailed Report of the Renowned District of Carolina Located in English America*. Most of those influenced by it might never even have seen it. Word of mouth would have been enough to spread Carolina's allure through illiterate villages.

This book had little power when first published. Its pages were stuffed with descriptions of Carolina, its landscape, vegetation, soil type, animal life and so on: all the things poor farmers would like to know. But even this was not enough to persuade people to leave their homeland en masse. Then, in 1709, the work was reissued, with a powerful new ingredient. This was a copy of a letter from London that described how Queen Anne had helped a small band of fifty Palatines emigrate to America in 1708. The beneficent queen had apparently paid for their upkeep and lodgings in London and for their passage to America, and even provided assistance until they were set up in the New World: 'The Queen would give them bread until they could grow it themselves.'[3] To the impoverished villagers, it seemed miraculous. They could sell up and sail to a new life, guaranteed by the Queen of England, no less. If only it had been that simple.

The book was at best a well-meaning propaganda puff for a colonial enterprise. It is now accepted that the author was a Lutheran pastor called Joshua Kocherthal, an obscure cleric from south of Heidelberg. In 1708, Kocherthal accompanied a small group of poor Palatines to London to seek help in emigrating to America. They came to the attention of Queen Anne, who charitably agreed to help, and the group was given free passage to America.

At around this time, Kocherthal met the owners of Carolina, or their representatives, and emerged as a promoter of their colonial enterprise. Carolina was under the control of an assemblage of Lords Proprietors, originally a group of eight men awarded a royal charter for the territory by Charles II in return for helping him to regain the throne. The meeting of the man of the cloth and the men of business gave rise to 'Queen Anne's Golden Book'. It would be far more successful than any of them could have imagined.

In February 1709, thousands of peasants began to arrive in Rotterdam in preparation for crossing the channel, with the expectation that the British would look after them from there on. Neither the Dutch nor the British were expecting them and by now the migrants were running out of money to pay for the crossing. As their numbers swelled, they built a series of *strassendorfen*, or one-street towns, balanced miserably on top of the dykes outside the city. The Rotterdam authorities provided what food and shelter they could. The British representative in Holland, James Dayrolle, sent dispatches home about these strange immigrants, who, having hardly the means to put bread in their mouths, expected to be carried to Carolina and resume their lives as farmers.

In early eighteenth-century England, as today, debate raged over immigration. While Britain was colonising North America, its own economy was in a slump. Some thought an influx of immigrants would revitalise it; others thought they might overwhelm the country. James Dayrolle was among those who favoured immigration and suggested that the German refugees might be a boon to the economy. This idea was taken up by the sympathetic Whig government. The fact that the refugees themselves kept saying they wanted to go to Carolina was ignored in the general whirlwind of debate.

Britain was at war on the Continent and Dayrolle arranged that troop ships should depart for home stuffed full of Palatines, doubtless singing with renewed energy. They swamped the poor London docklands area of St Catherine's and some of London's charitable inhabitants raised funds for the 'Poor Palatines'. Barns were rented in the villages of Camberwell and Kennington, and a large encampment was created on Blackheath. Charity kept the refugees barely above starvation. Disease was rife.

England debated what to do with 13,000 or more newcomers. The Tory opposition in Parliament was opposed to the idea of attempting to integrate thousands of foreigners into British society. But Dayrolle had the backing of the government and their influential supporter Daniel Defoe. Today, Defoe's fame rests on his novels, *Robinson Crusoe* and *Moll Flanders*. He was, however, primarily a journalist and propagandist, who took up fiction later in his career. As a one-time hosier, wine merchant and part-owner of a brick factory, Defoe was fascinated by most aspects of trade: as he said himself, trade was the harlot to which he most returned.

Defoe's ruminations on the economy led him into the immigration debate. As a Whig, Defoe was a reformer. Whigs favoured relaxed naturalisation laws that would make it easier for foreigners to become British subjects. On the other side, the Tories felt an influx of immigrants could take jobs from indigenous workers and become a burden to the state. There were also worries about the religious persuasion of newcomers, with Tories casting a baleful eye on dissenters.[4]

Defoe took up his pen in a pamphlet entitled *A Brief History of the Poor Palatine Refugees, Lately Arrived in England.* Defoe, who was well used to battling for political ideas, described his work as 'A full Answer to all objections made against receiving them; and plain and convincing proofs, that the accession of foreigners is a manifest advantage to Great Britain, and no detriment to any of Her Majesty's native subjects.'[5]

According to Defoe, if the Poor Palatines were given sufficient land to feed themselves, Britain would not have to provide for them. Other migrants, like the Huguenots, had arrived some time before and had added to the country's wealth by exporting the goods they made. By Defoe's estimate, 10,000 Palatines would increase the annual wealth of the nation by £80,000.

He continued, 'In truth, our own country England is not half peopled, Ireland not a quarter part, Scotland less . . . and yet we complain that Providence has sent us people to help us in these necessary services to the Public!' The nation described by Defoe did not sound like a country that had such masses of surplus people that they had to be transported to colonies overseas.

Defoe, like Dayrolle and everyone else, had completely forgotten that the Poor Palatines did not want to settle in Britain – they spoke about little else but Carolina. Defoe looked at all the possible options of where to settle the Palatines and discounted all schemes involving the colonies: a new settlement south of the River Plate was too expensive, as were Virginia and Maryland, and the same went for Jamaica and the Indies. For Defoe, the solution was to employ some of them in England and send the rest to Ireland.

After some months, Londoners began to grow weary of their foul-smelling visitors. They were accused of bringing disease. Worse, it become known that a good proportion of the migrants were Catholics. A mob threatened the Blackheath encampment but the Catholics were defended by their fellow refugees. It was clear that something had to be done. Government plans to disperse them around England were thwarted by provincial worthies. In the end, only a few hundred were resettled. The government in Ireland threw a lifeline, requesting 'German Protestants' to bolster religious hegemony. In September, 2,971 were shipped across the Irish Sea. However, the Germans did not take to toiling as labourers on Irish estates. By November 1710, only 1,200 remained in the country. The rest returned to London, remarkably fixed in their objective: they wanted to farm and they wanted to be free in Carolina.

Surprisingly, a plan finally was hatched to send some of them to Carolina. For the 600 who went, it must have seemed that all their prayers had been answered. If they had, it was by a god that liked to test his followers. During a voyage lasting thirteen weeks, half of the passengers died. The following year, sixty were killed during fighting with Tuscarora Indians. There were disagreements between the migrants and the owners of Carolina, with the settlers disputing the 250 acres per family they were allotted. Ultimately, some of the surviving migrants resettled in other colonies.

One other colonial plan showed promise: to use the Germans as indentured labour in a new tar and pitch industry in New York. The industry was to be set up to supply the maritime trade, smearing hulls and ropes to stop leaks and decay. The Germans would make a cheap and handy workforce whose labour would pay off their passage, secure a profit and eventually reward them with the land they craved in the New World. The power behind this scheme was a Scot named Robert Hunter, who fought in Europe under the Duke of Marlborough and was rewarded with the governorship of New York. Hunter saw the immigrant Palatine community as the perfect answer to the manpower needs of his industrial plan. If he had known how some of them were already reacting to their lot in Ireland, he might have reconsidered.

Of the Palatines remaining in England, 3,000 finally embarked on a fleet of nine ships. Even though they knew they were not bound for their beloved Carolina, they decided not to examine their gift horse too closely. The journey did not begin well. The emigrants were kept at anchor off Plymouth from the end of December until April the following year. Conditions became intolerable, with disease carrying off some of the younger and weaker migrants. The agreement with Hunter seems to have been thrashed out during these dreadful weeks. As far as the Governor was concerned, the Germans would work for seven years as indentured servants to repay the costs of their transport and keep, after which they would be given forty acres apiece. The Germans did not see it like that.

As the fleet set sail, the German refugee camps in London were closed down and destitute Palatine beggars wandered the streets. On 13 June 1710, the first ship reached New York. In all, 2,400 immigrants made it alive. Among them was that shameless opportunist Pastor Joshua Kocherthal. Records show that 470 either died en route or within the first month of landing. Matters did not end there. Within a year, a quarter of the total had died, most of them children.

Governor Hunter began arrangements for his tar and pitch industry. He intended to set up a large work camp in the Hudson River valley, north of New York town, where there was an abundant supply of suitable pine trees. These could be tapped for the resin, or pitch, that was in demand by navies around Europe to caulk the hulls of ships and render them watertight. Up until this time, Britain had relied upon other nations for these supplies. If Hunter could establish a British industry, not only would this dependence be broken but a profit could also be turned.

Overheads were paid for by the Board of Trade in London. The allowance was sixpence a day for persons over the age of ten and fourpence for those under ten. To cut expenditure, many immigrant children were sold by the British authorities as apprentices to families already living in New York town. In effect, these children became indentured slaves for the families who bought them. When they moved on to their new lodgings upstate, their parents would leave them behind, perhaps never to be seen again. Seventy children under the age of eleven were apprenticed, bound to strangers until the age of twenty-one. More than half of these children were orphans, the rest the children of widows or even members of large families. Some were as young as three.

In the autumn of 1710, Hunter's plans for industrialisation took root on the Hudson when a group of 1,500 Germans arrived in his camps. Instead of the hundred acres of land per person they had been dreaming about, each family was given a plot of 2,000 square feet to grow vegetables. This was not what the Germans had envisaged. The workforce looked around at the heavily wooded valley and compared it to other land in the area. They wanted to know why Hunter could not resettle them where the land was better for agriculture and a 'New Canaan' might be built. The good Paster Kocherthal was among them, ensuring their vision remained vivid. Disgruntlement turned to surly non-cooperative resistance.

Hunter found it difficult to impose his will upon the recalcitrant workforce. Many Germans carried guns provided by the British for defence against the indigenous tribes. Twice, Hunter had to bring armed troops to the camps to quell dissent. After one particularly tense stand-off, the Germans retreated into the forest and fired their guns in the air in an act of ineffectual defiance.

Some work did get done. Trees were tapped and prepared for the collection of resin. Heartened, Hunter unwisely moved more indentured Germans upcountry. The population of his encampments rose to 1,800. Expenditure was mounting but as yet no tar had been made. Soon, the £8,000 advance from the Board of Trade had gone.

In London, a Tory government replaced the Whigs and the mood changed. In *The Spectator*, Joseph Addison described the Palatine refugees as 'this race of vermin . . . this idle, profligate people'. Even the Lutheran pastors who had once befriended them chided them, saying that God had commanded the Children of Israel into exile whereas the Palatines left their land purely in search of property.

The Tories repealed the Whigs' naturalisation law. They stopped paying out for risky schemes involving migrant labour and Hunter found himself paying for his venture. The Germans grumbled on, though their bellies were filled. British bills for food and household supplies began to go unpaid. After a year, with not a barrel of tar produced, Hunter ran out of money and the venture folded. He felt he had no option but to free the Germans. They were at liberty to do what they had always wanted and take up farming.

By sheer bloody-minded stubbornness, the Germans had beaten the British colonial powers and escaped the indentured labour system. With an untypical burst of energy and initiative, the 'Poor Palatines' promptly negotiated with Mohawk chiefs, who gave them permission to settle and farm along the Schoharie Creek, north of Albany. For a second time, the migrants had sought and were given help by foreigners – the difference being that it cost the Mohawks nothing and they asked nothing in return. As the unwilling tar workers drifted up the Hudson Valley to reacquaint themselves with the trade they knew in a valley they did not, Governor Hunter's dreams of industrial profit faded into the shadows of the New York forests.

Elsewhere, the efforts of William Penn and others did not go in vain. Pennsylvania developed into a thriving colony that attracted large numbers of German immigrants. Its charms continued to be sung not only by salesmen in Europe but also by those who had already made the trip. In the 1720s, Johann Christoph Sauer wrote from Pennsylvania to describe a land bursting with goodness and charity. Thirty years later, however, he had changed his tune. In 1755, Sauer wrote to warn about those he termed 'Newlanders', who preyed upon new immigrants to Pennsylvania. German immigrants often depended upon a method known as the 'redemptioner' system to pay their passage. This system had evolved in the seventeenth century and under it an immigrant could have his or her fare paid upon arrival in the New World by a sponsor, friend or relative. This meant that the immigrant had a chance of paying their passage without having to enter into indentures and so might escape the colonial flesh markets. It was when sponsorship failed to materialise, as could often occur, or when the bill presented on arrival was much larger than envisaged when setting out, that the redemptioner became open to exploitation. According to Sauer, the Newlanders ferreted out those who had debts or no resources of their own and sold them into servitude to ruthless planters.

Sauer's warnings were corroborated by a young German music teacher who wrote a detailed account of the miseries awaiting emigrants without money to pay their way. Gottlieb Mittelberger's description referred to German emigrants in Pennsylvania but it could equally well have applied to emigrants from other parts of northern Europe in the period shortly before the American War of Independence.

In 1750, Mittelberger embarked on a ship named the *Osgood*, along with 500 fellow Germans. Accompanying him was a brand-new church organ destined for Pennsylvania. His detailed descriptions of their experiences should be compared with those of conditions endured by other Europeans and Africans on the Atlantic slave run:

> Both in Rotterdam and in Amsterdam the people are packed densely, like herrings so to say, in the large sea-vessels. One person receives a place of scarcely 2 feet width and 6 feet in length in the bedstead, while many a ship carries four to six hundred souls; not to mention the innumerable implements, tools, provisions, water-barrels and other things which likewise occupy such space.[6]

The passengers were so tightly packed that during stormy weather they tumbled over one another. 'Children cried out against their parents, husbands against their wives and wives against their husbands,' reported Mittelberger. Most of all, the passengers railed against 'the soul-traffickers' who had persuaded them to emigrate.

Slave ships on the run from Africa carried a cargo of up to 600 souls or so. In a later report to the British Parliament, the slave ship *Brooks* was depicted with a sleeping space for each adult male of only one foot, four inches across, and only one foot, two inches for a female. British convicts' berths were eighteen inches wide. So, with their 'scarcely 2 feet', the Europeans of Mittelberger's time were faring abominably but better than African or English slaves.

In one of the most powerful travel journals ever written, Mittelberger described the Atlantic journey in unflinching terms:

> There is on board these ships terrible misery, stench, fumes, horror, vomiting, many kinds of sea-sickness, fever, dysentery, headache, heat, constipation, boils, scurvy, cancer, mouth rot, and the like, all of which come from old and sharply salted food and meat, also from very bad and

foul water, so that many die miserably . . . Children from 1
to 7 years rarely survive the voyage.

During Mittelberger's own voyage, thirty-two children died and
their bodies were buried at sea. As there was no ordained minister
on board, Mittelberger conducted the burial services.

Having survived the voyage, Mittelberger recorded what
happened once they arrived in Pennsylvania. It is doubtful that
many of the redemptioners would have read Penn's intoxicatingly
optimistic charter for his province, written in 1683 – 'no People
can be truly happy, though under the greatest Enjoyment of Civil
Liberties' – but they would have been hoping for some relief from
the trials of the voyage. For many there was no release.

Those who were unable to pay for their passage or provide
security for payment from a friend or relative were kept on the
ship, still stinking from the ordeals of the crossing. As the vessel
rode at anchor, the familiar parade of agents and planters came
on board over a period of days and bargained over the length of
time the passengers should serve to pay their passage. The sick
had the worst of it, remaining on the ship for weeks. According to
Mittelberger, they frequently died without setting foot ashore.

Other cruel abuses awaited the redemptioners. If a husband or
wife had died at sea when the ship had made more than half the
journey, the surviving spouse had to sign themselves up not only
for their own passage but also for that of the deceased. When both
parents died more than halfway into the voyage, their orphaned
children had to stand for their parents' passages as well as their
own. Theoretically, an orphan could thus be enslaved for eighteen
years or so.

Mittelberger reported: 'It often happens that whole families,
husband, wife and children, are separated by being sold to different
purchasers, especially when they have not paid any part of their
passage-money.' Some parents felt compelled to sell their children
into bondage so that they might remain free, no doubt hoping that
they would in time raise enough money to redeem their children
and be reunited with them. As the parents often had no idea where
their children were going, they ran the risk of not seeing each other

again for many years or, as Mittelberger put it, 'perhaps no more in all their lives'.

Germans poured in, not just to Pennsylvania but also to New York, Maryland, New England and Carolina. Mittelberger calculated that during his four years in Philadelphia as many as 25,000 Germans arrived in the city. As he listened to their stories, he realised that merchants, or Newlanders, as they were known, were preying on German immigrants. They encouraged people of every rank and trade to emigrate, hoping they would fall into debt on the journey and then have to sell themselves as servants.

The new arrivals made a startling allegation. They claimed that European princes and rulers received a kickback from merchants for every subject they allowed to leave. For each person of ten years of age or more, their lord received a payment of three florins or a ducat. In Philadelphia, the merchants could make sixty, seventy or eighty florins for each person, in proportion to the passenger's debts incurred during the voyage.

For the prosperous, Pennsylvania was a land of bounty. Its inhabitants were almost free from taxation. The annual tax on a hundred acres of land was only a shilling. Trades and professions were not bound by guilds, so anyone could carry on whatever business they wished. If a lad learnt his art or trade in six months, he could become a master and marry whenever he chose.

Free men and women could marry redemptioners but would have to pay £5 to £6 for each year their bride or groom still had to serve. Mittelberger wryly noted that 'many a one who has thus purchased and paid for his bride, has subsequently repented his bargain, so that he would gladly have returned his exorbitantly dear ware, and lost the money besides'.

The inner man was equally well cared for. Mittelberger described how all types of religious sects were tolerated. Among those he listed were Lutherans, Catholics, Quakers, Anabaptists, Moravian Brethren, Pietists, Seventh Day Baptists, Dunkers, Presbyterians, Freemasons, Freethinkers, Jews, Mohammedans, Pagans, Negroes and Indians. Somehow, as one reads Mittelberger, images of ancient Greece float unbidden to the mind, with worthies discoursing upon democracy in the senate while their slaves labour in their estates.

By late 1755, Mittelberger was back home in Wittgenstein, where he received a package of letters from Philadelphia. He read that during the previous autumn more than 22,000 people had arrived in Philadelphia, mostly Württembergers, Palatines, Durlachers and Swiss. The sick were dying in great numbers. The rest were so poor that most had sold their children to pay their debts.

It is perhaps little wonder that Mittelberger found that in Pennsylvania, the land of religious tolerance, there were many who thought little of religion. 'Many do not even believe that there is a true God and devil, a heaven and a hell,' he said. The paradise that was being sought in the New World had more to do with what was in the minds of men who created its plantation than in providential promises arising from any golden book. As the German experience demonstrated, men could become free in America, but only if they could avoid the many snares and nets held out to trap the unlucky or unwary.

CHAPTER SIXTEEN

DISUNITY IN THE UNION

While Governor Hunter was grappling with the Palatines in New York, the authorities in England were drawing up plans to dump another batch of troublesome people on America. These were the Jacobites from what became known as 'the Fifteen' – the unsuccessful attempt in 1715 to dislodge the Hanoverian George I from the throne in favour of the Stuart claimant Prince James Edward Stuart, who would become known as the Old Pretender.

The rebellion was launched just a year after George had ascended to the throne. Large forces of Jacobite clansmen gathered in Scotland while in England an Anglo-Scottish army of Jacobites advanced into Lancashire. But the rebellion turned into a shambles. The push into England ended at the battle of Preston, where 1,500 Jacobite prisoners were taken. In Scotland, delay and indecision saw the Jacobites waste opportunity after opportunity and their forces disintegrate. In Christmas week 1715, the Old Pretender left France and landed in Scotland, for the first and only time in his life, in an attempt to rally his armies. But he was no military commander. While many among the Highland clans were for fighting on, James Edward prevaricated. By the end of the first week in February he had gone, never to return.

In the meantime, many ringleaders in both England and Scotland were rounded up and executed for treason. After the surrender in

Preston, the authorities had to decide what to do with the 1,468 prisoners, of whom 1,003 were Scots. Ultimately, the ordinary fighting men were given the choice of being tried for treason or accepting transportation.

The rank-and-file rebels were farmed out between the prisons of Lancaster, Liverpool and Chester. The aristocratic leaders were imprisoned in the Tower of London. Two famous escapes took place. The Earl of Winton, perhaps uniquely for a member of the nobility, had been apprenticed in his youth to a locksmith. He picked a lock and made off. Just as amusingly, the Earl of Nithsdale waddled out disguised as a pregnant woman.

The farce was short-lived. Thirty-three men were tried for treason, sentenced to death and hanged. The government felt sure this would encourage the remainder to accept the King's magnanimous gesture of an offer of their lives in return for transportation. The prisoners remained reluctant. There was probably a mixture of reasons why they did not immediately act to save their skins. Some no doubt thought it best to sit it out in the hope that any settlement made with their leaders would include clemency for the foot soldiers; others wanted to use what influence they had to gain a pardon; some were anxious to remain in the hope – no matter how slender – that they might see their families once more; and yet others had a legal gripe about being forced into indentures or transportation at all, for, as we have seen in Chapter Ten, transportation to the colonies was more of English making than Scottish.[1]

With so many prisoners awaiting their fate in several prisons, it was hardly surprising that an enterprising merchant should propose that he could ease the burden of the state. The British authorities had to deport the rebels whether they signed indentures or not. Sir Thomas Johnson, a merchant of Liverpool, wrote to the treasury offering to transport the rebels for forty shillings a head in return for being allowed to dispose of them for seven years' servitude apiece. By April 1716, the governors of the American colonies had been given instructions to receive the rebels. Any who had not signed seven-year indentures before they landed should be forced to do so. Many were reluctant not only to be transported but enslaved as well, as attested to in a letter from an officer imprisoned in Chester Prison on 28 April 1716.

> [We] were all offered indentures to sign for seven years in the plantations, as the said Sir Thomas should please to dispose of us. They have prevailed with a great many of the common sort to sign them, the last of whom were carried off to Liverpool this morning. But the gentlemen unanimously refuse to do the same, alleging they were no ways bound thereto by the nature of our petition presented to his Majesty, but only to simple transportation, which we were will[ing] to undergo at his Majesty's desire, whereupon we were severely threatened, and, without getting liberty to return to our rooms for our bed clothes and linen, and we were all turned into a dungeon or little better, and fed only with bread and water.[2]

Whatever the prisoners might expect, they were bound for servitude; after all, the officer in charge of the castle was none other than the son-in-law of Sir Thomas Johnson, whose government contract stipulated that he could sell them in the first place.

During the summer of 1716, Johnson and his associates transported some 600 prisoners to both the American mainland and the West Indies, to be indentured for seven years. During five months, twelve ships carried a total of 619 Jacobite rebels at a total cost to the Crown of £1,238, with the majority of them destined for South Carolina, Virginia, Jamaica, Maryland and Antigua. Thirty went to St Christopher and just one to Barbados.

As told by Margaret Sankey in wonderful detail in *Jacobite Prisoners of the 1715 Rebellion*, this was not the end of the troubles faced by the authorities. Many prisoners managed to escape before even crossing the Atlantic. Some bribed ships' crew members, others used subterfuge, while in one famous case, thirty prisoners, helped by at least one member of the crew, rebelled on board the *Hockenhill*, bound for St Christopher, and sailed from the Caribbean back to Europe, landing in Bordeaux, where they sold the cargo before making off. Other prisoners managed to escape indenture completely by bribing their way to freedom once they had arrived in the colonies. The *Elizabeth and Anne* set sail with 127 rebels but when it arrived in Virginia its complement was only 112. Investigations revealed the captain had been bribed to set the missing rebels ashore in England.

It appears that the deported rebels of 1715 may have done better in America than many of those transported to the West Indian colonies. By the early eighteenth century, conditions were easier in Virginia and a Scottish network had grown up among the colonists. Scottish settlers had been coming of their own volition for many years. The earliest had settled among the Dutch in New Netherlands and along the shores of the Delaware. Apart from the Covenanters and the Quakers from the lowlands, Highlanders also settled, predominantly along the Canadian borders. For those sent to South Carolina, things were not so good at first, as sporadic wars with the local Native Americans still persisted, but many thrived. Those sent to the West Indies, however, faced seven years' toil in the sugar factories or plantations, which was often considered a death sentence.

In 1745, Charles Edward Stuart – Bonny Prince Charlie – tried once more to retake the crown for the Stuart line. The story of the Young Pretender and the '45 is so well known that it hardly needs repeating here. It is enough to give the bare bones and say that this rising was of much more consequence than that of thirty years before. For a start, unlike the Old Pretender, the Young Pretender turned up to lead his armies, arriving in Scotland in July 1745 to run a campaign that would last nine months. Charles expected that not only would the clans gather to support him but also that further large-scale support would be forthcoming in England. He also believed he would have considerable French assistance, for they had nearly mounted an invasion in support of him the previous year.

As things worked out, after an advance into England that almost reached Derby, Charles had to retreat. Ultimately, the French saw which way the military wind was blowing and cancelled their invasion fleet. Charles stood at Culloden with an army of little more than 5,000, composed of two-thirds Catholic

Highland clansmen and one-third Episcopalian Scots. They faced a much stronger English force of 8,000. The battle went against the Jacobites. The superior forces commanded by the Duke of Cumberland (the son of Hanoverian King George II) quickly overwhelmed the Scots. The Prince's lack of skill as a commander did not help.[3]

The bloody aftermath is perhaps better known than the battle itself. Cumberland ordered all prisoners and the wounded to be killed. Charles Stuart escaped capture by hiding and ultimately escaping in disguise to France. In all, some 3,500 were imprisoned following Culloden.[4] Many clan leaders were banished, having been granted the historic Scottish punishment that allowed the person under sentence to choose their destination. Some of their clansmen no doubt followed them to the Continent, while others were able gradually to drift back home.

Of the remainder, two merchants, Samuel Smith of London and Richard Gildart of Liverpool, were licensed to transport rebels to the colonies. Gildart and Smith were to be paid £2 10s upon proof of shipment, with the balance of £2 10s upon notice from the colonies that their prisoners had arrived. Shortly afterwards, the merchants were empowered to offer pardons to rebels who gave themselves up to transportation and indenture for seven years. Although the total number of pardons issued was 866, it seems only 610 were actually transported.

The reason more were not transported was probably because the powers in London decided that breaking up the clan system would be a much more effective and long-term solution to destroying support for the House of Stuart. Some of those sent to Maryland who refused to sign indentures were eventually bought and set free by Catholic planters whose sympathies were at odds with the wishes of the government in England. In this way, many Scottish rebels went on to thrive in their new country, establishing plantations of their own, while others finally returned home to Scotland. The fate of some of the transported rebels of the risings of 1715 and of the '45 was undoubtedly grim indeed, especially in the sugar islands, while the fate of others turned out to be much superior to that intended by those who had so recently passed sentence upon them.

The bitter aftermath of the Jacobite risings would send echoes through not only history but also works of fiction for many years to come, as would the fate of another group of people who suffered being sent to the colonies – the kidnapped.

CHAPTER SEVENTEEN

LOST AND FOUND

In 1722, the prolific Daniel Defoe wrote a novel in which the hero is kidnapped. Defoe liked his fiction to have contemporary themes and he knew that kidnapping sent shivers down delicate spines as much as it had in the preceding century.

The eponymous Colonel Jack is a London orphan who becomes a pickpocket. After graduating to highway robbery, Jack is forced to flee to Scotland. Finding his options growing thin, he enlists in the army and soon deserts. A ship's captain says he will take him to London. Once at sea, Jack discovers he has been kidnapped and is bound for Virginia.

After thirty-two days at sea, the ship reaches its destination, where Jack is sold: 'I was disposed of, that is to say sold, to a rich planter . . . brought to the plantation and put in among about 50 servants, as well Negroes . . .'

Jack is fictional but the detail in his tale has the tang of the Atlantic and the smell of Virginian fields about it. He reflects upon what brought him 'into this miserable condition of a slave'. At the time of writing, Defoe would have known that since Bacon's Rebellion European and African colonial workers were subject to different conditions, with Africans now enslaved for life. The fact that Defoe continued to refer to white servants as slaves indicates an understanding that slavery could exist in different forms. In *Moll Flanders*, published in the same year as

Colonel Jack, he again referred to indentured servants as slaves.

Jack repents his ways and is given his freedom. He becomes a plantation owner and grows critical of how servants are treated. As a woman is taken ill and is carried into a shelter for sick workers, Jack observes: 'I think they should call it the condemned hole, for it was really only a place for people to die in, not a place to be cured in.' He reflects that 'masters in Virginia are terrible things'.

Occasionally, real life could mirror fiction and fortune shine on those taken against their will to be sold into the colonies. On the Isle of Skye, two wily lairds concocted a scheme to make money by selling some of their tenants. In 1739, Sir Alexander MacDonald and Norman MacCleod sold 100 men, women and children to merchants who planned to resell them in the American slave markets, where the unlucky islanders were to be presented as criminals. The scheme fell apart when the ship carrying them put in at Donaghadee in the north of Ireland for supplies and the innocent islanders escaped. Following an official inquiry they were given their liberty; MacDonald and MacCleod were not prosecuted.[1]

For others, freedom came even after they had crossed the Atlantic. In an unusual case in 1753, a planter called Ann Dempsey petitioned the Philadelphia court to release one of her servants from indenture. This woman had proved to her mistress's satisfaction that she had been taken from Ireland against her will. Ms Dempsey was a paragon among the servant-owning classes.

A very late example of someone taken against their will comes from London in 1775 and involves seventeen-year-old Elizabeth Brickleband. Her name first turns up in the customs lists of those emigrating, entered as Elizabeth Brittleband.[2] It seems reasonable to assume that it is the same person, for in either form the name is unusual. The lists of émigrés are the nearest thing that has survived of a record of emigration levels in the latter part of the seventeenth century. In 1773, records were ordered to be kept because of government fears that a depressed economy was giving rise to a level of emigration and depopulation that could not be sustained.

Elizabeth is listed as leaving for Baltimore in June, one of ninety-nine 'redemptioners' on board the brig *Nancy*. The records add a few years to her age, listing her as twenty-one. This could be significant. Whoever entered her name could have wished to disguise her true identity by making her older and deliberately misspelling her surname. Her mother must have been a resourceful and tenacious woman, for she not only discovered that her daughter had been kidnapped but also managed to track down the culprits who had taken her.

The guilty ones were a married couple called John and Jane Dennison, 'office-keepers' with a 'lock-up house'. Sadly, by the time Mrs Brickleband discovered who had taken her daughter, she was too late – the *Nancy* had already sailed, carrying her daughter towards an uncertain future. Although Elizabeth's fate is unknown, we do know what happened to her abductors. Thanks to the efforts of Elizabeth's mother, they were put on trial, but not before they attempted to buy Mrs Brickleband off with the reported – though unlikely to be forthcoming – sum of £500, saying that if they went to trial they would be hanged. Elizabeth's mother was not to be bought. From the court records we see that John and Jane Dennison, together with their clerk Quirforth, were charged with 'conspiring to send into foreign countries one Elizabeth Brickleband'.[3]

The Dennisons and their clerk admitted that they had signed up 'near an hundred people' for which they had been paid £9 7s 6d – scarcely the level of income that would enable them to lavish large bribes to avoid being taken to trial. In the event, the trio need hardly have worried. They got off lightly. John Dennison was jailed for one month on the condition he posted security with the court against his good behaviour for one year. Mrs Dennison and Quirforth appear to have been judged the ringleaders. They were sentenced to three months apiece and ordered to find security for two years – not the sentences one might have expected for abducting a young woman and selling her into slavery in the colonies, to be separated from home and family for ever. The courts appeared to take no sterner view of spiriting in the eighteenth century than they had in the seventeenth. No wonder, then, that spiriting was such good business and persisted for so long both in reality and in the popular imagination.

John Jamieson was an example of an even younger victim. He went missing from his home at Old Meldrum in Scotland in 1741, at the age of eleven. His father William heard that the merchant 'Bonny' John Burnett had shipped John to Maryland. Aberdeen magistrates refused to sign a warrant for Burnett's arrest, so William obtained the backing of his landlord, the Earl of Aberdeen. Under pressure from the Earl, Burnett promised to return young John. But the Earl died, Burnett went bankrupt and John was never seen again.

As far as their parents were concerned, most kidnapped children vanished off the face of the earth. Miraculously, a very few reappeared. Peter Williamson and James Annesley were among those that did. Though James was taken from Aberdeen in north-east Scotland and James from the backstreets of Dublin, their stories shared interesting characteristics – both not only came back but also wrote about their experiences and set out to seek justice. There was another confluence in their stories: James Annesley, newly returned to Britain, published his memoirs in 1743, the same year that Peter Williamson was snatched.

Peter Williamson's memoir is a remarkable account of experiences that must have been shared by others who were rounded up to fulfil the insatiable labour demands of the colonial tobacco and sugar industries. It is filled with high adventure. The hero was kidnapped, suffered shipwreck, sold into slavery, captured by Native Americans and finally managed to return home to Scotland. Even if parts of Williamson's account are fabricated or exaggerated to excite the reader, it provides insights into the nature of 'spiriting' in the eighteenth century and of conditions in the colonies.

Williamson's story begins in 1740, when, at the age of ten, he was sent to live with his aunt in Aberdeen after his mother had died and his father, a crofter in Aboyne, found himself with too many children to look after. Three years later, while playing by the dockside, Williamson was inveigled on board a ship lying by the quay. Two men told him stories of a new life beyond the seas and easily turned the young boy's head. The ship that carried him away was aptly named the *Planter*. After that, like so many thousands of others, he might never have been heard of again if it were not for

his remarkable resourcefulness. Williamson was a victim of a trade
in youngsters that was endemic in Scotland. Young people were
daily rounded up in the towns and country to feed the colonial
trade. The practice of scooping up fresh labour by any means, fair
or foul, was well established, there being no effective force against
it, nor any real remedy for it. In his memoirs, Williamson described
the racket:

> Almost all the inhabitants of Aberdeen knew the traffic . . .
> which was carried on in the market places, in the High Street,
> and in the avenues of the town in the most public manner. The
> trade in carrying off boys to the plantations in America and
> selling them there as slaves was carried on with an amazing
> effrontery . . . and by open violence. The whole neighbouring
> country were alarmed at it. They would not allow their
> children to go to Aberdeen for fear of being kidnapped.
> When they kept them at home, emissaries were sent out by
> the merchants who took them by violence from their parents
> [and] if a child was missing, it was immediately suspected
> that he was kidnapped by the Aberdeen merchants.[4]

The picture Williamson paints appears extreme but at the time
groups of children were regularly gathered up against their parents'
wishes and forcibly held in Aberdeen for transportation to America.
To a considerable extent, the town authorities and merchants were
part of the illicit trade. There were holding houses in which the
children were corralled until a ship could be found for them. There
were people who supplied them with food and drink. And the local
magistrates were geared up to process large numbers of children in
groups 'in a parody of indenturing'.

Williamson's later investigations revealed that he had been
abducted by agents working for one of several members of the
town's business community involved in the trade, one James
Smith, a saddler. No child from either the town or the surrounding
countryside seems to have been safe from the merchants' agents.
They operated openly and with impunity. When parents who had
lost their children came looking for them in the town, their elation

at finding them still incarcerated awaiting embarkation was short lived on their discovery that they were powerless to bring their children home. The spirits were in league with the local justices and parents were faced with bills for the food consumed by the children while they had been incarcerated. For poor rural crofter and urban worker alike, these bills were too much and they had to watch with horror as their children were led onto ships and taken away from them for ever. As Williamson put it:

> It is absurd to imagine that any parent, tho' in ever so necessitous a condition, would dispose of their own flesh and blood to strangers who make a prey of innocent children to accumulate their ill-gotten wealth and support their grandeur by conveying the unhappy victims to the remotest parts of the globe where they can have no redress for the injuries done to them.

In the summer of 1743, the world very nearly heard the last of young Peter Williamson when he was taken on board the ship of Captain Robert Ragg:

> They conducted me between decks to some others they had kidnapped . . . I had no sense of the fate that was destined for me and spent my time in childish amusements with my fellow sufferers in the steerage, being never suffered to go up on deck while the vessel was in harbour, which was until such a time as they had got in their loading with a complement of unhappy youths for carrying on their wretched commerce.

In all, sixty-nine children were loaded onto the *Planter*, bound for Virginia. The voyage was in itself an adventure in which the ship was grounded and wrecked off the eastern coastline of America:

> We struck a sand bank near the Capes of Delaware but bailed out and the crew left us to perish. We were taken on shore to a sort of camp and then taken on a vessel bound to Philadelphia. The original vessel was entirely lost.

Having survived shipwreck, young Peter's worries were only beginning:

> When we arrived and landed at Philadelphia, that captain soon had people enough who came to buy us. He made the most of his villainous loading after his disaster and sold us at about £16 a head.

Williamson was now a servant, sold for a period of seven years, but he had some luck. The man who bought him was a fellow Scot called Hugh Wilson, who, according to Williamson, was 'a humane, worthy, honest man'. Wilson was childless and he took to Peter, looking after him and not setting him to work until he had time to recover from his journey. In return for an extra year of indenture, Wilson sent Peter to school. The bond between the two was certainly strong, for when Wilson died he left the boy '£200 currency', his best horse and a saddle. Williamson, then aged seventeen, travelled around, working where he could, until he fell for the daughter of a well-established planter and settled down on land by the Delaware River given him by his new father-in-law. 'I settled there and was happy in a good wife,' he reports. But fate had not done with Peter Williamson. One evening at eleven o'clock in 1754, while his wife was away visiting her relations, Williamson was at home when his farm was attacked by Native Americans.

> They tried to get in and I threatened them with a loaded gun. They threatened to burn me alive if I did not come out. They rushed me, disarmed me, bound me to a tree and plundered and destroyed everything and burned the whole.

The incident was indicative of the recurring campaigns by Native Americans to drive out the Europeans throughout the colonial period. Peter Williamson now found himself the object of continuing animosity from those who were there first. He became their prisoner.

> I was threatened with a tomahawk to be killed if I did not go with them, was loaded with a great pack and travelled at night. At daybreak they tied me to a tree and forced blood out of my fingernails and then lit a fire near the tree and danced round me.

Williamson continues with descriptions of the treatment meted out by the Native Americans to other planters:

> They then scalped John Adams' wife and four children before his eyes and took the old man off, sometimes stripping him naked and painting him or plucking hairs from his head . . . [and] scorched his cheeks with hot coals.

Williamson escaped and made his way to his father-in-law's house, only to be told that his wife had died while he was in captivity. With no home or family to tie him, Williamson joined the British Army and campaigned against the Native Americans who had deprived him of his livelihood. Finally, his regiment returned to England, where Williamson was discharged. He then began a different campaign – against those who had kidnapped him and so many other children:

> We were driven through the country like cattle to a Smithfield market and exposed to sale in public fairs like so many brute beasts. If the devil had come in the shape of a man to purchase us, his money would have been as readily accepted as of the most honest and humane man in the world. These children are sometimes sold to barbarous and cruel masters from whom they often make an elopement to avoid the harsh usage they often meet with, but as there is scarce a possibility of making a total escape, they are generally taken and brought back; and for every day they have been absent they are compelled to work a week, for every week a month, and for every month a year. They are besides obliged to pay the cost of advertising and bringing them back which often protracts their slavery four or five times longer.

From other accounts of life for indentured servants quoted in this book, we know that Williamson's description is accurate. So bad was the treatment of many that advertisements for runaways were posted regularly (several examples will be found in the penultimate chapter). And, as we have already seen, servants did have their indentured period lengthened – often disproportionately – for misbehaviour or running away. So bad was the lot of some that they took their own lives: 'Some of these poor deluded slaves, in order to put an end to their bondage, put a period to their lives,' wrote Williamson in one of his most plaintive passages.

Williamson set out to shame those involved in the kidnapping business in his home town of Aberdeen. He published several books, containing different versions of his memoirs and his views on the indentured servant trade. Most important among his writings is his early indictment of those involved in his own abduction. He implicated the town's magistrates and named names. The magistrates in turn found Williamson guilty of libel, fined him and clapped him in gaol. Although they ordered his book to be burned, it quickly gained notoriety and was widely circulated around Scotland and England. Williamson even edited and added to its various editions. He continued his campaign by launching a counter-offensive against the Aberdeen magistrates. The case was heard in the Court of Session in Edinburgh and caused a sensation when Aberdeen's legal and mercantile elite denied all wrongdoing, while Williamson's case was supported by the appearance of witnesses who corroborated the events he described.

The magistrates shot themselves in the foot and provided in their defence the very evidence that would damn them. In their pomposity, they claimed that while a trade in children was widespread, none under the age of ten was indentured and that only those who would benefit would be signed up for a better life abroad. For their good-natured work, they were paid up to £10 a child. The court awarded damages of £100 to Williamson and was careful to stipulate that the money should not come from the town's funds, thus firmly putting the strain on the defendants' own pockets.

Williamson's odyssey was not an isolated one. Others were

snatched, transported across the ocean and made it home again. In the same year he disappeared from the dockside in Aberdeen, a strange pamphlet appeared in London entitled *Memoirs of an unfortunate young nobleman return'd from a thirteen years slavery in America where he had been sent by the wicked contrivances of his cruel uncle.*[5]

The writer was James Annesley, who claimed to be the rightful heir to the Irish title of Lord Altham. Annesley said his tale was: 'A story founded on truth and addresses equally to the head and the heart'. It is certainly intriguing and it illustrates how easily kidnapping and transportation could be used to get someone out of the way, either for revenge or profit. Human nature being what it is, one can imagine that many such instances must have taken place.

Annesley alleged that his uncle had him kidnapped to usurp his inheritance and steal his estates. Whatever the veracity of the memoir, Annesley's account, like Williamson's, opens a window into the conditions those spirited away would find themselves contending with in the colonies.

A controversy arose over whether or not Lord Altham had a son, James, born in 1715, his rightful heir. Altham's existence was a rackety one, with large estates but a trail of debts and mortgages over his lands. He loved to drink and hunt and was famous for keeping a pack of hounds that were said to be so hungry they would eat each other.

Not long after the disputed heir was born, Lord Altham separated from his wife and took a mistress, who in turn took a disliking to the boy. Although his lordship loved his son, he loved his mistress more. Being weak, he had the child packed off to live first with servants and then at a boarding school. James ran away and earned a precarious livelihood running errands for the students of Trinity College.

Lord Altham died in 1727. If he truly had a son, then that boy should have come into his inheritance – but step forward evil Uncle Richard, Altham's equally disreputable brother. Richard strode off in the dead man's shoes into his estates, treating James as an impostor. But many people knew the story of young Annesley.

From evidence given in the court case many years after the crime, the facts appear plain enough.

When Lord Altham died, his estranged son became an embarrassment. He turned up at his father's funeral and wept a great deal. Uncle Richard – who stood to inherit the title if his awkward nephew was out of the way – was reported as saying he would have the boy transported. In April 1728, Richard hired several villains and went to the house where the child, now aged barely twelve, lodged in Dublin. James was accused of stealing a silver spoon. The child was taken to George's Quay, rowed to King's End, about a mile from the city, and put on board a ship named, not without irony, the *James*. The ship's passenger list shows a James Annesley, servant, on board. One month before, one James Hennesley was indentured before the town clerk of Dublin on 28 March. It is tempting to see this as the same person. However it might be, young James sailed for the colonies, just as so many youngsters had done before.

The story of his American adventures was originally published in *The Gentleman's Magazine* and has since been rehearsed by more modern writers. It seems that the *James* sailed to Newcastle, which is probably modern New Castle on the Delaware River. He was sold to a planter named Drummond, who was a tyrannical fellow and set his new slave to felling timber. Finding the boy's strength unequal to the heavy work, Drummond beat him severely and the toil and brutality told upon James's health. He found an ally in an old female servant who had also previously been kidnapped. This woman had some education and sometimes wrote short pieces of instructive history on bits of paper and passed them to James. The lad neglected his work to read them in the field, thereby incurring more of Drummond's wrath. After four years, his old friend died and James decided to run away. He armed himself with a stolen billhook and set out. He was seventeen years of age.[6]

James wandered in the woods for three days until he came to a river and followed it to a town. He decided to wait for night to fall before entering the town and trying to steal some food. As he waited in the woods, two horsemen approached, one with a woman seated behind him. It appeared the party comprised a man with his wife or mistress and his servant. They dismounted and laid out a picnic. Annesley, by now distraught with hunger, betrayed himself. After nearly being run through with a sword, he managed to convince the party that he was harmless. Over supper, Annesley convinced his new friends that he was a wronged man rather than simply yet another runaway slave among many. The others told Annesley they were going to Appoquinimink to embark on a ship for Holland, and that they would buy him a passage.

The party of four had gone only a short way through the woods before they were apprehended by a group of horsemen who had been sent to track them down. They were bound and taken to Chester gaol. According to a nineteenth-century version:

> It appeared that the young lady was the daughter of a rich merchant, and had been compelled to marry a man who was disagreeable to her; and that, after robbing her husband, she had eloped with a previous lover who held a social position inferior to her own. All the vindictiveness of the husband had been aroused; and when the trial took place, the lady, her lover, and the servant, were condemned to death for the robbery.

Somehow, Annesley persuaded the authorities that he was not involved in the robbery or the elopement. The court was not convinced of his innocence in all things, however, and decided he should be put in the stocks in the marketplace, where he could be seen by all and identified if he had committed any offence. By now, it is obvious to the reader that Annesley was not by nature a lucky man.

After several weeks in the stocks, he was spotted by his owner Drummond, who had come to town on business. Annesley, who had two years remaining of his servitude, found his period doubled to four. Back on the plantation at New Castle, Drummond's cruelty increased to such a pitch that the local justices ordered him to sell Annesley to another planter. The wretched Annesley toiled away for three more years until he decided again that he had had enough and took off once more. Before he could reach a ship, he was recaptured. The single remaining year of his bondage was increased to five.

Annesley sank into a depression. He tells how his new master's wife took pity on him and often brought him into the family home, whereupon her daughter Maria fell in love with the handsome young servant. By now, Annesley had built up his tale with enough qualities to make his story sell. But he was not yet done. He described how Maria had a rival, a young Iroquois slave girl, whose advances he rejected. The girl ran to the river and, like a tragic romantic heroine, threw herself in and drowned.

This appeared to be the most fortunate stroke of luck for Annesley, for when the story was told to Maria's father he decided it was best if Annesley left his service. He announced he would give him his liberty but unfortunately reneged on his promise and sold Annesley to another planter.

Many more adventures followed, all no doubt designed to keep the readers of *The Gentleman's Magazine* entertained. Annesley was tracked by the brothers of the Indian girl, who had sworn to avenge her fate, and narrowly escaped being murdered. After many further dramatic episodes, Annesley decided to make one final attempt to get home.

Astonishingly for one so dogged by ill-luck, he was successful. He sailed on a trading ship to Jamaica, where he went on board a British warship and declared himself to be a kidnapped nobleman. His brave claim came to the attention of the commanding officer of the flotilla, Admiral Vernon. The admiral decided the young man's story was plausible and gave him passage to England, where he arrived in October 1741.

Uncle Richard was in a pickle: a man had turned up out of the blue claiming to be his nephew and clamouring for his inheritance. It is said that the uncle attempted to have the pretender jailed for murder.[7] If so, it did no good. James brought an action at the Dublin Court of Exchequer for his uncle's 'ejectment'.

Annesley's claim gave rise to one of the longest and most famous legal struggles ever seen in Ireland. It was so protracted that it has been called the Irish equivalent of Jarndyce v. Jarndyce, after the legal quarrel in *Bleak House*. Dickens' description of a drawn-out dispute that never came to a conclusion could well describe the Annesley case, which has echoes in other works of fiction, including Robert Louis Stevenson's *Kidnapped* and *Guy Mannering* by Walter Scott. All of Dublin society was hooked upon it and readers of *The Gentleman's Magazine* savoured it in London.

The case began on 11 November 1743. Howell's *State Trials* declared it: 'the longest trial ever known, lasting fifteen days, and the jury (most of them) gentlemen of the greatest property in Ireland, and almost all members of parliament'. The jury unanimously found for Annesley.[8] All Dublin was thrilled, believing a great injustice had been righted. The defending side lodged an appeal but the judgment was upheld. However, for the unluckiest man alive, this could not be the end of things. Following his great success, James petitioned the King for his seat in the House of Lords but delay after delay took place.

In the meantime, a former servant of the Annesleys was tried for perjury. In the initial hearing, Mary Heath had given evidence that Lady Altham had not given birth to a child in 1715. The jury did not believe her. At her subsequent trial, Mary Heath was found not guilty, a verdict that contradicted the earlier court's decision. If no son and heir had been born, Annesley was an imposter and his claim to the title was void. By now, Annesley had run out of the means to continue. He died aged forty-four, his claim to the title unresolved. Justice was just as expensive and elusive a prize to grasp in the eighteenth century as it can be today.

Not many years after Annesley and Williamson returned from their enforced migrations, kidnappings in British seaports began to subside. The quays in Aberdeen, Bristol and London where the spirits once prowled became busier with fleets bringing African slaves to the thriving colonies. By the Victorian age, European kidnapping would become, like the kidnappers themselves, the stuff of fable, replaced by the systematic mass abduction of Africans that has left such a stain on America's plantations. But in the seventeenth century, the British government was about to give white servitude a major boost.

CHAPTER EIGHTEEN

'HIS MAJESTY'S SEVEN-YEAR PASSENGERS'

On 23 December 1769, the *Virginia Gazette* carried extracts of a letter from a gentleman in Boston to a friend in London. Heavy with irony, it made a point about slavery:

> Through all the provinces the common cry is liberty and independence. Virginia and Maryland, with some reason form a pretension to independency. The bulk of the inhabitants or their progenitors forfeited their rights as subjects in England and were banished to America to expiate the crime they had committed in Europe. They suffered after their emigration . . . for seven, fourteen years or their life . . . But they should not forget that they came over as slaves; that there are many daily arriving in that capacity and that two thirds of the inhabitants, white or black are now actually slaves.

The observations were distorted; but as America approached the parting of the ways with England, many exiled whites from Britain were indeed arriving daily and being thrust into slavery. They were 'His Majesty's Seven Year Passengers': convicts sentenced to seven or fourteen years or sometimes life 'transportation to His Majesty's American plantations'. For much of the previous century, convicts had been shipped over spasmodically in relatively modest numbers and sold as servants. Now they poured into New York, Boston, Philadelphia and Charleston to be marketed. In the final decade of British rule, at least 900 a year were arriving and possibly even more. The convict trade was big business. The merchant who transported most of them in the early 1770s claimed that it was twice as profitable as the black slave trade.

The year 1718 marked the start of the mass emptying of England's gaols into America on the scale first envisaged more than a century earlier. The trigger was the ending of the War of the Spanish Succession in 1714. This unleashed thousands of unemployed soldiers on a country already suffering a crime wave, and prisons began to overflow. It might have been expected that convict transportation would be used immediately to ease the situation but there was increasing resistance in the colonies to the admission of convicts and merchants were reluctant to take them because few fetched a good enough price on the American servant market.[1] As a result, the numbers of transported villains dwindled. In the years immediately after the war ended, judges at London's Old Bailey sentenced no one to transportation.

An Act of Parliament passed in 1717 transformed the situation. It was entitled 'An Act for the further preventing Robbery, Burglary, and other Felonies, and for the more effectual Transportation of Felons, and unlawful Exporters of Wool; and for declaring the law upon some Points relating to Pirates'. Despite the references to pirates and wool this measure was all about convict transportation. When it passed into law, the act's preamble stated that it had two prime objectives: 'to deter criminals and supply the colonies with servile labour'.

The act overrode colonial restrictions on the convict trade, empowered judges to make far greater use of transportation and turned the business of shipping convicts to America into a gold mine for the merchants contracted to do it. They were to be officially endowed with property rights in the men and women who were turned over to them from the gaols and to get a subsidy for every convict landed in America. The subsidy – up to £5 a head – meant that whatever price the convict fetched the merchant couldn't lose.

A slave trader, Jonathan Foreward, secured the most lucrative contract, for convicts from London and the Home Counties. He was one of the merchants operating on the notorious triangular route – taking English manufactures to West Africa, where he acquired shiploads of slaves, whom he then shipped to the New World, where he was paid for his human cargo in sugar or tobacco. On the last leg, he shipped these commodities home. Foreward offered to take convicts for a subsidy of £3 a head, which undercut the opposition substantially. That won him the contract but it was a loss leader. Soon after the first shipments of English villainy, Foreward secured a huge increase in the subsidy to £5 per convict.

The sentencing formula had been devised in Ireland and had been in operation there for some fifteen years. Under an act passed by the Irish Parliament in 1703, courts were authorised to commute the death sentence for relatively minor offences to a sentence of transportation for seven or fourteen years or sometimes life. Those guilty of stealing one cow (but not two) qualified, as well as those guilty of stealing nine (but not ten) sheep and those who had stolen other property worth less than twenty shillings. That act would be used to send countless thousands from Ireland to the New World.

In England, the value of any property stolen would similarly determine who was executed and who transported under the new act. Here, too, the sentences available were seven or fourteen years or life. On 23 April 1718, the first felons judged under the new act heard their fate pronounced in Justice Hall at the Old Bailey. They consisted of fifteen women and thirteen men all guilty of minor property crime. Most seem to have been the small fry of the English underworld or to be in the dock because of one of those mad, bitterly regretted lapses that mark people criminal for ever. They included a tavern skivvy condemned for taking home some plates of leftover food, a couple of young shoplifters, a man who had stolen a coach cushion, and a drunk who seems to have gone off with the tankard he had supped from. For these crimes, they were each to be sold in America. The heaviest villain amongst them was a lone burglar.[2]

The contract bound the merchant to ship to America everyone

sentenced to transportation 'without excepting or refusing any by reason of age, lameness or any other infirmities whatsoever . . .' Once the felon was in America, it was left to the merchant to decide how to dispose of him or her. Rich felons could pay the merchant off and become free men or women as long as they didn't return to England. The rest – the vast majority – were sold off as servants for whatever the merchant could get.

For the convicts, the journey began, as it ended, in chains. The merchant contractor would have paid for the first group of twenty-eight 'transports' to have been 'ironed' and lodged in Newgate, probably in a huge cell beneath ground level. When the contractor's ship was ready, the transports faced a half-mile tramp to the river amid the jeers of Londoners who always collected at the sight of manacled men and women. Foreward used the *Eagle*, a vessel that he diverted from the African slave run. He described her as 'most suitable' for convicts. On board, the convicts were held between decks, chained together in 'messes' of six.

From the outset, convict ships were beset by mutinies.[3] In 1718, thirty prisoners took over a ship bound for the plantations and got ashore in France. In 1735, forty Irish convicts ran their vessel aground off Nova Scotia, murdered the entire crew and vanished. In 1751, transports from Liverpool shot the captain, took the vessel to South Carolina and fled. Foreward's successor as chief convict contractor said that 'an extraordinary number of seamen' was always necessary 'to prevent the felons rising upon them'. Moreover, their wages were 'always very great by reason of the nature of such a cargo'.[4]

The journey took two months or more. Merchants did not get a subsidy on dead convicts, so some instructed their captains to keep their reluctant passengers healthy by incorporating ventilators into the hull and ordering regular washing. But such considerate men were exceptional. There was money to be made by cutting supplies and squeezing more bodies into the ship, whatever the conditions. In 1767, George Selwyn MP was shocked when he visited a convict ship preparing to sail to Maryland.

I went on board and all the horror I had an idea of is short of what I saw this poor man in chained to a board in a hole not above 16 feet long, more than fifty with him, a collar and padlock about his neck and chained to five of the most dreadful creatures I ever looked on.[5]

In the early part of the century, dysentery, smallpox, freezing temperatures and typhoid carried off as many as one in three incoming convicts. On the *Owner's Goodwill* in 1721, fifty convicts embarked and only thirty-one disembarked. On the *Rappahannock* in 1726, there were only sixty survivors out of 108 who embarked. On the *Foreward* in 1728, ninety-six embarked and twenty-seven of them perished.

Such appalling losses in human life were not confined to convict ships. The voyage of the *Seaflower* is among the most poignant of all the stories. On 31 July 1741, the *Seaflower* put out of Belfast bound for Philadelphia with 106 passengers. She encountered heavy weather, sprang her mast and was then becalmed for several weeks. Supplies of food ran out and crew and passengers began to die. By the time she made Boston on 31 October – thirteen weeks after starting out – sixty-four were dead, including the captain. Six of the dead had been eaten by the survivors.

Among the convict carriers some captains were notorious for their greed and sadism. One was Barnet Bond, the master of the *Justitia*. A merchant who employed Bond was so furious at the loss of human life – and his profits – that he sued Bond for murder. The captain was alleged to have cut convicts' water rations and literally watched them die of thirst though there was plenty of water aboard. He then grabbed anything of value the dead had been carrying. A witness said Bond declared himself 'heir to all the felons who should die under his care'. He got off the charge.[6]

After greeting the incoming ship in Annapolis or Boston, the merchant's priority was advertising his cargo. Notices of arrival of the convict servants were placed in the *Boston Gazette* or the *Virginia Gazette*. Posters, known as tear sheets, were pinned to the walls of the local coffee houses.

Last week arrived here from Bristol the *Snow Eugene*, Captain Jonathan Tallimay, with 69 of His Majesty's seven-year passengers, 51 men and 18 women.

Just imported from Bristol in the ship *Randolph*, captain John Weber Price, 115 convicts, men, women and lads: among whom are several tradesmen who are to be sold on board the said ship, now in Annapolis Dock, this day, tomorrow and Saturday next.

One advertisement notifying a sale of newly arrived servants gave pride of place to other, presumably more desirable goods. It appeared in the *Boston Gazette* in the late 1720s, headed 'Plaids from Glasgow'. The text read 'Plaids of sundry sorts, both fine and ordinary, choice linens of several sorts, bed tickens, handkerchiefs and muslins, with some young men and women's time of service . . .' Would-be buyers examined the human merchandise, paying minute attention to every limb and tooth. The convicts were, in a real sense, perishable goods. If a woman couldn't stand up to the work or was diseased, the £8 or £10 spent on buying her was wasted. With men costing £13 and upwards, the buyer was even keener on ensuring they were sound. Those undergoing inspections or witnessing others being inspected usually drew the same parallel. Convict servant William Green recalled: 'They search us there as the dealers in horses do those animals in this country by looking at our teeth, viewing our limbs to see if they are sound and fit for their labour.'[7]

Another ex-convict, James Revel, put the scene in verse:

> Examined like horses, if we're sound
> What trade are you my lad says one to me
> A tin man Sir, that will not do says he.
>
> Some felt our hands and viewed our legs and feet
> And made us walk to see if we were complete
> Some viewed our teeth to see if we were good
> Or fit to chew our hard and homely food.[8]

In 1758, a London weaver observed a sale of convict servants in Williamsburg:

> They all was set in row, near 100 men and women and the planter come down the country to buy . . . I never see such parcels of poor wretches in my life some almost naked and what had clothes was as black as chimney sweeps, and almost starved by the ill-usage of their passage by the captain, for they are used no better than many negro slaves and sold in the same manner as horses or cows in our market or fair.[9]

The true parallel was with other humans. What happened to white convicts on their entry to the New World was the same as what happened to Africans. Both were advertised for sale, both were inspected and probed and both were taken off in chains by new masters or by an agent who would find them new masters.

Apart from the chains, non-criminal servants were often sold in much the same way. John Harrower, a forty-year-old indentured servant from Scotland, kept a diary of his arrival in Fredericksburg, Virginia, in 1774. On 16 May, he wrote:

> This day severals came on board to purchase servants' indentures and among them there was two soul drivers. They are men who make it their business to go on board all ships who have in either servants or convicts and buy sometimes the whole and sometimes a parcel of them as they can agree, and then they drive them through the country like a parcel of sheep until they can sell them to advantage, but all went away without buying any.[10]

The mainland colonies tried to block the resumption of convict sales. They couldn't overturn a British law but they could sabotage it. Maryland took the lead and in 1719 it enacted a law requiring everyone buying convicts to lodge a good-behaviour bond of £100 per convict. The Privy Council squashed this wrecking move inside two months.

Virginia's burgesses attempted similar tactics. They ordered ships' captains to give a security of £100 for each convict sold and buyers to lodge a £10 bond for their purchase's good behaviour. This, too, was vetoed by the Privy Council, so Virginia's leaders temporised, arguing that if convicts must come they should be settled on the western frontier. The merchant Joshua Gee proposed giving them frontier land and using them as a bulwark against Native Americans. The influential Reverend Hugh Jones suggested workhouses for them on the frontier where they could work and become self-sufficient.[11]

None of it came to anything, and convicts poured in. The vast majority went to the Chesapeake provinces, followed a long way behind by Pennsylvania. Many of these unwilling immigrants were immediately thrust into heavy labour – on the plantations, in mining, forestry and industry. Others, the skilled amongst the convicts, were bought to be assistants in shops, printing works and a hundred different small enterprises. According to a convict agent from Baltimore, Maryland alone absorbed some 600 convicts a year for decade after decade. The province's Governor Horatio Sharpe commented: 'I could heartily wish that they [convicts] were sent to any other part of His Majesty's plantations but while we purchase them they will send them.'

Quite simply, thanks to the subsidy, convicts were cheap labour and too good a bargain to miss. They were a third of the price of black slaves and, while more expensive than regular indentured servants, the free-willers, they invariably had far longer to serve. Baltimore records show that convicts were twenty-five to twenty-nine per cent more expensive than other indentured servants but their length of servitude was more than twice that of the average indentured period.[12]

Neverthless, the market for free-willers was buoyant. Fewer were arriving from England, where the economy was picking up, but many more were coming from Ireland and Scotland, where poverty and want were widespread. The nature of the exodus from Ireland in the eighteenth century differed significantly from what had preceded it. In the 1600s, people were forcibly transported mainly to clear the land of its Catholic population to make way for

Protestant English and Scots. Now, in the 1700s, punishment and poverty were the two driving forces.

Ireland contributed convicts and free-willers. As was happening to people up and down the Rhine, the Irish were the target of the hard sell on the wonders of life in the New World. Merchants published advertisements, bogus letters were planted in the press and tracts extolling America were passed hand to hand. The *Dublin Weekly Journal*, for instance, carried an advert in January 1735 offering Irish Protestant emigrants to New York a special deal. Land purchased from the Mohawk Indians could be rented by them for one shilling and nine pence farthing per hundred acres. Then there was a widely circulated letter that was purportedly written to a County Tyrone clergyman extolling the money-making merits of New York. It was written phonetically in a Scots dialect: '. . . if your son Samuel and John Boyd wad but come here they wad get mair money in ane year for teaching in a Latin School, nor your sell wad get for three years preaching whar ye are . . .'

The letter described the 'bonny country' then gave the very high wage rates for various trades and the very low price of land, and urged: 'I beg of ye all to come here.' The letter was signed 'James Murray' but was most probably a fake, a piece of propaganda got up by planters or shipping agents. But the propaganda worked. In 1728, the head of the Anglican church in Ireland, Archbishop Boulter, complained that canvassing by American agents had persuaded large numbers to emigrate from Ulster, 'deluded with stories of great plenty and estates to be had for going for in these parts of the world'. He continued: 'there are now seven ships at Belfast that are carrying off 1,000 passengers hither'. However, the Archbishop then put his finger on what was really sending so many across the ocean – dire poverty. Referring to the Belfast migrants, he added: 'if we knew how to stop them, as most of them can neither get victuals nor work at home, it would be cruel to do it'.

There are few reliable figures for those shipped from Ireland. However, it is estimated that 15,000 convicts were deported between 1718 and 1775. In the 1740s, the Irish Parliament commissioned a report into the deportations of felons and vagabonds. The suspicion was that merchants engaged to transport the convicts were taking their subsidy and dumping their cargoes in England, Wales or even somewhere else in Ireland. This investigation got nowhere and the records that exist provide only snapshots of the Irish convict trade. What there is, however, tends to confirm that it was considerable. For example, over just two days in September 1766, seventeen women and ninety-two men, all evidently felons, were indentured before the Lord Mayor of Dublin prior to transportation. (The practice of taking emigrants, free-willers or criminals before the mayor had been established in an attempt to stamp out kidnapping and false indenturing.) They were then taken in fifteen carts from prison to Sir John Rogerson's Quay, where they were put on board the *Hicks*, from Whitehaven, 'bound for His Majesty's plantations in America'.

There were brief moments of comedy in the convict deportations from Ireland. The *Dublin Mercury* for 9–13 June 1767 ran this story about a transported felon:

> Among the unfortunate transports shipped out last Monday was one poor fellow, who being skilled in modern fashions of hair dressing, had unluckily made too free with some of his employer's trinket: one thing he proposed to himself, might be a useful introduction to his being employed by the ladies in America, who will, like the ladies of their sister Kingdoms, not be outdone in mode of fashion.

By now, large-scale users of labour, ranging from Virginia's great planters to the first generations of industrialists, were all turning to Africa as a major source of slaves. But they remained in the market for convicts and free-willers. In what was still a transitional period in racial segregation, they had no qualms about using mixed-race labour gangs. The picture of black slaves existing alone at the bottom of the heap does not hold. For a long time, white servants were with them at the bottom and treated with equal inhumanity. Indeed, there are indications from various sources that whites were in some cases treated worse than blacks. It was William Eddis, England's Customs Surveyor in Annapolis, who reckoned that African slaves were better treated than Europeans on the plantations because they were more valuable, a lifelong property, whereas European servants mostly had a term to their service. Planters exercised 'an inflexible severity' over white servants, he said. 'Generally speaking, they groan beneath a worse than Egyptian bondage.' In fact, nothing suffered by whites equated with the most unspeakable cases of cruelty to blacks: whites were never 'limbed' nor castrated. Nevertheless, the death rate suggests that Eddis was broadly right about their treatment. Fifty per cent of convict servants were dead inside seven years.[13]

Tidewater aristocrats, who came to be so completely identified as African-American slave owners, were among those who bought convicts. Eighteen-year-old petty thief John Lauson was acquired by one of them. According to his own account, he was bought on the quayside by a planter from Rappahannock and slaved for fourteen years. Lauson was in a plantation labour gang of twenty-four, eighteen of them Africans and six Europeans. According to Lauson, his treatment was indistinguishable from that meted out to the Africans. They were chained together, they lived together, slept together, worked together and were whipped together.[14]

White slavery wasn't confined to rural America. The archive of the Hampton-Northampton ironworks near Baltimore provides day-to-day evidence of an inter-race slave workforce in operation over decades. The ironworks were owned by the Ridgely family. Between 1750 and 1800, the Ridgelys bought 300 or so white servants, most apparently convicts, and put them to work alongside black slaves. Professor R. Kent Lancaster researched the archive and emerged with a picture of endless sweat and harsh discipline. Everywhere there was hard physical labour – feeding the furnaces, working the forge, mining the ore, felling trees for fuel, hauling the ore and 'in slack times' being put on farm work. Time books catalogued near perpetual toil. Colliers worked a twenty-six-day month, with only Sundays free, year after year. The only time off at Christmas was on 28 December, which the clerk described as 'Chillimas Day'. 'Indentured servants were exploitable for a limited time only and that time could not be wasted on the niceties of holidays,' Professor Lancaster explains.[15]

The Ridgelys made money not just by working servants but also from buying and selling them. Professor Lancaster uncovered a profitable little deal done by Captain Charles Ridgely in 1769. He bought eleven men for £12 each and nine women at £9 each. Within two months he had sold seven of the women for between £10 and £15 a head and eight or nine men for between £17 and £30 a head.

Men and women continually tried to escape. A document dated 1772 and headed 'Description of White Workers' contained profiles of eighty-eight men and women labourers and had been compiled for use if, or rather when, they escaped. When a man called Francis Barrett vanished in the summer of 1775, Captain Ridgely used his profile in the 'description' file for a runaway notice in the *Maryland Gazette*. This described Barrett and noted that he 'had also an iron collar on'. The collar was apparently fitted after a previous escape attempt and 'left on to facilitate his return to the furnace site'.

The servants' legal right to take grievances to court is revealed as virtually worthless. Time and again over fifty years, Ridgely servants went to court, usually claiming they were being held beyond their time, and there is only a single instance of the court finding against the company. Moreover, every unsuccessful servant litigant found him/herself listed as a 'runaway' and penalised – very probably by serving extra time.

Giveaway references to neck rings (iron collars), a company jail and whipping appeared in the archive. There was also a letter from an English doctor denouncing the Ridgelys for cruelty to their servants. The Ridgelys were typical, judging from David Waldstreicher's study *Runaway America*: 'Much available evidence suggests that the risks to and the possibilities for profit drove masters to treat their bondsmen with a cruelty and lack of care more often associated with the slave societies of the Caribbean.'[16]

One of the justifications of earlier English moves to dump the unwanted in America was redemption of their souls. The idea of villains finding salvation in the tough climes of Virginia was voiced by Sir Humphrey Gilbert, James I, John Donne and a galaxy of others. However, it did not feature in the 1717 Transportation Act nor were convicts offered a glimpse of eventual salvation after arriving in America. In 1749, Virginia's burgesses decided that even when a convict's term was served, and even if he or she became a successful landowner, they would be second-class citizens for ever. Ex-convicts were denied the right to vote and in this they were grouped with children and slaves.

In contrast, the lot of non-convict servants seemed to improve. They were still being imported but in smaller numbers. In 1753, the Virginia Assembly imposed a five-year maximum on the time in servitude to be served by poor immigrants arriving without indentures. The same law tried to deter masters from dumping servants who fell ill, laying it on every owner as an obligation to care for sick or lame servants during their whole period of service. But in other ways nothing changed. Indentured servants were still chattels and the Virginia Assembly reminded them of their place. In the 1750s, it extended earlier legislation ordering complete obedience to masters. Servants who disobeyed their owners' 'just and lawful commands, and resist or offer violence to master, mistress or overseer' had a year more of servitude added for each offence. Punishments for runaway servants were also increased – yet again.

As for the prospects of servants after they eventually attained freedom, they appear to have diminished as colonies developed and became more stratified. In *Down and Out in Early America*, Gary B. Nash quotes data showing this to be the case in Maryland after the 1660s and in Pennsylvania after the 1740s. Nearly three out of four servants freed in Pennsylvania ended up on the public dole and 'only a handful ever became property holders'.[17]

In many eyes, all servants – and not just convict servants – were scum. So thought the Reverend Hugh Jones, a professor in the 1720s and 1730s at America's first great seat of learning, the William and Mary College:

> The servants and inferior sort of people, who have either been sent over to Virginia, or have transported themselves thither, have been, and are, the poorest, idlest, and worst of mankind, the refuse of Great Britain and Ireland, and the outcast of the people.

The Reverend Jones thought the convicts among them had nothing to complain about: 'Their being sent thither to work as slaves for punishment, is but a mere notion, for few of them ever lived so well and so easy before.'[18]

Was there an especially southern bias against servants? The Columbia University historian Richard Hofstadter thought so. He suggested that the plantation practice of buying both convict and non-convict servants, and so putting honest unfortunates and hardened criminals together, caused them to be 'lumped all together as rogues who deserved no better than what was meted out to them'.[19]

However, in New England where few convicts were sold and there were not many free-willers, there was just as much distaste for servants, judging from a withering article in the *Boston Gazette* in 1725. The main target was Irish servants, who were then overtaking the English on the migrant ships:

> The masters of servants going to Ireland knowing the great want of servants here pick up all the vagabonds they can find to make up a cargo. Fellows and wenches brought up to no other employment than the picking [of] St Patrick's vermin and driving them out of their strongholds . . . they serve us for no other purposes than to plague their masters and mistresses and to debauch their children. This gives us an ill opinion of foreigners, especially those coming from Ireland when the truth of it is the best of them stay at home . . . and generally the very scum of the nation, both freemen and servants visit the plantations.

Few servants were in a position to argue their own case and we know very little about them as individuals. One exception is Elizabeth Sprigs, whose pathetic letter home in 1756 was as desperate and futile as that penned by that other indentured servant, Richard Frethorne, 134 years earlier:

> Honored Father,
> My being for ever banished from your sight, will I hope

260

pardon the boldness I now take of troubling you with these, my long silence has been purely owing to my undutifulness to you, and well knowing I had offended in the highest degree, put a tie to my tongue and pen, for fear I should be extinct from your good graces and add a further trouble to you, but too well knowing your care and tenderness for me so long as I retained my duty to you, induced me once again to endeavour if possible, to kindle up that flame again. O Dear Father, believe what I am going to relate the words of truth and sincerity, and balance my former bad conduct my sufferings here, and then I am sure you'll pity your distress daughter. What we unfortunate English people suffer here is beyond the probability of you in England to conceive, let it suffice that I one of the unhappy number, am toiling almost day and night, and very often in the horses drudgery, with only this comfort that you bitch you do not half enough, and then tied up and whipped to that degree that you'd not serve an animal, scarce any thing but Indian corn and salt to eat and that even begrudged nay many Negroes are better used, almost naked no shoes nor stockings to wear, and the comfort after slaving during masters pleasure, what rest we can get is to rap ourselves up in a blanket and lie upon the ground, this is the deplorable condition your poor Betty endures, and now I beg if you have any bowels of compassion left show it by sending me some relief, clothing is the principal thing wanting, which if you should condescend to, may easily send them to me by any of the ships bound to Baltimore Town.

Honored Father
Your undutiful and disobedient child
Elizabeth Sprigs[20]

Her father did not reply because he never received his daughter's letter. England and France were at war and a French man-of-war captured the vessel taking the letter to England. Then the Royal Navy captured the Frenchman and all the paperwork it carried was sent to the Admiralty. Elizabeth Sprigs' letter lay in the Admiralty vaults unread for 300 years. We can only speculate about the young woman's fate.

There is an amazing resource that tells us a lot more about the eighteenth-century servant. It is the hundreds of runaway ads placed in the colonial press by masters hunting escaped servants. In the nineteenth century, the quarry was the runaway black slave; in much of the eighteenth century, the runaway was more likely to be white. There is no more vivid an insight into this class of people than the wanted notices posted by their masters. The selection below is from the *Maryland Gazette*, the *Virginia Gazette* and the *Pennsylvania Gazette*. It covers regular indentured servants and convict servants.

There were always many Irish amongst the escapers:

> TWENTY POUNDS REWARD. Run away from . . . Alexandria, Fairfax County, Virginia, a convict servant man, named John Murphey, born in Ireland, about 28 Years of Age, by trade a joiner, a low set fellow, about 5 feet 4 inches high, struts in his walk, has a pale complexion, large black beard and eyebrows, wide mouth, and pleasant countenance, sings extraordinarily well, having followed it in the playhouses in London, talks proper English, and that in a polite manner . . . It is imagined he has forged a pass, and likely will deny his name, trade and place of nativity.
>
> N.B. All Masters of Vessels are forbid to take him off at their Peril. (August 1760)

> RUN away from the subscriber, living in Lancaster . . . a Native Irish Servant Woman, named Katey Norton, who came from the County of Wicklow, in Ireland, last Fall, she is about 25 or 26 years of age, of a dark complexion, has black hair, talks in the Irish dialect, rocks in her walk, and is pretty sharp in talking . . . she is a cunning hussey, and no doubt will pass a while for an honest woman, as she has good clothes with her, and can behave herself. Whoever takes up said woman, and brings her to the subscriber, in Lancaster, shall have three pounds reward, and reasonable Charges, paid by me ROBERT FULTON. (July 1763)

There were many English-born runaways, too, including one who presumably had something on her master:

> Run away, last night, from the workhouse in Chester, a servant girl that belonged to Thomas Blair in West New Jersey; she was advertised some time ago in this Gazette by the name of Elizabeth Burk, but changes her name often . . . is about 18 years of age, of small stature, dark complexion, and speaks much through her nose. Had on . . . a blue calimancoe gown, striped linsey petticoat, and a black silk bonnet, was bare footed... Four pounds reward, and reasonable charges.
>
> N.B. I desire that all persons would take notice of this advertisement, and secure the girl, wherever found, as it will ruin me if she is not got; and not to believe what she says, as she will certainly tell many lies. (July 1, 1756)

Some runaways looked like murderers:

> RUN away, on the 20th instant, four convict servant men (Englishmen) . . . Francis Wignall . . . a stout able fellow, and about 5 feet 10 inches high . . . Stephen Devoux . . . a grim looking lusty fellow, and much pitted with the smallpox . . . James Trump . . . a yellow complexion, has a remarkable scabbed head, and wears on it a striped worsted cap and felt hat. John Henes . . . walks very lame, occasioned by one leg being much shorter than the other Reward 20s shillings per servant. (June 1766)

Some runaways were murderers:

> Whereas, Alexander Jamieson and John Skerum, two servant men, belonging to me, as they were returning from Norfolk, in a small schooner . . . did barbarously murder Mr. Tobias Horton, their Skipper, (his body having been since found on the Bay Shore, nigh Windmill Point) and ran away with the Vessel . . . As Jamieson has been used to go by water, they

will probably pass for sailors, and endeavour to make their escape, by getting on board some vessels, outward bound; wherefore it is expected all commanders will strictly examine their crew before sailing, to prevent, if possible, the escape of such barbarous murderers. (September 1745)

A great many servants carried scars, most from disease but some from whippings:

Ran away . . . last month, a convict servant man, named Edward Ormsby: He is an Irishman, of a low stature, has an impediment in his speech . . . 'Tis suppos'd he is gone away in company with a mulatto woman, known by the name of Anne Relee, alias Bush; who being whipt last court held for the County of King George, may possibly have the marks on her back. Two pistols reward besides what the law allows. (April 1737)

James Brannon . . . an Irishman born, about 20 years of age . . . much afflicted with the kick kicksey and jaundice, and, if observed is much scarring about the arms, and many other parts of his body . . . (October 1753)

RAN away from the Subscriber, in Richmond County . . . two servants, a man and a woman. The man, named Brian Cagan, is a tall thin man, about fifty years of age, wears his own black hair . . . Had on, when he went away, a dark brown coat, a blue great coat, and a pair of blue plush breeches . . . The woman named Mary Ramshire, is of a middle age and stature, a fresh complexion, has several scars on her face, and one on her arm. Five pounds reward besides what the law allow. (June 1738)

Many servants fled in groups and they must have been easy to spot unless they got to New York or Boston and lost themselves in the crowds:

> RAN away, on Tuesday Night . . . four servant men, viz.
> John Tomlins, a tall, thin fellow, about 26 Years old, very
> much disfigur'd with the Small-Pox . . . John Minor, a tall
> well-set fellow, about the same age, he had on a light drab
> coat and breeches, with a white wig . . . Thomas Lee, a tall,
> thin man, a convict, has lost one of his Fingers . . . George
> Barry, a lad about 16 or 17 years of age, a convict. (April
> 1738)

Frequently, such advertisements featured black slaves and white
servants, who, as in the 1600s, were still fighting back together,
often by running away together:

> RAN away, on Saturday the 15th instant, at night, from Mr.
> Humphry Brooke, in King William County, a servant man,
> nam'd John Harris, a Welshman . . . A Negro man, nam'd
> Abraham, belonging to Col. George Braxton. And a Negro
> man, nam'd Windsor, belonging to the subscriber . . . The
> Negroes are both Virginia born, and are sensible fellows.
> They went away by water, and 'tis suppos'd will endeavour
> for Carolina, the Eastern Shore, or up the Bay. (July 1738)

> RUN away . . . a Negro man named Temple, about 35 years
> old, well set, about 5 feet 6 inches high, has a high forehead,
> and thick bushy beard; he took a gun with him . . . Likewise
> run away . . . two indented servants, imported from London
> last September, viz. Joseph Wain aged 22 years, about 5 feet
> 4 inches high, round shouldered, stoops pretty much in his
> walk, has a down look, and understands ploughing. William
> Cantwell of Warwuckshire, aged 19, about the same height,
> and stoops a little. (May 1766)

Some of the runaways appear to have been lovers who, of course,
faced a year or two extra service if they were ever caught in the act
by their master:

> RUN away . . . a Servant Man, named Nathaniel McDowell,

about 30 Years of Age . . . wears his own black Hair, round Face, and rough Features . . . As it is known an Intimacy has subsisted between him and a neighbouring Woman, the Wife of Alexander Logan, who left her Husband about the same Time, and took her Child with her, a promising Boy, six Years old, with white Hair, it is thought they are gone together, and that they will go to Philadelphia. Three pounds reward. (May 1763)

RAN away . . . a servant man, named Patrick Flood: He is a pretty tall lusty fellow, of a black swarthy complexion . . . He took with him a young bay mare, with a star in her forehead, and one white foot. He went in company with one Sarah Carrol, who formerly travelled to Carolina, where they are both suspected to be gone . . . She is a tall slender woman, with a wry Look, and a swarthy Complexion. Four pistols reward. (March 1738)

FIVE PISTOLES REWARD. RAN away from the Subscriber, in Fairfax County . . . an English indented servant woman, named Elizabeth Bushup, about 23 Years of age, of a low stature, fair skin, black eyes, black hair, a scar on her breast, and loves drink . . . It is suspected she was carried away, by Capt. Tipple's boatswain, from Potowmack River to Patuxent, where the ship lies, or that he has left her at the mouth of the river. Whoever takes up the said servant, and brings her to her master, shall have five pistoles reward, besides what the law allows, and five pistoles more if it can be proved that the said boatswain conceals her. (November 1745)

Of all the escapees, the most spectacular was surely Sarah Wilson, a servant to one of the Queen's maids of honour. She was arrested in London in 1771 after the disappearance of some of the Queen's jewels and she was transported to Maryland. The *London Magazine* reported that on landing she was 'exposed to sale and purchased . . . but escaped'. Wilson assumed the title of the Princess Susanna Carolina Matilda, non-existent sister to the Queen, and in a whirlwind tour of the eastern seaboard conned colonial American society. The *London Magazine* told the story:

> She travelled from one gentleman's house to another under these pretensions, making astonishing impressions in many places, affecting the mode of royalty so inimitably that many had the honour to kiss her hand. To some she promised governments, to others regiments, with promotions of all kinds in the treasury, army, and the royal navy. At length, however, an advertisement appeared, and a messenger arrived from her master, who raised a loud hue and cry for her serene highness.

The game was up. She was caught in Charleston and one of history's more colourful impostors was dragged back to the man who bought her. She was forced to serve for another two years.[21]

Hostility to convict servants grew as more and more were imported and crime levels increased. The *Virginia Gazette* complained in 1751:

> When we see our papers filled continually with accounts of the most audacious robberies, the most cruel murders, and infinite other villainies perpetrated by convicts transported from Europe, what melancholy, what terrible reflections it must occasion! What will become of our posterity? These are some of thy favours Britain. Thou art called our Mother Country; but what good mother ever sent thieves and villains to accompany her children; to corrupt some with their infectious vices and murder the rest? What father ever endeavour'd to spread a plague in his family? . . . In what can Britain show a more sovereign contempt for us than by emptying their jails into our settlements; unless they would likewise empty their jakes [privies] on our tables!

That same year, Virginia's attorney general was given a wage rise because of the increase in the number of criminals he was prosecuting. It was not unreasonable for him to blame British convicts for his extra workload.

In the 1750s, Benjamin Franklin, America's most gifted populist, planted himself at the head of those demanding an end to the convict trade. Writing in his paper, the *Pennsylvania Gazette*, he famously suggested that in return for convicts, rattlesnakes should be sent to every member of the British Parliament, both peers and MPs:

> Rattle-snakes seem the most suitable returns for the human serpents sent us by our mother country. In this, however, as in every other branch of trade, she will have the advantage of us. She will reap equal benefits without equal risk of the inconveniencies and dangers. For the rattlesnake gives warning before he attempts his mischief; which the convict does not.[22]

More attempts were made to restrict the trade. In 1754, Maryland slapped a twenty-shilling-per-head duty on convicts. But such was the British government's enthusiasm for transportation that merchants knew they could safely defy the colony's law.

The issue burst into flame again in the 1760s, this time ignited by fear of epidemics. Outbreaks of yellow fever, smallpox, typhoid and other infectious diseases were an increasingly worrying feature of the packed migrant ships coming into Boston, Baltimore and other ports along the eastern seaboard. In the 1740s, a quarantine post was established at Fisher Island outside Philadelphia. But when Virginians and Marylanders wanted the right to quarantine ships, including convict ships, merchants pressurised the Crown to stamp on the idea.

The disease most feared was endemic to English prisons, a truly fearful strain of typhoid known as 'gaol fever'. Sir Francis Bacon described it as the 'most pernicious infection, next to the plague'. The symptoms were a sudden headache, followed by chills and stomach pains that could drag on for about three weeks or kill within hours. On one notorious day in the spring of 1750, gaol fever hit the Royal Courts of Justice in the heart of London and reportedly killed more than fifty people within a day, including four judges, the Lord Mayor of London, four counsel, the under-sheriff and forty jurors.

Numerous outbreaks and suspected outbreaks occurred in America following convict shipments. They culminated in July 1767, when the fever infected a plantation outside Baltimore, reportedly killing thirty African-American slaves as well as the owner of the plantation. A newly arrived convict was the presumed carrier and the *Maryland Gazette* set a panic rolling with a vivid report on 'the fury of this malignant ravaging pestilence' that was spread by 'a casual visit, it seems, from one of the Felons, sometime since imported in a Convict ship'. The Chesapeake was gripped by rumours of other outbreaks. As one of the Tidewater grandees put it, 'A bare suspicion of that terrible disorder is enough to make a whole county tremble.'[23]

The Maryland Assembly demanded quarantine controls and Governor Horatio Sharpe urged London to allow restrictions. 'That scores of people have been destroyed here by the jail fever first communicated by servants from on board crowded infectious Ships is notorious,' he wrote. But London was not interested in allowing anything to impede the westward flow of convicts. Proposed restrictions were watered down and then vetoed by London. A bitter statement from Maryland's assemblymen followed, blaming the Crown and greedy convict contractors who had lobbied against restrictions. The statement condemned the contractors for esteeming 'the health of the inhabitants light in the scale against a grain of their profit' and for lobbying in England 'against a country, from which they have extracted so much wealth, and at the expense of so many lives'.

Benjamin Franklin now returned to the attack. He penned an article for the *London Chronicle*, labelling transportation as 'the most cruel insult offered by one people to another'. It was, he wrote, 'an unexpected barbarity in your Government to empty your gaols into our settlements and we resent it as the highest of insults'. None of this made any difference. The convict trade was now so profitable, with convicts fetching such good prices, that in 1772 the British government decided to end the subsidy.

The following year, approaching 1,000 convicts were sold. It took war and independence to end the trade. The British government stopped shipments when the first serious fighting of the American War of Independence broke out at Arlington and Concorde in April 1775.

The business of acquiring new convict servants went on until the very last minute and so did the pursuit of the runaways. On 21 April, two days after the war began, planters posted notices in the *Virginia Gazette* offering rewards for ten runaways. Two of the escapees were 'Negro slaves'. The other eight were white servants. Among the servants sought were a twenty-year-old joiner from Bristol, Thomas Pearce, and the rather older William Webster, a Scots brick maker. The man pursuing them at this hour of national need was the Virginia planter and soldier George Washington.

CHAPTER NINETEEN

THE LAST HURRAH

With the surrender of the British Army at Yorktown in 1781, the colonial era was over and so, one might have imagined, was America's role as a dump for Britain's convicts. American ports had turned away British convict ships at the start of the war. It was surely inconceivable that the new nation, the United States of America, proudly independent, would ever allow a single British convict in again.

However, in the summer of 1783, as British and American envoys were meeting in the Palace of Versailles to put the final touches to the peace treaty ending the war, an extraordinary plot was hatched in London. The men involved planned to smuggle convicts into the United States by disguising them as ordinary migrants. They persuaded themselves that if the Americans found out they might even come to welcome the trade again.

The plotters weren't irresponsible freebooters or impetuous young bloods. They were headed by the joint leader of Britain's coalition government, Lord North, who had presided over many of the misjudgements that led to the end of British rule in America. Other ministers in the coalition were behind him. And when the King, George III, was brought in on the plot, he gave it his full, indeed his delighted, support.

This desperate venture was triggered by fears of the crime wave expected after the mass demobilisation of troops when the peace was signed. It was recognised that the gaols would not be able to cope. As we have seen, after every major war a prison crisis loomed when ex-soldiers, 'sixpence a day heroes', returned home and spread crime across the country. This time the crisis developed even while the war was raging. During the six years of conflict, the safety valve – transportation to America – had been jammed shut.

Well before the war ended, prison overcrowding became acute. The prisons had to accommodate almost 1,000 extra inmates a year who would formerly have been transported. Everywhere, prisons began to burst at the seams. In five years, Newgate's population doubled.

The wretched inadequacy of Britain's prisons was laid bare by the penal reformer John Howard. He shook England with his monumental study of the prison system. He had inspected several hundred gaols and presented a picture of disease, corruption and cruelty in cramped and fetid buildings. There were prisoners in windowless cells taking turns to breathe at tiny ventilation holes; prisoners in medieval dungeons where food was dropped through grates in the ceiling; prisoners knee-deep in water; prisoners chained on their backs to the floor; and sick prisoners left unattended to die. Howard reported that 'vast numbers' of convicts perished from smallpox, cholera and gaol fever. He was especially concerned about this form of typhoid and estimated that more convicts died from it each year than the total numbers executed. The most shocking part of it was that the infection was endemic in Britain's prisons, and Britain's alone. Howard's researches had taken him to gaols in most corners of western Europe (only the Bastille wouldn't allow him in) and in none had he found gaol fever. Contrasting the prisons of Europe and England, Howard declared that he was 'put to the blush for my native country'.[1]

The Crown's solution to the new crisis was the prison ship. The 1776 Hulks Act authorised felons to be lodged in 'hulks', or prison ships, on the Thames. This was a strictly short-term expedient: the act's provisions lasted just two years. In government circles, there was no doubt that the Yankee rebels would soon be crushed and the convicts would be on their way again. But the hulks were to be a feature of British life for eighty years.

The county's leading convict contractor, Duncan Campbell, secured the contract for the first hulks. Campbell was a merchant with extensive sugar interests in Jamaica who had handled all convict transportations from London and the Home Counties for the previous six years. The first of the hulks was the *Justitia*, which Campbell had employed shipping convicts to America and his sugar back on the return voyage. He anchored the ship in the Thames at Galleons Reach, Woolwich, and demasted her. Her landward portholes were blocked and her lower deck was converted to house 130 chained convicts. The Hulks Act laid down that they should be put to 'severe labour', so Campbell put his convicts to work extracting sand and gravel from the river bed and extending the foreshore around what became the Woolwich Arsenal.

As soon as war began, hulks also became Britain's chosen solution to the problem of housing prisoners of war in America. Decommissioned ships moored in the British navy base in New York's Wallabout Bay held thousands of American, French and Spanish prisoners. Some 11,500 men are said to have perished in and around the base as a result of deliberate cruelty, ill-treatment and outright murder. Today, they are commemorated in the Prison Ship Martyrs' Monument, standing 149 feet high in Fort Greene Park.

In England, the first batch of eighty felons brought from Newgate climbed aboard the *Justitia* in August 1776. A year later, Campbell was commissioned to operate a second hulk at Woolwich and later a third there, the *Censor*. He would also be contracted to operate hulks in Plymouth and Portsmouth. The press would label them 'Campbell's academies of crime'.

People were in turn fascinated, horrified and frightened by the floating prisons. At first, the *Justitia* was a tourist attraction. Crowds flocked to Woolwich to watch the prisoners labouring on the foreshore. Most prison inmates of the time were described as raucous and intimidating; not so the convicts from the hulks. The *Scots Magazine* ran a story depicting the men as 'miserable wretches', utterly cowed. 'So far from being permitted to speak to anyone, they hardly dare speak to one another.' The men wore fetters on each leg that were tied to the waist or throat. They laboured silently from dawn till dusk.

Londoners brought up on the comforting refrain from 'Rule Britannia' that 'Britons never, never, never will be slaves' now saw Englishmen in chains, used as slaves. As the historian Dan Byrnes puts it: 'The English were invited to watch at home what their transports did in the colonies.'[2] The sight was a jolt. The *London Magazine* called the sight of an Englishman 'transformed into a galley slave' humiliating.

What sightseers were witnessing was the mirror of what had been happening to blacks and whites sold by British merchants to toil in American plantations for 170 years – until Campbell built a wall to block the view.

Campbell would have preferred to hide the fact that the hulks were death traps. But just two months after the first convicts came aboard the *Justitia*, John Howard came calling. He depicted the prisoners as half-clothed, cold and badly underfed and called the conditions alarming. Convicts couldn't use the hammocks provided because of the weight of their chains.

John Howard's findings prompted a Parliamentary inquiry. This revealed that in the first eighteen months, out of a total of 632 convicts deposited on the hulks, 176 died. The mortality rate was even higher subsequently. In the winter of 1778–9, convicts on the *Censor* and *Justitia* were dying at a rate of more than twenty a month.

The sight and smell of the hulks were daily reminders of the crisis. 'Hulk after hulk, hung with bedding, clothes, weed and rotting rigging, lined the river like a floating shantytown.'[3] Although portholes on the shore side of each hulk were blocked, as were the hatches, the stink is said to have carried a hundred yards.

Pressure to do something was coming from all sides. 'All our gaols are overglutted,' declared Edmund Burke. 'Half the British navy converted into *Justitia* galleys would scarce suffice to contain all our English penitents.'[4]

By January 1783, matters were desperate. A frightening memorandum was sent to Lord North containing a warning from the keepers of London's gaols. Unless overcrowding was tackled, 'the consequences may be fatal not only for the persons confined but also to the people of the town'. A subsequent memorandum records that their Lordships [the government] agreed it was 'highly important' to resolve the problem of 'the great number of convicts in Newgate' and 'settle question of transportation to America'.[5]

A few months later, Lord North's secret plot was hatched. It coincided dangerously with the delicate last stages of the peace talks in Versailles between Britain and the United States and her European allies. North secured the services of an ambitious risk taker, the London merchant George Moore. Moore was willing to take a first shipment of nearly 150 convicts and try to sell them in America for a government payment of £500. Much later in the game, Moore would ask for twice the price but in the early stages he was convinced that he was on to a good thing. His plan was to pass off the convicts as innocents migrating as indentured servants.

Moore's contact in America was an influential Baltimore merchant, George Salmon, who had previously imported Irish convicts into Maryland. Salmon was bullish about the prospects. 'I don't know any thing would bring more money here,' he wrote, 'than a parcel [of] servants or convicts which was formerly a good business.'[6]

The two merchants planned an elaborate subterfuge, with false trails, switched destinations, changed courses and the renaming of the ship. As well as the £500, they were to keep whatever profits came from selling the convicts as servants.

What they proposed was not illegal. No ban on convicts had yet been imposed in Maryland. Salmon and Moore assumed they could sell quite a number of convicts before any ban could be imposed. Salmon was also confident of buying off other influential men in Maryland. He would distribute 'porter and cheese' among friends in the assembly.

The King's go-ahead for the plan was essential. It turned out to be a formality. George III had not forgiven Americans for their 'treason' in taking up arms against him. When Lord North approached him with details of the plot, the King appears almost to have salivated with glee at the idea of scoring over his former subjects. George wrote to Lord North, 'Undoubtedly the Americans cannot expect nor ever will receive any favour from me, but permitting them to obtain men unworthy to remain in this Island I shall certainly consent to.'[7]

Moore's ship, the *George*, was to take the initial shipment. Her name was changed to the *Swift*. The captain, Thomas Pamp, was told that in the event of being challenged he was to say that the *Swift* was taking the convicts to Nova Scotia. Events moved quickly. Eighty-seven male and female convicts from Newgate Prison were the first to be loaded on board. In choosing them, George Moore would have made sure they were skilled craftsmen, since they always fetched a good price.

They were a mixed bunch. Charles Thomas had been convicted of stealing one wooden tub, valued at a penny, and twelve pounds' weight of butter, valued at five shillings. Charles Keeling was a former midshipman who admitted stealing a sword. Christopher Trusty was convicted of highway robbery after being caught red-handed holding up a coach. Jane Warwickshall was a widow who had been promised leniency for helping constables find some property stolen by her son. In the event, she was sentenced to fourteen years' transportation. Her son and his partner in crime each got seven.[8]

The *Swift* made her way downstream to pick up fifty-six more convicts from Campbell's hulk the *Censor*. But things were already going wrong. A London merchant whose sympathies were with the Americans got wind of a scheme to ship convicts. He alerted John Jay, leader of the American peace delegation in Paris. It was to take Jay many weeks to get the news to Baltimore. In the meantime, the *Swift* could have reached America and unloaded her convicts with the American authorities none the wiser. But the voyage was beset with mishaps.[9]

Captain Pamp made the mistake of allowing the convicts to learn that that if they were not sold in America, they would be sold in Africa. The morning after hearing the news, the convicts mutinied. A group of six somehow slipped their chains. Led by the highwayman Christopher Trusty and the former midshipman Charles Keeling, they stormed the captain's cabin, where the firearms were kept. With Trusty brandishing a sword over Captain Pamp's head, the convicts took command of the vessel and released the rest of the prisoners. It was a frightening experience, and not just for the crew. Some of the convicts accosted Jane Warwickshall and it seems that only the intervention of Charles Keeling saved her from being raped and then the captain being robbed. Keeling grabbed a blunderbuss and threatened to use it on his fellow convicts.[10]

The *Swift* was now between Rye and Dungeness. She carried two longboats and the convicts fought between themselves to get a place on them. Several ended up in the sea and drowned. Forty-eight eventually squeezed aboard the boats, leaving about a hundred still on the *Swift*. Among those who got away were Trusty, who knocked down two or three others to get himself a place, and Charles Keeling. Those left behind found the rum supply and got progressively drunk as they waited for the longboats to return to take them off. The weather now played a hand, for the convicts were persuaded that the wind was so heavy that the ship's survival depended on the crew locked below being allowed back on deck to sail her. The convicts agreed and some of the crew were released. They took the first chance to turn the tables and regained control of the *Swift* from their drunken captors. Next morning, with the convicts now safely locked below again, Pamp hailed a passing frigate and she escorted them into Portsmouth.

A manhunt for the forty-eight escapees was set in motion, stretching all the way from the south coast to London. Every constable and magistrate in Kent, Sussex and the metropolis was alerted. According to some reports, much of Kent was now terrorised by the escapers. In fact, half were quickly recaptured, some after ferocious resistance. The rest vanished.

Two weeks after the mutiny, twenty-four recaptured men, chained to each other, went on trial in the Old Bailey's Justice Hall on the capital charge of 'returning from transportation'. Captain Pamp sent his first mate, Thomas Bradbury, to give evidence while he prepared the *Swift* to resume her mission with ninety convicts still aboard.

The court case nearly blew the plot out of the water. Charles Keeling claimed from the dock that the *Swift*'s real destination was America. He said that the mutiny had been sparked by the threat that they would be dumped in Africa if the American plan went wrong. Bradbury, the mate, denied knowledge of any plan to land in American territory. Sticking to the script laid down by the men behind the plot, he insisted that Nova Scotia in Canada was the destination. Naturally, his word was accepted before that of a convict and the hearing moved on. The moment of danger was past.

All twenty-four escapees were found guilty but only six of them were hanged at Tyburn. Of the others, seventeen had their death sentences commuted to transportation for life and one to transportation for fourteen years. Among those who escaped death was Charles Keeling. His life was saved by testimony regarding his behaviour in preventing a rape. Not so fortunate was Christopher Trusty. He was hanged.[11]

The following month, the *Swift* sailed again, carrying about a hundred convicts. News of her departure was reported in the *Maryland Gazette*, putting her destination as Nova Scotia. The plot was evidently holding and on Christmas Eve the *Swift* and her convicts sailed unhindered into Baltimore. Briefly, everything continued to go to plan. Would-be buyers went on board to inspect the merchandise and accepted – or chose to accept – the convicts as free-willers. They appear to have paid sky-high prices, £35 a head according to one report; nearly twice that according to another.[12] Presumably the buyers included those who knew exactly what was going on but were happy to turn a blind eye. The trade in white flesh seemed to have resumed as if there had never been a war.

Most Marylanders remained blissfully unaware that convicts were again being dumped on them. This is evident from a gloating piece in the *Maryland Gazette* in January 1784, which built upon the paper's earlier report that the *Swift* was shipping convicts to Nova Scotia. The Canadian province was earmarked as a refuge for Americans loyal to King George and the *Gazette* rejoiced over them sharing a future with convicts. It wrote of 'respectable loyalists . . . being obliged to herd with the overflowings of Newgate'.

Enthused by his first sales, George Salmon wrote to his partner in England, George Moore, telling him to send more convicts. However, winter suddenly descended on Baltimore and everything stopped. Arctic conditions iced in the *Swift*. Then the news leaked out that the *Swift*'s so-called servants were in fact convicts. There was uproar. Angry buyers and indignant patriots blockaded the *Swift* so no one could get on or off her. According to one of the convicts, a horse thief called George Townsend, some buyers dumped the men they'd purchased in the woods, presumably to freeze to death. Sixty convicts were stuck on board the ice-bound ship, more and more going down with fever, others threatening to escape.[13] Salmon now faced losing money, and he contemplated dumping the convicts in the woods. In February, he wrote to Moore:

> I thought several times it would be almost as good to let the villains go on shore and so have done without them . . . If I find I cannot sell them for some price or another I shall turn them adrift.

After five freezing weeks, a sharp local agent managed to smuggle George Townsend off the *Swift* and find a gullible buyer, a Quaker. The agent, who probably paid less than £20 for Townsend, asked ninety guineas and got sixty. When the Quaker realised Townsend was a convict, he put him on board an England-bound vessel, though, as a returned transport, he would be sentenced to hang.

Outrage at the British 'move' to dump convicts spread and in March Salmon instructed Moore not to send a second shipment.[14] But his letter arrived too late. Moore had dispatched another convict ship called the *Mercury* in March 1784, with 179 men and women. This time he took care to guard against mutiny. Special barriers were erected on deck to hold back any mutineers – but the precautions were not sufficient. As the *Mercury* cleared the English Channel, she was taken over by her convicts. The ship was in convict hands for six days before she was recaptured. The resulting delay was fatal. By the time she arrived off the American coast, every port in the USA seems to have been alerted. None would admit her. The *Mercury* eventually deposited some very sick convicts in Belize.

It took five years before the importation of convicts was banned by law across the USA and in that period seven convict ships secretly brought their cargoes to America and at least two successfully landed them. However, the *Mercury* debacle sounded the death knell for the convict trade. It forced the British Parliament to accept that America would never again be the dumping ground for Britain's convicted criminals. In 1785, a Parliamentary committee concluded 'with regret . . . that the ports of the United States have been closed against the importation of convicts'. Australia had by then been selected as the alternative. Two years later, a fleet set out for Botany Bay in New South Wales, carrying a cargo of 750 convicts. Among them were some of those that Britain had desperately tried to offload in America in a last hurrah for the American white slave trade.

Although the convict trade was over, white slavery was not. As with convicts, shipments of free-willers were barred during the war. With the advent of peace, servant ships were back in New York and Boston before the ink was dry on the peace treaty, carrying men and women for sale. The reappearance of the trade scandalised some Americans. In January 1784, while Messrs Pamp and Salmon were in Baltimore trying to pass off the convicts from the *Swift* as free-willers, a group of men liberated a consignment of the genuine articles from a ship just docked in New York. The *Independent Gazette* reported that these New Yorkers considered the indentured system to be 'contrary to . . . the idea of liberty this country has so happily established' and, having freed the servants, they were raising a public subscription to pay for their passage. Hopes of universal liberty were misplaced, however. The prime enslavers, the planter elite from Virginia, were senior partners in the coalition of interests that won the war and would now mould America. The richest planter of them all – slave holder and servant holder – was to be the first president of the new United States, George Washington.

Washington's attitude was put to the test at the beginning of the war, when the British Governor of Virginia, Lord Dunmore, promised freedom to servants and slaves who joined his side and fought for King George. The prospect of losing their prime assets enraged the planters, not least Washington. He described Lord Dunmore as an 'arch traitor to the rights of humanity'.[15]

It would take thirty years before the indentured-servant trade disappeared. It did so as unobtrusively as it came in, dying out slowly and without fuss. No principled campaign was fought to end it, as happened with black slavery. Economics killed it. The trade in white servants simply lost its profitability. Advances in ship design made the journey quicker and cheaper and therefore within reach of more of the poor. At the same time, ethnic self-help groups emerged offering loans to would-be migrants from back home. The result was that fewer people needed to mortgage their best years in pursuit of a new life in a new world. By 1820, the trade was gone and those who connived at it – some of them great names in America and Britain – were remembered for other things.

What of the legacy of their victims? Did those convicts and free-willers and others dealt with so grossly by the indentured-servant system leave some definable trace of themselves in the fabric of the society they helped to build? The answer is undoubtedly yes, for America grew from their experience just as much as it did from that of others whose stories are more readily told. Is it too fanciful to see something of the harsh conditions of those early settlements, of the backbreaking work in farm and factory, within the present-day American psyche, with its proud insistence on the work ethic? And in its rigorous penal codes, with the death penalty still available in so many states, is it too much to see something of those stern early disciplinarians? One tends to think not.

Early America was created out of a series of convulsive efforts that so often depended upon the sacrifice of those who cleared the trees and tilled the soil. These men and women played their peculiar part in the creation of the dual facets of the American dream: the right to individual freedom and the opportunity to make something of oneself. Thousands upon thousands of enslaved workers gave up their freedom, or had it taken from them, in order that others could make money, while hoping upon hope that one day it would be their turn, too.

NOTES

INTRODUCTION

1 John Van der Zee, *Bound Over: Indentured Servitude and American Conscience* (1985).
2 A. Roger Ekirch, *Bound for America: The Transportation of British Convicts to the Colonies, 1718–1775* (1987).
3 Walter Hart Blumenthal, *Brides from Bridewell: Female Felons Sent to Colonial America* (1962).
4 Peter Wilson Coldham, *Emigrants in Chains: A Social History of Forced Emigration to the Americas, 1607–1776* (1992).
5 Lerone Bennett Jr, *Before the Mayflower: A History of the Negro in America 1619–1964* (1964).
6 Gary B. Nash, 'Poverty and Politics in Early American History' in Smith, Billy G. (ed.), *Down and Out in Early America* (2004).
7 Thomas Jefferson, *Notes on the State of Virginia* (1785).
8 Sydney George Fisher, *Men, Women and Manners in Colonial Times* (1898).

CHAPTER ONE

1 Raphael Holinshed, *The Chronicles of England, Scotland, and Ireland* (1802).
2 E.E. Rich, 'The Population of Elizabethan England' in *The Economic History Review*, New Series, Vol. 2, No. 3 (1950).

3 L.W. Cowie, 'Bridewell', *History Today*, 23 (1973).

4 Nassau W. Senior, and Edwin Chadwick, et al., *The Poor Law Commissioners Report of 1834: Copy of the Report Made in 1834 by the Commissioners for Inquiring into the Administration and Practical Operation of the Poor Laws* (1885).

5 John Ranelagh, *Ireland: An Illustrated History* (1981).

6 Humphrey Gilbert, *A Discourse for the Discovery of a New Passage to Cathaia* (1972).

7 *Canadian Dictionary of National Biography Online*, www. biographi.ca/EN/ShowBio.asp?BioId=34374&query=humphr ey%20AND%20gilbert

8 Gilbert, *Discourse.*

9 C.W. Eliot, *Voyages and Travels Ancient and Modern* (2006).

10 W.G. Gosling, *The Life of Sir Humphrey Gilbert: England's First Empire Builder* (1911).

11 Kevin Major, *As Near to Heaven by Sea: A History of Newfoundland and Labrador* (2001).

12 Gosling, *Life of Sir Humphrey Gilbert.*

13 David Beers Quinn, *Set Fair for Roanoke: Voyages and Colonies, 1584–1606* (1985).

14 Annette Kolodny, *The Lay of the Land: Metaphor as Experience and History in American Life and Letters* (2002).

CHAPTER TWO

1 Alexander Brown, *Genesis of the United States: A Narrative of the Movement in England, 1605–1616, which Resulted in the Plantation of North America by Englishmen* . . . (1964).

2 John Brereton, *A Brief and True Relation of the Discovery of the North Part of Virginia . . . 1602* (1973).

3 Martin Pring, 'A Voyage Set Out From the City of Bristol', in Burrage, Henry S. (ed.), *Haklyut 1534–1608* (1906).

4 Lord John Campbell, *The Lives of the Chief Justices of England* (1876).

5 Ibid.

6 T.B. Macaulay, *The History of England*, Vol. 2 (1863).

7 Campbell, *Lives of the Chief Justices.*

8 Thomas Fuller, *Worthies of England* (1840).

9 James Sullivan, *History of the District of Maine* (1795).

10 Don Pedro de Zuniga, communication to King Philip, 1607, in Brown, *Genesis of the United States.*

11 Peter Wilson Coldham, *Child Apprentices in America from Christ's Hospital, London, 1617–1788* (1990).

12 John A. Poor, *The First Colonisation of New England* (1863).

13 W.F. Poole, *The Popham Colony: A Discussion of its Historical Claims* (1866).

14 John Aubrey, *Brief Lives Chiefly of Contemporaries* (1931).

15 William Stirling, *An Encouragement to Colonies* (1624).

16 Douglas Walthew Rice, *The Life and Achievements of Sir John Popham, 1531–1607: Leading to the Establishment of the First English Colony in New England* (2005).

17 Sullivan, *History of the District of Maine.*

18 William Strachey, *History of Travel into Virginia Britannia* (1953).

19 George Chalmers, *Parliamentary Portraits; or, Characters of the British Senate* (1795).

20 B.F. de Costa, *Relation of a Voyage to Sagadahoc* (1880).

21 Ferdinando Gorges, *A Brief Narration of the Original Undertakings of the Advancement of Plantations into the Parts of America* (1658).

22 John Wingate Thorton, *Colonial Schemes of Popham and Gorges* (1863).

CHAPTER THREE

1 John Smith, *The True Travels, Adventures and Observations of Capt John Smith* (1630).

2 Hugh Brogan, *Penguin History of the United States of America* (1985).

3 Richard Hakluyt, *Richard Hakluyt's Voyages in Search of the North West Passage* (1973).

4 Smith, *True Travels.*

5 George Percy, *A Discourse of the Plantation of the Southern Colony in Virginia by the English, 1606* (1625).

6 Smith, *True Travels.*

7 David Beers Quinn, 'Theory and Practice: Roanoke and Jamestown', the Brewster Lecture in History 1985, Sydney Jones Library, University of Liverpool.

8 Cited in Alexander Brown, *Genesis of the United States: A Narrative of the Movement in England, 1605–1616, which Resulted in the Plantation of North America by Englishmen . . .* (1964).

9 Ibid.

10 Giles Milton, *Nathaniel's Nutmeg: How One Man's Courage Changed the Course of History* (2000).

11 Peter Force, *Tracts Relating to the Origin, Settlement, and Progress of the Colonies in North America,* Vol. 3 (1836), see Library of Congress.

12 Robert Johnson, *The New Life of Virginia* (1612).

13 Ibid.

14 Terence O'Brien, 'The London Livery Companies and the Virginia Company', *Virginia Magazine,* April 1960.

15 William Strachey, *A True Reportory of the Wreck and Redemption of Sir Thomas Gates, Knight, Upon and From the Islands of the Bermudas* (1965).

16 George Percy, A *Discourse of the Plantation of the Southern Colony in Virginia by the English* (1606).

17 Smith, *True Travels.*

18 Alice Morse Earle, *Curious Punishments of Bygone Days* (1896).

19 Cited in Elmer I. Miller, *The Legislature of the Province of Virginia: Its Internal Development* (1907).

20 Sir Thomas Dale, letter to Lord Salisbury (King James I's Secretary of State), 27 August 1611, in Brown, *Genesis of the United States.*

21 A Broadside by the Virginia Council, 1609, in Brown, *Genesis of the United States.*

22 Richard Hall, *Empires of the Monsoon: A History of the Indian Ocean and its Invaders* (1996).

23 Frank Welsh, *A History South of Africa* (1998).

24 Mary Johnston, *Pioneers of the Old South: A Chronicle of English Colonial Beginnings* (1918).

25 Beamish Murdoch, *A History of Nova Scotia or Arcadie* (1867).

26 Don Diego de Molina, letter of 1613, in Tyler, Lyon Gardiner, *Narratives of Early Virginia, 1606–1625* (1907).

27 Count de Gondomar, communication to King Philip, in Brown, *Genesis of the United States*.

28 Susan Kingsbury, *An Introduction to the Records of the Virginia Company of London* (1905).

29 Ralph Hamor, *Discourse of the Present State of Virginia and the Success of the Affairs There till 18 June 1614* (1957).

30 Peter Wilson Coldham, *Emigrants in Chains: A Social History of Forced Emigration to the Americas, 1607–1776* (1992).

CHAPTER FOUR

1 John Stow, *A Survey of the Cities of London and Westminster* (1720).

2 *Court Records of Bridewell Royal Hospital 1618–1638*, Bridewell Archives, Kent.

3 Hugh Lee to Wilson/Cecil, 26 March 1609, *Calendar of State Papers*, Public Records Office, SP/89/3.

4 Hugh Cunningham, *Children and Childhood in Western Society Since 1500* (1995).

5 Alexander Brown, *Genesis of the United States: A Narrative of the Movement in England, 1605–1616, which Resulted in the Plantation of North America by Englishmen . . .* (1964).

6 Susan Kingsbury, *An Introduction to the Records of the Virginia Company of London* (1905).

7 Elizabeth McLure Thomson, *The Chamberlain Letters* (1966).

8 R.C. Johnson, 'Transportation of Children from London to Virginia 1618–22', in Reinmuth, Howard F., *Early Stuart Studies* (1970).

9 T.B. Macaulay, *History of England* (1863).

10 Theodore Rabb, *Jacobean Gentleman: Sir Edwin Sandys 1561–1629* (1998).

11 Hubert Hall, *History of the Customs Revenue in England* (1885).

12 John Smith, *The Complete Works of Captain John Smith* (1986).

13 H.E. Marshall, *This Country of Ours: The Story of the United States* (1917).

14 Kingsbury, *Records of the Virginia Company.*

15 Ted Nace, *Gangs of America: The Rise of Corporate Power and the Disabling of Democracy* (2003).

16 Kingsbury, *Records of the Virginia Company.*

17 L.W. Grant and James Munro (eds), *Acts of the Privy Council of England*, Vol. 1 1613–1680 (1908).

18 Kingsbury, *Records of the Virginia Company.*

19 John Donne, *The Sermons of John Donne* (1984).

20 John Rolfe, letter to Sir Edwin Sandys, 1619, in Kingsbury, *Records of the Virginia Company.*

21 Engel Sluiter, 'New light on the 20 and odd Negroes', *William and Mary Quarterly*, April 1997.

22 Hugh Fred Jope, *The Flying Dutchman* (1993). Private publication cited in Hashaw, Tim, 'Malunga: The African Origins of the American Melungians', *Electra Magazine*, July/August 2001.

CHAPTER FIVE

1 Theodore Allen, *The Invention of the White Race* (1994).

2 Indenture Between Four Adventurers of Berkeley Hundred and Robert Coopy of Nibley, *Thomas Jefferson Papers*, Series 8, http://memory.loc.gov/ammem/collections/jefferson_papers/

3 Smith of Nibley correspondence, *Thomas Jefferson Papers*, ibid.

4 Ibid.

5 Charles E. Hatch Jr, *America's Oldest Legislative Assembly and its Jamestown Statehouses* (1956).

6 James Curtis Ballagh, *White Servitude in the Colony of Virginia: A Study of the System of Indentured Labor in the American Colonies* (2004).

7 Philip Alexander Bruce, *Economic History of Virginia in the Seventeenth Century: An Inquiry Into the Material Condition of the People, Based Upon Original and Contemporaneous Records* (1896).

8 William W. Hening, *The Statutes at Large: Being a Collection of All the Laws of Virginia from the First Session of the Legislature* (1823).

9 Bruce, *Economic History of Virginia.*

10 Susan Kingsbury, *An Introduction to the Records of the Virginia Company of London* (1905).

11 Ibid.

12 Theodore K. Rabb, *Jacobean Gentleman: Sir Edwin Sandys 1561–1629* (1998).

13 Wesley Frank Craven, *Dissolution of the Virginia Company: The Failure of a Colonial Experiment* (1932).

14 Kingsbury, *Records of the Virginia Company.*

15 Ibid.

16 Edmund S. Morgan, *American Slavery, American Freedom: The Ordeal of Colonial Virginia* (1975).

17 Ted Nace, *Gangs of America: The Rise of Corporate Power and the Disabling of Democracy* (2003).

18 John Smith, *The True Travels, Adventures and Observations of Captain John Smith* (1630).

CHAPTER SIX

1 Richard Frethorne's letters to his parents, March 1623, in Kingsbury, Susan, *An Introduction to the Records of the Virginia Company of London* (1905).

2 Edmund S. Morgan, *American Slavery, American Freedom: The Ordeal of Colonial Virginia* (1975).

3 Wesley Frank Craven, *Dissolution of the Virginia Company: The Failure of a Colonial Experiment* (1932).

4 Jacqueline Jones, *American Work: Four Centuries of Black and White Labor* (1998).

5 Thomas Jefferson, *Notes on The State of Virginia* (1801).

6 Theodore W. Allen, *The Invention of the White Race* (1994).

7 Morgan, *American Slavery, American Freedom.*

8 Craven, *Dissolution of the Virginia Company.*

9 Abbot Emerson Smith, *Colonists in Bondage: White Servitude and Convict Labor in America, 1607–1776* (1947).

10 Morgan, *American Slavery, American Freedom.*

11 John Hammond, *Leah and Rachel or the Two Fruitful Sisters Virginia and Maryland* (1656).

12 James Morton Smith (ed.), *Seventeenth Century America: Essays in Colonial History* (1959).

13 Anon., *The Life of Thomas Hellier* (1678).

14 Ibid.

15 Edmund S. Morgan, 'The First American Boom 1618–1630', *William and Mary Quarterly*, April 1971.

16 Charles McKew Parr, 'The Voyages of David de Vries', *William and Mary Quarterly*, July 1970.

17 Mary Johnston, *The Old Dominion: An Account of Certain Prisoners of Hope* (1899).

18 Thomas J. Wertenbaker, *The Planters of Colonial Virginia* (1922).

19 Bernard Bailyn, *The Peopling of British North America: An Introduction* (1988) and *Voyagers to the West: A Passage in the Peopling of America on the Eve of the Revolution* (1988).

20 Wesley Frank Craven, *The Virginia Company of London: 1606–1624* (1997).

CHAPTER SEVEN

1 John Winthrop sermon, 'A Model of Christian Charity', 1630, in Rosenbaum, Stuart (ed.), *Pragmatism and Religion: Classical Sources and Original Essays* (2003).

2 Thomas Morton, *New English Canaan* (1637). See also Connors, Donald F., *Thomas Morton* (1969) and Dunn, Richard S., *Puritans and Yankees: The Winthrop Dynasty of New England, 1630–1717* (1962).

3 Morton, *New English Canaan*.

4 Ibid.

5 William Bradford, *History of the Plymouth Plantation* (1901).

6 Thomas Dudley, letter to Bridget Countess of Lincoln, 1631, in Young, Alexander, *Chronicles of the First Planters of the Colony of Massachusetts Bay, from 1623–1636* (1846).

7 Ibid.

8 Timothy Paul Grady, *On the Path to Slavery: Indentured Servitude in Barbados and Virginia During the Seventeenth*

Century (2000), http://scholar.lib.vt.edu/theses/available/etd-02252000-09590007/

9 Lawrence William Towner, *A Good Master Well Served: Masters and Servants in Colonial Massachusetts 1620–1750* (1998).

10 Grady, *On the Path to Slavery.*

11 John West, letter to Commissioners for Plantations, *Calendar of State Papers*, Colonial, Vol. IX, No. 7, National Archive.

12 Philip Alexander Bruce, *Economic History of Virginia in the Seventeenth Century: An Inquiry Into the Material Condition of the People, Based Upon Original and Contemporaneous Records* (1896).

13 William Tucker, will dated London, 12 Oct 1642, http://homepages.rootsweb.com/~bianco/Resources/riddle.html

14 Grady, *On the Path to Slavery.*

15 Archives of Maryland, Vol. 10, 1649–50, http://www.msa.md.gov/megafile/msa/speccol/sc2900/sc2908/html/index.html

16 John Van der Zee, *Bound Over: Indentured Servitude and American Conscience* (1985).

17 Maryland Calendar of Wills, Vol. 1, http://www.usgennet.org/usa/md/state/wills/01/addenda.html

18 Ibid.

19 Abbot Emerson Smith, *Colonists in Bondage: White Servitude and Convict Labour in America, 1607–1776* (1947).

CHAPTER EIGHT

1 W. Bullock, *Virginia Impartially Examined* (1649).

2 Ibid.

3 Morgan Godwin, *The Negro's and Indian's Advocate: Suing for Their Admission Into the Church* (1680).

4 Abbot Emerson Smith, *Colonists in Bondage: White Servitude and Convict Labor in America, 1607–1776* (1947).

5 Walter Hart Blumenthal, *Brides from Bridewell: Female Felons Sent to Colonial America* (1962).

6 Peter Wilson Coldham, 'The Spiriting of London Children to Virginia, 1648–1685', *The Virginia Magazine of History and Biography*, Vol. 83, No. 3, July 1975.

7 Ned Ward, *The London Spy* (1699).

8 Ibid.

9 Legal affidavits quoted by D. George, *London Life in the 18th Century* (1930).

10 Miscellaneous sheets 74/515 L2 British Library.

11 Tudor and Stuart proclamations, 2613a, Bodleian Library.

12 Peter Coldham, *Emigrants in Chains: A Social History of Forced Emigration to the Americas, 1607–1776* (1992).

13 Smith, *Colonists in Bondage.*

CHAPTER NINE

1 Fernand Braudel, *Civilization and Capitalism 15th–18th Century* (1984).

2 Theodore W. Allen, *The Invention of the White Race* (1994).

3 T.W. Moody, *The Londonderry Plantation: 1609–1641* (1939).

4 High Court of Admiralty Miscellany, Bundle 30/636, Public Records Office.

5 The Papal Nuncio in Ireland, Giovanni Battista Rinuccini, writing in 1654; quoted in MacInerny, *Irish Slaves in the West Indies,* (1909).

6 T.B. Macaulay, *History of England* (1863).

7 John Prendergast, *The Cromwellian Settlement of Ireland* (1865).

8 Charles George Walpole, *A Short History of the Kingdom of Ireland* (Kegan Paul, 1882).

9 The term 'tory' comes from the Irish *tórai*, or outlaw. Many tories were former soldiers, or irregulars, fighting on the Irish Confederate side against the Cromwellians, some of whom later turned to crime. A later term for a rural bandit was 'rapparee', from the Irish *rápaire*. These were sometimes Jacobite guerrillas fighting against the Williamite forces, who also sometimes turned to crime once hostilities had ended.

10 MacInerny, *Irish Slaves in the West Indies.*

11 Walpole, *Short History of the Kingdom of Ireland.*

12 Cotton Mather, *Memorable Providences, Relating to Witchcraft and Possession* (1689).

CHAPTER TEN

1 George Pratt Insh, *Scottish Colonial Schemes 1620–1686* (1922).

2 H.C.B. Rogers, *Battles and Generals of the Civil Wars 1642–1651* (1968).

3 Quoted in Abbot Emerson Smith, *Colonists in Bondage: White Servitude and Convict Labour in America, 1607–1776* (1947).

4 Robert Wodrow, *The History of the Sufferings of the Church of Scotland from the Restoration to the Revolution* (1836–1838).

5 John H. Thomson (ed.), *A Cloud of Witnesses for the Royal Prerogatives of Jesus Christ; or, The Last Speeches and Testimonies of Those Who Have Suffered for the Truth in Scotland, Since the Year 1680* (1871).

6 J. Calderwood, 'Collection of Dying Testimonies', 1806, in Thomson, ibid.

7 Ibid.

8 *Register of the Privy Council of Scotland*, Third Series, Vol. VII.

9 Ibid.

CHAPTER ELEVEN

1 Edmund S. Morgan, *American Slavery, American Freedom: The Ordeal of Colonial Virginia* (1975).

2 Lerone Bennett Jr, *The Shaping of Black America* (1975).

3 Audrey Smedley, *Race in North America: Origin and Evolution of a Worldview* (1993).

4 Morgan, *American Slavery, American Freedom*.

5 Massachusetts Body of Liberties 1641, in *The Colonial Laws of Massachusetts* (1889).

6 Act of 1670, in William W. Hening, *The Statutes at Large: Being a Collection of All the Laws of Virginia from the First Session of the Legislature* (1823).

7 Henry Read McIlwaine (ed.), *Minutes of the Council and General Court of Colonial Virginia, 1622–1632* (1924).

8 Frank W. Sweet, 'The Invention of the Colour Line', http://www.backintyme.com/essay050101.htm

9 Act of 1662, in Hening, *Statutes at Large*.

CHAPTER TWELVE

1 Maurice Bloomfield (trans.), 'Hymns of the Atharva Veda', in *Sacred Books of the East*, Vol. 42 (1897).

2 Robert H. Schomburgk, *The History of Barbados* (1971).

3 Hilary Beckles, *White Servitude and Black Slavery in Barbados, 1627–1715* (1989).

4 Ibid.

5 Richard Ligon, *A True and Exact History of the Island of Barbados* (1657).

6 Ibid.

7 Figures extrapolated from data published by the International Institute of Social History, including Global Price and Income Group, *English Prices and Wages, 1209–1914,* and van Zanden, Jan Luiten, *Wages and the Cost of Living in Southern England, 1450–1700.*

8 Eric Williams, *Capitalism and Slavery* (1944).

9 For an informative and enlightening discussion of this point, see Beckles, *White Servitude and Black Slavery.*

10 Governor Atkins, *Colonial Office Papers*, 1/37, No. 51, Public Records Office.

11 Ligon, *A True and Exact History.*

12 Thomas Burton, *Parliamentary Diary, Member in the Parliaments of Thomas & Richard Cromwell, 1656–59,* (1828).

13 Ibid.

14 Cited in P.E. Moran, *Historical Sketch of the Persecutions Suffered by the Catholics of Ireland* (1862).

CHAPTER THIRTEEN

1 Theodore W. Allen, *The Invention of the White Race* (1994).

2 Edmund S. Morgan, *American Slavery, American Freedom: The Ordeal of Colonial Virginia* (1975).

3 This was one of many illuminating replies Berkeley gave to questions put by the Council for Foreign Plantations in 1671. Among other things he claimed that new hands did not often die now 'whereas heretofore not one of five escaped the first year'. Personal narratives from the Virtual Jamestown Project, http:// etext.lib.virginia.edu/etcbin/jamestown-browse?id=J1062

4 Allen, *Invention of the White Race.*

5 Edmund Jennings Lee, *Lee of Virginia 1642–1892: Biographical and Genealogical sketches of the descendants of Colonel Richard Lee* (1895).

6 Moncure Daniel Conway, *Barons of the Potomack and the Rappahannock* (1892).

7 The Assembly passed an act requiring that 'every master shall provide servants with a competent diet, clothing, lodging, and shall not exceed the bounds of moderation in correcting them and a servant may make complaint to the commissioner and have remedy for his grievances'. Act of 1662, in Hening, William W., *Statutes at Large.*

8 Archives of Maryland 1661, http://query.mdarchives.state. md.us/search?site=aom_coll&sort=date%3AD%3AL%3Ad1&ou tput=xml_no_dtd&ie=UTF-8&oe=UTF-8&client=mdarchives_ FE&proxystylesheet=mdarchives_FE&filter=0&q=bradnox

9 Act of 1661, in Hening, *Statutes at Large.*

10 Jill Nock Jeffery, 'More a Monster than a Man', *Shore Historian*, Fall 2001.

CHAPTER FOURTEEN

1 'A True Narrative of the Rise, Progress and Cessation of the Late Rebellion in Virginia by His Majesty's Royal Commissioners 1671', Collected Papers, XLI, 79, Public Records Office.

2 Peter Wilson Coldham, *Emigrants in Chains: A Social History of Forced Emigration to the Americas, 1607–1776* (1992).

3 Robert Beverley, *The History and Present State of Virginia* (1947).

4 James Davie Butler, 'British Convicts Shipped to American Colonies', *American Historical Review*, Vol. 2, No. 1, October 1896.

5 An Act of 1672 for the Apprehension and Suppression of Runaways, Negroes and Slaves, in Hening, William, W., *Statutes at Large*

6 William L. Shea, *The Virginia Militia in the Seventeenth Century* (1983).

7 H.E. Marshall, *This Country of Ours* (1917).

8 Wilcomb E. Washburn, *The Governor and the Rebel: A History of Bacon's Rebellion in Virginia* (1957).

9 Warren M. Billings (ed.), *The Old Dominion in the Seventeenth Century: A Documentary History of Virginia, 1606–1689* (1975).

10 Peter Thompson, 'The Thief, the Householder, and the Commons: Languages of Class in Seventeenth-Century Virginia', *William and Mary Quarterly*, April 2006.

11 Sir William Berkeley, *A Discourse and View of Virginia* (1662).

12 Edmund S. Morgan, *American Slavery, American Freedom: The Ordeal of Colonial Virginia* (1975).

13 John Goode, *Virginia Cousins: A Study of the Ancestry and Posterity of John Goode of Whitby* (1887).

14 'T.M.', 'The Beginning, Progress, and Conclusion of Bacon's Rebellion in Virginia, in the Years 1675 and 1676', in Force, Peter, *Tracts Relating to the Origin, Settlement, and Progress of the Colonies in North America*, Vol. 1 (1836).

15 Thomas Grantham, *An Historical Account of some Memorable Actions Particularly in Virginia as Performed by Sir T.G.* (1716).

16 Marshall, *This Country of Ours*.

17 Charles A. Goodrich, *A History of the United States of America* (1825).

18 Howard Zinn, *A People's History of the United States* (1980).

19 Theodore W. Allen, *The Invention of the White Race* (1994).

20 Frank W. Sweet, *Legal History of the Color Line* (2005).

CHAPTER FIFTEEN

1 Quoted in Philip Otterness, *Becoming German: The 1709 Palatine Migration to New York*, (2004). The authors are indebted to this work for the depth of understanding it contains covering the events in the first part of this chapter.

2 Joshua Kocherthal, *A Complete and Detailed Report of the Renowned District of Carolina Located in English America*, (1706–1709).

3 Ibid.

4 Otterness, *Becoming German*.

5 Daniel Defoe, *A Brief History of the Poor Palatine Refugees, Lately Arrived in England* (1709).

6 Gottlieb Mittelberger, *Journey to Pennsylvania* (1960).

CHAPTER SIXTEEN

1 Margaret Sankey, *Jacobite Prisoners of the 1715 Rebellion* (2005).

2 Quoted in Peter Wilson Coldham, *Emigrants in Chains: A Social History of Forced Emigration to the Americas, 1607–1776* (1992).

3 John Prebble, *The Lion in the North* (1973).

4 John Prebble, *Culloden*, (1962).

CHAPTER SEVENTEEN

1 Cited in A. Roger Ekirch, 'The Transportation of Scottish Criminals to America During the Eighteenth Century', *Journal of British Studies*, Vol. 24, No. 3.

2 Treasury Papers 47, Public Records Office.

3 London Sessions Papers, April 1776, www.oldbaileyonline. org.

4 Peter Williamson, *The Life and Adventures of Peter Williamson* (1757).

5 James Annesley, *Memoirs of an Unfortunate Young Nobleman*, British Library, 243.I.4.

6 For an interesting account of the Annesley affair, see *Famous Claimants*, a rattling read published in London, 1873.

7 There are several records of the Annesley trial, the clearest is that edited by Andrew Lang in *Notable English Trials*, William Hodge and Co. (1912).

8 T.B. Howell (ed.), *Collection of State Trials* (1828).

CHAPTER EIGHTEEN

1 J.M. Beattie, *Crime and the Courts in England 1660–1800* (1986).

2 Proceedings of the Old Bailey, April 1718, http://www. oldbaileyonline.org/html_units/1710s/t17180423-5.html

3 A. Roger Ekirch, *Bound for America: The Transportation of British Convicts to the Colonies, 1718–1775* (1987).

4 Ibid.

5 George Selwyn, letter quoted in Blumenthal, Walter Hart, *Brides from Bridewell: Female Felons Sent to Colonial America* (1962).

6 Peter Wilson Coldham, *Emigrants in Chains: A Social History of Forced Emigration to the Americas, 1607–1776* (1992).

7 Ibid.

8 James Revel, *The Poor Unhappy Felon's Sorrowful Account of his Fourteen Years' Transportation at Virginia in America* (1800).

9 Scott Christianson, *With Liberty for Some: 500 Years of Imprisonment in America* (1998).

10 John Harrower, *The Journal of John Harrower an Indentured Servant in the Colony of Virginia* (1963).

11 Hugh Jones, *Present State of Virginia: From Whence is Inferred a Short View of Maryland and North Carolina* (1724).

12 Christianson, *With Liberty for Some.*

13 William Eddis, *Letters from America* (1792).

14 John Lauson, *The Felon's Account of His Transportation at Virginia in America* (1969).

15 R. Kent Lancaster, 'Almost Chattel: The Lives of Indentured Servants at Hampton-Northampton, Baltimore County', *Maryland Historical Magazine*, Vol. 94, No. 3, Fall 1999.

16 David Waldstreicher, *Runaway America: Benjamin Franklin, Slavery and the American Revolution* (2004).

17 Gary B. Nash, 'Poverty and Politics in Early American History', in Smith, Billy G. (ed.), *Down and Out in Early America* (2004).

18 Jones, *Present State of Virginia.*

19 Richard Hofstadter, *The United States: The History of a Republic* (1967).

20 Elizabeth Sprigs, letter to John Sprigs, White Cross Street, London, 22 September 1756, http://www.digitalhistory. uh.edu/learning_history/servitude_slavery/servitude_ account1.cfm

21 Blumenthal, *Brides from Bridewell*.

22 Benjamin Franklin, 'Rattlesnakes for Felons', *Pennsylvania Gazette*, 9 May 1751.

23 Charles Carter, letter to Landon Carter, 1770. Carter Archives, Charlottesville, VA, University of Virginia Library, 1967.

CHAPTER NINETEEN

1 John Howard, *The State of the Prisons in England and Wales with an Account of Some Foreign Prisons* (2000).

2 Dan Byrnes, *The Blackheath Connection*, www.danbyrnes.com.au.

3 National Maritime Museum, *Port Cities* (2006).

4 Edmund Burke, quoted in William Cobbett, *Parliamentary History of England* (1812).

5 A. Roger Ekirch, 'Great Britain's Secret Convict Trade to America 1783–84', *American Historical Review*, LXXXIX, 1984.

6 George Moore, *Letterbooks*, Mitchell Library, Sydney.

7 Sir John Fortescue, *Correspondence of King George III* (1927).

8 Proceedings of the Old Bailey, 10 September 1783, http://www.oldbaileyonline.org/html_units/1780s/t17830910-20.html

9 A. Roger Ekirch, *Bound for America: The Transportation of British Convicts to the Colonies, 1718–1775* (1987).

10 *Proceedings of the Old Bailey*, 10 September 1783.

11 Ibid.

12 Convict George Townsend claimed in court that he was sold for 60 guineas. See *Proceedings of the Old Bailey*, 19 July 1785, http://www.oldbaileyonline.org/html_units/1780s/t17860719-38.html

13 Ekirch, *Bound for America*.

14 Moore, *Letterbooks*, and www.danbyrned.com.au.

15 *George Washington Papers*, http://oll.libertyfund.org/Texts/LFBooks/Washington0268/Collection/HTMLs/0026_Pt02_Chap02.html

SELECT BIBLIOGRAPHY

Akenson, Don, *An Irish History of Civilization* (Granta, 2005)

Alderman, Clifford Lindsey, *Colonists for Sale: The Story of Indentured Servants in America* (Macmillan, 1975)

Allen, Theodore W., *The Invention of the White Race* (Verso, 1994)

— *Rum, Slaves and Molasses: The Story of New England's Triangular Trade* (Crowell-Collier Press, 1973)

Andrews, K.R., N.P. Canny and P.E.H. Hair (eds), *The Westward Enterprise: English Activities in Ireland, the Atlantic and America, 1480–1650* (Liverpool University Press, 1978)

Aubrey, John, *Brief Lives Chiefly of Contemporaries* (Davies, 1931)

Bailyn, Bernard, *The Peopling of British North America: An Introduction* (Vintage, 1988)

— *Voyagers to the West: A Passage in the Peopling of America on the Eve of the Revolution* (Vintage, 1988)

Ballagh, James Curtis, *White Servitude in the Colony of Virginia: A Study of the System of Indentured Labor in the American Colonies* (Kessinger Publishing, 2004)

Bancroft, George, *History of the United States: From the Discovery of the Continent to the Present Time* (Appleton, 1885)

Beattie, J.M., *Crime and the Courts in England 1660–1800* (Oxford University Press, 1986)

Beckles, Hilary, *White Servitude and Black Slavery in Barbados 1627–1715* (University of Tennessee Press, 1989)

Beier, A.L., *Masterless Men: The Vagrancy Problem in England, 1560–1640* (Methuen, 1985)

Bennett Jr, Lerone, *Before the Mayflower: A History of the Negro in America 1619–1964* (Johnson Publishing Co., 1964)

— *The Shaping of Black America* (Johnson Publishing Co., 1975)

Beverley, Robert, *The History and Present State of Virginia* (University of North Carolina Press, 1947)

Bezis-Selfa, John, *Forging America: Ironworkers, Adventurers, and the Industrious Revolution* (Cornell University Press, 2003)

Billings, Warren M. (ed.), *The Old Dominion in the Seventeenth Century: A Documentary History of Virginia, 1606–1689* (University of North Carolina Press, 1975)

Binder, Fredrick M. and David M. Reimers, *The Way We Lived: Essays and Documents in American Social History, Vol. 1, 1607–1877* (D.C. Heath & Co., 1992)

Blumenthal, Walter Hart, *Brides from Bridewell: Female Felons Sent to Colonial America* (Prentice Hall, 1962)

Bond, R.P., *Queen Anne's American Kings* (Clarendon Press, 1952)

Bottigheimer, Karl, *English Money and Irish Land* (Clarendon Press, 1971)

Boyd, Paul S. (ed.), *The Oxford Companion to United States History* (Oxford University Press, 2001)

Bradford, William, *History of the Plymouth Plantation* (Boston, 1901)

Branch-Johnson, William, *The English Prison Hulks* (Phillimore, 1957)

Braudel, Fernand, *Civilization and Capitalism 15th–18th Century* (Collins, 1984)

Brenner, Robert, *Merchants and Revolution: Commercial Change, Political Conflict, and London's Overseas Traders, 1550–1653* (Princeton University Press, 1991)

Brereton, John, *A Briefe and True Relation of the Discovery of the North Part of Virginia . . . 1602* (Da Capo Press, 1973)

Bridenbaugh, Carl, *The Beginnings of the American People: Vexed and Troubled Englishmen, 1590–1642* (Oxford University Press, 1968)

Brogan, Hugh, *Penguin History of the United States of America* (Penguin, 1985)

Brown, Alexander, *Genesis of the United States: A Narrative of the Movement in England, 1605–1616, which Resulted in the Plantation of North America by Englishmen* . . . (Russell & Russell, 1964)

Brown, J.M., *A Brief Sketch of the First Settlement of the Country of Schoharie by the Germans* (New York, 1823)

Brown, Kathleen M., *Good Wives, Nasty Wenches, and Anxious Patriarchs: Gender, Race, and Power in Colonial Virginia* (University of North Carolina Press, 1996)

Bruce, Philip Alexander, *Economic History of Virginia in the Seventeenth Century: An Inquiry Into the Material Condition of the People, Based Upon Original and Contemporaneous Records* (Macmillan and Co., 1896)

Bullock, W., *Virginia Impartially Examined* (Hammond, 1649)

Burton, Thomas, *Parliamentary Diary, Member in the Parliaments of Thomas & Richard Cromwell, 1656–59, Vol. 4* (Henry Colborn, 1828)

Campbell, Lord John, *The Lives of the Chief Justices of England* (Carswell, 1876)

Cecil, Robert, *The Cecil of Chelwood Papers*, British Library catalogue of additions to the manuscripts, additional manuscripts 51071–51204 (British Library, 1991)

Chalmers, George, *Parliamentary Portraits; or, Characters of the British Senate* (Bellamy, 1795)

Cheyney, Edward P., 'Some English Conditions Surrounding the Settlement of Virginia', *American Historical Review*, 12 (April 1907)

Christianson, Scott, *With Liberty for Some: 500 Years of Imprisonment in America* (Northeastern University Press, 1998)

Clarke, Aidan, *Prelude to Restoration in Ireland: The End of the Commonwealth, 1659–60* (Cambridge University Press, 1999)

Cobb, S.H., *The Story of the Palatines: An Episode in Colonial History* (Putnam, 1897)

Coldham, Peter Wilson, *Child Apprentices in America from Christ's Hospital, London, 1617–1788* (Genealogical Publishing, 1990)

— *Emigrants in Chains: A Social History of Forced Emigration to the Americas, 1607–1776* (Sutton, 1992)

Condon, E. O'Meagher, *The Irish Race in America* (Ford's National Library, 1887)

Connors, Donald F., *Thomas Morton* (Twayne Publishers, 1969)

Conway, Moncure Daniel, *Barons of the Potomac and the Rappahannock* (Grolier Club, 1892)

Craven, Wesley Frank, *Dissolution of the Virginia Company: The Failure of a Colonial Experiment* (Oxford University Press, 1932)

— *The Virginia Company of London: 1606–1624* (Clearfield, 1997)

Cunningham, Hugh, *Children and Childhood in Western Society Since 1500* (Longman, 1995)

Cunnington, Phyllis Ellis and Catherine Lucas, *Costume of Household Servants: From the Middle Ages to 1900* (Barnes and Noble Imports, 1974)

Dawkins, Richard, *The God Delusion* (Bantam Press, 2006)

de Costa, B.F. (ed.), *Relation of a Voyage to Sagadahoc* (J. Wilson, 1880)

Defoe, Daniel, *A Brief History of the Poor Palatine Refugees, Lately Arrived in England* (J. Baker, 1709)

Demos, John, *A Little Commonwealth* (Oxford University Press, 1970)

Dickson, R.J., *Ulster Emigration to Colonial America, 1718–1775* (Ulster Historical Foundation, 1966)

Dixon, N.W., *Palatine Roots: The 1710 German Settlement in New York* (Picton Press, 1994)

Doddridge, Joseph, *Notes on the Settlement and Indian Wars: On the Western Parts of Virginia and Pennsylvania 1763–1783* (Albany, 1876)

Donne, John, *The Sermons of John Donne* (University of California Press, 1984)

Drake, Samuel, *Making of Virginia and the Middle Colonies: 1578–1701, With Many Illustrations and Maps* (Gibbings, 1894)

Dunn, Richard S., *Puritans and Yankees: The Winthrop Dynasty of New England, 1630–1717* (Princeton University Press, 1962)

Earle, Alice Morse, *Curious Punishments of Bygone Days* (H. Stone and Co., 1896)

Ekirch, Roger A., *Bound for America: The Transportation of British Convicts to the Colonies, 1718–1775* (Oxford University Press, 1987)

Eliot, C.W., *Voyages and Travels Ancient and Modern* (Cosimo, 2006)

Ellis, Peter Beresford, *Hell or Connaught: The Cromwellian Colonization of Ireland 1652–1660* (Blackstaff Press, 1975)

Fisher, Sydney George, *Men, Women and Manners in Colonial Times* (J.P. Lippincott, 1898)

Fortescue, Sir John, *Correspondence of King George III* (Macmillan, 1927)

Foster, R.F., *Modern Ireland 1600–1972* (Allen Lane, 1988)

Fuller, Thomas, *The Holy State and The Profane State* (Pickering, 1840)

— *Worthies of England* (Nuttall, 1840)

Galenson, David W., *White Servitude in Colonial America* (Cambridge University Press, 1981)

George, D., *London Life in the 18th Century* (Routledge, 1930)

Gilbert, Humphrey, *A Discourse for the Discovery of a New Passage to Cathaia* (Marston Scholar Press, 1972)

Godwin, Morgan, *The Negro's and Indian's Advocate: Suing for Their Admission Into the Church* (London, 1680)

Goode, John, *Virginia Cousins: A Study of the Ancestry and Posterity of John Goode of Whitby* (J.W. Randolph, 1887)

Goodrich, Charles A., *A History of the United States of America* (Bellows Falls, 1825)

Gorges, Ferdinando, *A Brief Narration of the Original Undertakings of the Advancement of Plantations into the Parts of America* (1658)

Gosling, W.G., *The Life of Sir Humphrey Gilbert: England's First Empire Builder* (Constable, 1911)

Grady, T.P., On the Path to Slavery: Indentured Servitude in Barbados and Virginia During the Seventeenth Century, scholar.lib.vt.edu/theses/available/etd-02252000-09590007/unrestricted/etd.pdf

Grant, L.W. and James Munro (eds), *Acts of the Privy Council of England* (Colonial, 1908)

Griffiths, Paul, *Youth and Authority: Formative Experiences in England, 1560–1640* (Clarendon Press, 1996)

Guild, June Purcell, *The Black Laws of Virginia: A Summary of the Legislative Acts of Virginia Concerning Negroes from Earliest Times to the Present* (Whittet & Shepperson, 1936)

Hakluyt, Richard, *Richard Hakluyt's Voyages in Search of the North West Passage* (Hakluyt Society, 1973)

Hall, Hubert, *History of the Customs Revenue in England* (Elliot Stock, 1885)

Hall, Richard, *Empires of the Monsoon: A History of the Indian Ocean and its Invaders* (HarperCollins, 1996)

Hammond, John, *Leah and Rachel or the Two Fruitful Sisters Virginia and Maryland* (London, 1656)

Hamor, Ralph, *Discourse of the Present State of Virginia and the Success of the Affairs There till 18 June 1614* (Virginia State Library Publications, 1957)

Harlow, Vincent, *A History of Barbados 1625–1685* (Clarendon Press, 1926)

Hatch, Charles E. Jr, *America's Oldest Legislative Assembly and its Jamestown Statehouses* (National Park Service Interpretive Series History, 1956)

Hening, William W., *The Statutes at Large: Being a Collection of All the Laws of Virginia from the First Session of the Legislature* (Richmond, 1823)

Herrick, Cheesman A., *White Servitude in Pennsylvania: Indentured and Redemption Labor in Colony and Commonwealth* (Negro Universities Press, 1969)

Hofstadter, Richard, *The United States: The History of a Republic* (Prentice Hall, 1967)

Holinshed, Raphael, *The Chronicles of England, Scotland and Ireland* (London, 1802)

Hooper, William Eden, *History of Newgate and the Old Bailey* (Underwood, 1935)

Horn, James, *A Land as God Made it: Jamestown and the Birth of America* (Basic Books, 2005)

Howard, John, *The State of the Prisons in England and Wales with an Account of Some Foreign Prisons*, in Forsythe, W.J. (ed.), *The State of Prisons in Britain 1775–1900*, Vol. 1 (Routledge, 2000)

Howson, Gerald, *Thief Taker General: The Rise and Fall of Jonathan Wild* (Hutchinson, 1970)

Hyde, H. Montgomery, *John Law: The History of an Honest Adventurer* (W.H. Allen, 1969)

Insh, George Pratt, *Scottish Colonial Schemes 1620–1686* (Maclehose & Co., 1922)

Jefferson, Thomas, *Notes on the State of Virginia* (Philadelphia, 1801)
— *Thomas Jefferson Papers*, Library of Congress, http://memory. loc.gov/ammem/collections/jefferson_papers/

Johnson, Robert, *The New Life of Virginia* (London, 1612)

Johnston, Mary, *Pioneers of the Old South: A Chronicle of English Colonial Beginnings* (Yale University Press, 1918)
— *The Old Dominion: An Account of Certain Prisoners of Hope* (Constable and Co., 1899)

Jones, Hugh, *Present State of Virginia: From Whence is Inferred a Short View of Maryland and North Carolina* (London, 1724)

Jones, Jacqueline, *American Work: Four Centuries of Black and White Labor* (W.W. Norton, 1998)

Jones, M.A., *American Immigration* (University of Chicago Press, 1960)

Kellow, Margaret M.R., 'Indentured Servitude in Eighteenth-Century Maryland', *Social History*, 17 (November 1984)

Kelso, William M., *Kingsmill Plantations 1619–1800: Archaeology of Country Life in Colonial Virginia* (Academic Press, 1984)

Kingsbury, Susan, *An Introduction to the Records of the Virginia Company of London* (Library of Congress, 1905)

Kocherthal, Joshua, *A Complete and Detailed Report of the Renowned District of Carolina Located in English America* (Frankfurt, 1706–1709)

Kolchin, Peter, *American Slavery 1619–1877* (Penguin, 1993)

Kolodny, Annette, *The Lay of the Land: Metaphor as Experience and History in American Life and Letters* (Scholarly Book Services Inc., 2002)

Lang, Andrew (ed.), *The Annesley Case* (W. Hodge & Co., 1913)

Lause, Mark, *Young America: Land, Labour and the Republican Community* (University of Illinois Press, 2005)

Lauson, John, *The Felon's Account of His Transportation at Virginia in America* (Toucan Press, 1969)

Ligon, Richard, *A True and Exact History of the Island of Barbados* (London, 1657)

Linnell, Rosemary, *The Revenge of Indian Peter: The Incredible Story of Peter Williamson* (Book Guild, 2006)

Lockhart, Audrey, *Some Aspects of Emigration from Ireland to the North American Colonies between 1660 and 1775* (Arno Press, 1976)

Macaulay, T.B., *The History of England* (Longmans, 1863)

McIlwaine, Henry Read (ed.), *Minutes of the Council and General Court of Colonial Virginia, 1622–1632* (Virginia, 1924)

MacInerny, M.H., *Irish Slaves in the West Indies* (Dublin, 1909)

Major, Kevin, *As Near to Heaven by Sea: A History of Newfoundland and Labrador* (Viking, 2001)

Manhattan, Avro, *Catholic Imperialism and World Freedom* (Watts & Co., 1952)

Marshall, H.E., *This Country of Ours: The Story of the United States* (George H. Doran, 1917)

Martin, James Kirby (ed.), *Interpreting Colonial America: Selected Readings* (Harper & Row, 1978)

Menard, Russell R., *Migrants, Servants and Slaves: Unfree Labor in Colonial British America* (Ashgate Varorium, 2001)

Miller, Elmer I., *The Legislature of the Province of Virginia: Its Internal Development* (Columbia University Press, 1907)

Milton, Giles, *Nathaniel's Nutmeg: How One Man's Courage Changed the Course of History* (Sceptre, 2000)

Mittelberger, Gottlieb, *Journey to Pennsylvania* (1756), edited and translated by Oscar Handlin and John Clive (Belknap Press, 1960)

Moody, T.W., *The Londonderry Plantation 1609–1641* (Mullen, 1939)

Moraley, William, *The Infortunate: The Voyage and Adventures of William Moraley* (Pennsylvania State University Press, 1992)

Moran P.F., *Historical Sketch of the Persecutions Suffered by the Catholics of Ireland* (Dublin, 1862)

Morgan, Edmund S., *American Slavery, American Freedom: The Ordeal of Colonial Virginia* (W.W. Norton & Co., 1975)

Morgan, Kenneth, *Slavery and Servitude, 1607–1800* (Edinburgh University Press, 2000)

Morris, Richard B., *Government and Labor in Early America* (Columbia University Press, 1946)

Morton, Thomas, *New English Canaan* (Amsterdam, 1637)

Murdoch, Beamish, *A History of Nova Scotia or Arcadie* (J. Barnes, 1867)

Nace, Ted, *Gangs of America: The Rise of Corporate Power and the Disabling of Democracy* (Berrett-Koehler, 2003)

Nash, Gary B., 'Poverty and Politics in Early American History' in Smith, Billy G. (ed.), *Down and Out in Early America* (2004)

O'Callaghan, S., *To Hell or Barbados* (Brandon Press, 2000)

Oldham, Wilfrid, *Britain's Convicts to the Colonies* (Library of Australian History, 1990)

Olson, Alison Gilbert, *Making the Empire Work: London and American Interest Groups 1690–1790* (Harvard University Press, 1992)

Osgood, Herbert L., *The American Colonies in the Seventeenth Century* (Columbia University Press, 1926)

Otterness, Philip, *Becoming German: The 1709 Palatine Migration to New York* (Cornell University Press, 2004)

Percy, George, *A Discourse of the Plantation of the Southern Colony in Virginia by the English* (1606)

Poole, W.F., *The Popham Colony: A Discussion of its Historical Claims* (Wiggin and Lunt, 1866)

Poor, John A., *The First Colonisation of New England* (Anson and D. Randolph, 1863)

Prebble, John, *Culloden* (Athaneum, 1962)

— *The Lion in the North* (Penguin, 1973)

Prendergast, John, *The Cromwellian Settlement of Ireland* (Longman, 1865)

Pring, Martin, 'A Voyage Set Out From the City of Bristol', in Burrage, Henry S. (ed.), *Haklyut 1534–1608* (Scribners, 1906)

Purchas, Samuel, *Hakluytus Posthumus* (Maclehose, 1905–07)

Quinn, David Beers, *Set Fair for Roanoke: Voyages and Colonies, 1584–1606* (University of North Carolina Press, 1985)

Rabb, Theodore K., *Jacobean Gentleman: Sir Edwin Sandys 1561–1629* (Princeton University Press, 1998)

Ranelagh, John, *Ireland: An Illustrated History* (Collins, 1981)

Reinmuth, Howard F., *Early Stuart Studies* (University of Minnesota Press, 1970)

Revel, James, *The Poor Unhappy Felon's Sorrowful Account of his Fourteen Years' Transportation at Virginia in America* (London, 1800)

Rice, Douglas Walthew, *The Life and Achievements of Sir John Popham, 1531–1607: Leading to the Establishment of the First English Colony in New England* (Fairleigh Dickinson University, 2005)

Rivers, M. and Foyle, *England's Slavery or Barbados Merchandise* (London, 1659)

Rogers, H.C.B., *Battles and Generals of the Civil Wars 1642–1651* (Seeley Service and Co., 1968)

Rosenbaum, Stuart (ed.), *Pragmatism and Religion: Classical Sources and Original Essays* (Urbana, 2003)

Sainsbury, W. Noel (ed.), *Calendar of State Papers, Colonial Series: America and West Indies*, Vol. 1, 1574–1660 (London, 1860–9)

Salinger, Sharon V., *To Serve Well and Faithfully: Labor and Indentured Servants in Pennsylvania, 1682–1800* (Cambridge University Press, 1987)

Sankey, Margaret, *Jacobite Prisoners of the 1715 Rebellion* (Ashgate, 2005)

Schomburgk, Robert H., *The History of Barbados* (Frank Cass Publishers, 1971)

Scott, William Robert, *The Constitution and Finances of English, Scottish and Irish Joint Stock Companies to 1720* (Cambridge University Press, 1910–12)

Secundus, *The London Spy Revived by Demonitas* (London, 1736)

Senior, Nassau W., Edwin Chadwick, et al., *The Poor Law Commissioners Report of 1834: Copy of the Report Made in 1834 by the Commissioners for Inquiring into the Administration and Practical Operation of the Poor Laws* (London, 1885)

Seward, Desmond, *The First Bourbon: Henri IV, King of France and Navarre* (Constable, 1971)

Shea, William L., *The Virginia Militia in the Seventeenth Century* (Louisiana State University Press, 1983)

Smedley, Audrey, *Race in North America: Origin and Evolution of a Worldview* (Westview, 1993)

Smith, Abbot Emerson, *Colonists in Bondage: White Servitude and Convict Labor in America, 1607–1776* (University of North Carolina Press, 1947)

Smith, Billy G. (ed.), *Down and Out in Early America* (Pennsylvania State University Press, 2004)

Smith, James Morton (ed.), *Seventeenth Century America: Essays in Colonial History* (University of North Carolina Press, 1959)

Smith, John, *The Complete Works of Captain John Smith* (University of North Carolina Press, 1986)

— *The True Travels, Adventures and Observations of Capt John Smith* (T. Slater, 1630)

Smith, Warren B., *White Servitude in Colonial South Carolina* (University of South Carolina Press, 1961)

Stirling, William, *An Encouragement to Colonies* (Stansby, 1624)

Stith, William, *The History of the First Discovery and Settlement of Virginia* (Williamsburg, 1747)

Stow, John, *A Survey of the Cities of London and Westminster* (London, 1720)

Strachey, William, *History of Travel into Virginia Britannia* (London, 1953)

— *A True Reportory of the Wreck and Redemption of Sir Thomas Gates, Knight, Upon and From the Islands of the Bermudas* (University Press of Virginia, 1965)

Stratton, Eugene Aubrey, *Plymouth Colony: Its History and People, 1620–1691* (Ancestry Publishing, 1986)

Sullivan, James, *History of the District of Maine* (Boston, 1795)

Sweet, Frank W., *The Legal History of the Colour Line* (Backintyme, 2005)

Thomson, Elizabeth McLure, *The Chamberlain Letters* (John Murray, 1966)

Thorton, John Wingate, *Colonial Schemes of Popham and Gorges* (Balch, 1863)

Towner, Lawrence William, *A Good Master Well Served: Masters and Servants in Colonial Massachusetts, 1620–1750* (Garland Pub., 1998)

Tyler, Lyon Gardiner, *Narratives of Early Virginia, 1606–1625* (1907)

Van der Zee, John, *Bound Over: Indentured Servitude and American Conscience* (Simon and Schuster, 1985)

Waldstreicher, David, *Runaway America: Benjamin Franklin, Slavery and the American Revolution* (Hill & Wang, 2004)

Walpole, Charles George, *A Short History of the Kingdom of Ireland* (Kegan Paul, 1882)

Washburn, Wilcomb E., *The Governor and the Rebel: A History of Bacon's Rebellion in Virginia* (University of North Carolina Press, 1957)

Welsh, Frank, *A History of South Africa* (HarperCollins, 1998)

Wertenbaker, Thomas J., *The Planters of Colonial Virginia* (Princeton University Press, 1922)

Williams, Eric, *Capitalism and Slavery* (Chapel Hill, 1944)

Williams, Joseph J., *Whence the 'Black Irish' of Jamaica?* (Dial Press, 1968)

Williamson, Peter, *The Life and Adventures of Peter Williamson* (Glasgow, 1757)

Wodrow, Robert, *The History of the Sufferings of the Church of Scotland from the Restoration to the Revolution* (Blackie, 1836–38)

Young, Alexander, *Chronicles of the First Planters of the Colony of Massachusetts Bay, from 1623–1636* (Boston, 1846)

Zinn, Howard, *A People's History of the United States* (Longman, 1980)

INDEX